VINCENT VAN GOGH

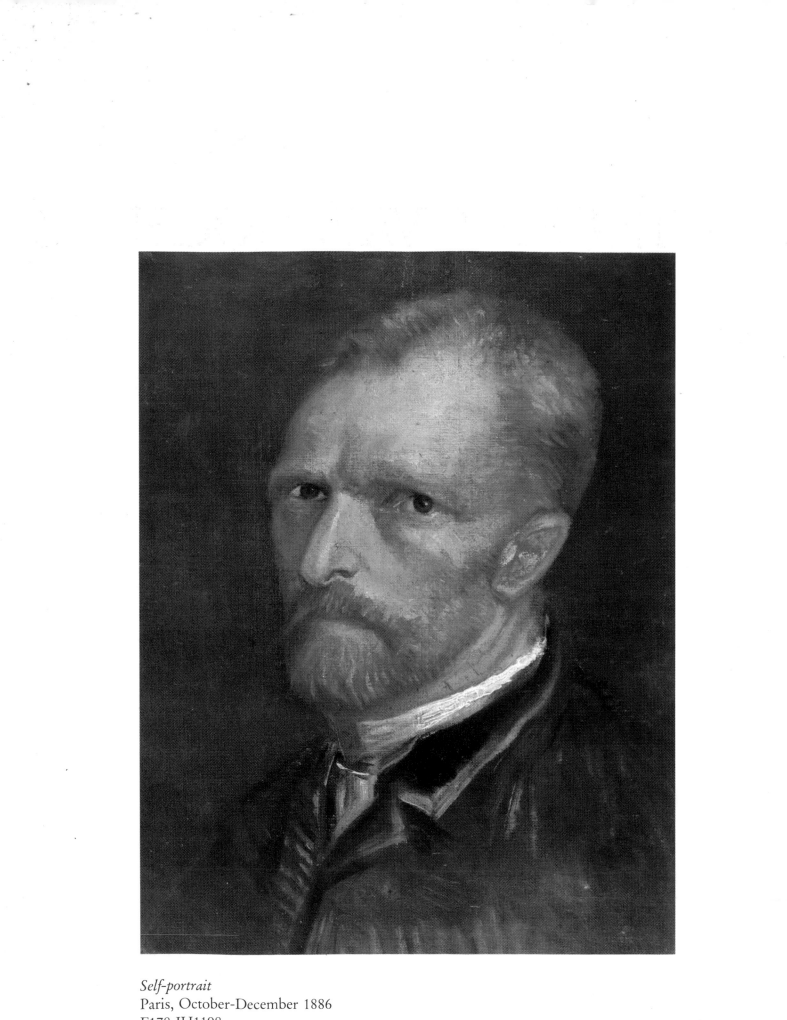

Self-portrait
Paris, October-December 1886
F178 JH1198
Canvas, 39.5 x 29.5 cm
The Hague, Gemeentemuseum

VINCENT VAN GOGH

Hans Bronkhorst

Weidenfeld and Nicolson, London

Author's Note

- The numbers in the text refer to the letters from Vincent Van Gogh to his brother, Theo.

- The numbers preceded by a W refer to letters from Van Gogh to his sister, Wil.

- The numbers preceded by a B refer to the letters from Van Gogh to Emile Bernard.

- The letters referred to can be found in: *Collected Letters of Vincent Van Gogh*, Wereldbibliotheek, Amsterdam 1974.

- The numbers in the text preceded by JH refer to the complete catalogue, *Van Gogh en zijn weg* by Jan Hulsker, Meulenhoff, Amsterdam 1979.

- The captions to the illustrations include, in addition to the JH numbers, F numbers which refer to the catalogue by J.B. de la Faille, Meulenhoff International, Amsterdam 1970.

- In addition to the sources mentioned here, a large number of other works were consulted: these are listed in the bibliography. The author would like to express his gratitude to Anita Vriend, Librarian at the Rijksmuseum Vincent Van Gogh, Amsterdam, for her help in the literary research.

– In addition, special thanks to Tony Daalder-Vos of the Stedelijk Museum in Amsterdam, who, on behalf of the Vincent van Gogh Stichting/Rijksmuseum Vincent van Gogh, assisted in assessing and correcting the illustrations of Van Gogh's works which are not always easy to reproduce.

First published in Great Britain in 1990 by
George Weidenfeld & Nicolson Limited
91 Clapham High Street, London SW4 7TA

First published in paperback 1991

Translated from the Dutch by Tony Langham and Plym Peters

Coordination and production: Smeets Illustrated Projects, Weert
Filmset: Grafische Industrie Puntkomma B.V., Veldhoven, The Netherlands
Print: Royal Smeets Offset b.v., Weert, The Netherlands

© Royal Smeets Offset b.v., Weert, The Netherlands

Contents

Chronological survey

The main events in the life of Vincent Van Gogh

1853	Vincent Willem Van Gogh was born in Zundert in the Netherlands on 30 March, the eldest of six children of a Protestant pastor.
1857	Vincent's brother, Theo Van Gogh, was born on 1 May. He was to be a great support to the artist throughout his life.
1864	Vincent was at a boarding school in Zevenbergen from 1 October 1864 to the summer of 1866.
1866	From 15 September 1866 to 19 March 1868 - less than two full school years - he was a pupil at the Rijks Hogere Burgerschool Willem II in Tilburg, where he gained good marks. He then left school, possibly because his father found it too expensive.
1869	For almost four years, from August 1869 to June 1873, he was employed by the art dealer Goupil in The Hague. A plaque now marks the building on de Plaats where he worked.
1872	In August Vincent started writing regularly to his younger brother Theo. He continued to do so for eighteen years until his death, a correspondence which totals at least 650 letters.
1873	In June Vincent was transferred from The Hague to a branch of Goupil's in London.
1874	In October he was given a post at Goupil's main office in Paris, where he worked for a few months before returning in December to the London branch.
1875	In the middle of May he was back in Paris, where he worked for nearly a year, until he was dismissed on 1 April 1876.
1876	In the spring, Vincent took a teaching post in Ramsgate, England. He then became a teacher and assistant pastor in Isleworth.
1877	In January he returned to the Netherlands, where he became a bookkeeper at Blussé and Van Braam, a bookshop in Dordrecht.
1877	In May he moved to Amsterdam to live with his uncle Jan Van Gogh, a Vice-Admiral and marine commander. He had Greek and Latin lessons from M.V. Mendes da Costa. Initially he hoped to take the state entrance examination to the faculty of theology at the University of Amsterdam. However, he gave up his study of classical languages and abandoned the plan to go to university, as his father had done.
1878	At the end of August he enrolled at the Evangelical College in Brussels.
1878	In November he was appointed to the post of assistant pastor in Wasnes in the Belgian Borinage, but was dismissed after some six months for being over-zealous. He then settled in Cuesmes, again in the Borinage, as an evangelist. It was here that he started to draw.
1880	He moved to Brussels and decided to become an artist. He applied himself to drawing and became friendly with Count Anthon van Rappard, a proficient artist five years younger than himself.

1881	In April he moved to Etten, where he lived at his parents' parsonage, and developed his talent for drawing. He fell in love with his cousin, Kee Vos-Stricker, who had recently been widowed. She rejected him with the words: 'Never, no, never.' In December Vincent had a serious argument with his father and decided to leave.
1881	He moved to The Hague, where he studied watercolour painting with Anton Mauve. A prostitute, Sien Hoornik, and her child moved in with him. In The Hague he started painting as well as drawing. Less than two years later he moved to Drenthe.
1883	From September to December Vincent worked first in Hoogeveen and then in Nieuw-Amsterdam.
1883	In December he moved to his parents' parsonage in Nuenen, where he stayed for almost two years. During this period he painted *The Potato Eaters*.
1885	Vincent's father, Th. Van Gogh, died of a heart attack on 26 March.
1885	On 28 November Vincent arrived in Antwerp. He lived at 194 Lange Beeldekensstraat. He studied at the Academy of Fine Arts, but this was a failure and some three months later he moved to Paris.
1886	At the beginning of March Vincent moved in with his brother in Paris. During this period he discovered Impressionism. He started painting with lighter colours. He stayed in Paris for two years and during this time he did about 110 paintings.
1888	On 20 February he travelled to Arles and moved into the Yellow House. From October to December 1888 Gauguin also lived there. Vincent produced almost 200 paintings in Arles.
1889	His brother, Theo, married Jo Bonger on 18 April.
1889	On 8 May Vincent was admitted to the Saint-Paul-de-Mausole asylum in Saint-Rémy-de-Provence.
1890	On 16 May 1890, after spending a year in the asylum, he travelled to Auvers-sur-Oise via Paris, where he visited Theo and Jo. In Auvers he became friends with Dr Paul Gachet.
1890	On 27 July Vincent shot himself, and two days later, on 29 July, he died of internal bleeding, aged thirty-seven. He was buried in the churchyard in Auvers.
1891	Theo died on 21 January, only six months after his brother. He was buried in Utrecht, but in 1914 his remains were moved to Auvers, where he now lies next to his brother, Vincent.
1914	Jo Van Gogh-Bonger published the first Dutch edition of Vincent's letters: *Vincent Van Gogh, Brieven aan zijn broeder*, three volumes, Wereldbibliotheek, Amsterdam.

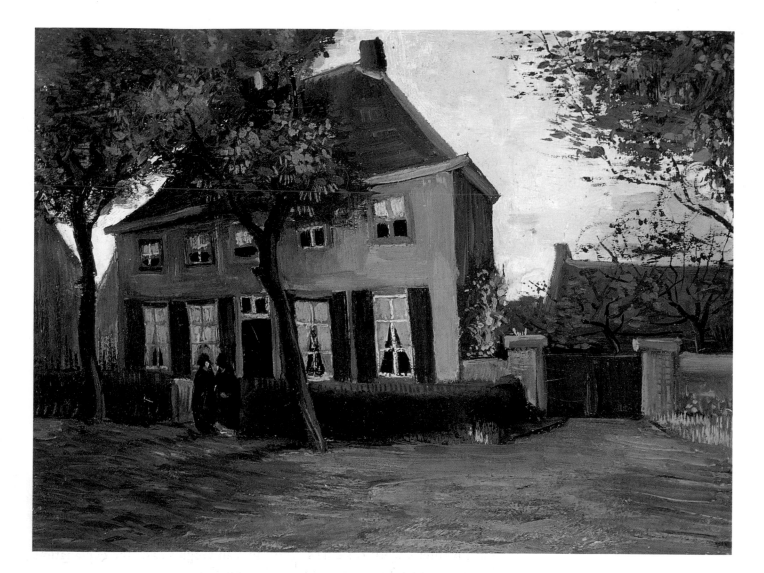

The Parsonage at Nuenen
Nuenen, October 1885
F182 JH948
Canvas, 33 x 43 cm
Amsterdam, Rijksmuseum
Vincent van Gogh

Chapter 1

A friend of the people

Vincent Van Gogh only lived to the age of thirty-seven, the same age as the great Italian painters, Raphael and Caravaggio, and his contemporary and Parisian friend, Toulouse-Lautrec. He has become one of the most popular painters in the history of art, and his paintings are sold for astronomical sums at auction. But it is not only for such sensational reasons that his work is universally loved. Van Gogh was honest in his dealings with people, and his strong social commitment appealed to many. This is how he wished to paint: not so much beautifully, but with genuine feeling. He wanted to produce art for the people, a wish that has been realized in the twentieth century.

Van Gogh only really became an artist in the last ten years of his life. During this period, between 1880 and 1890, he worked feverishly, and with a great deal of self-criticism, producing 2,125 works of art, of which there are about 825 paintings and 1,300 drawings, sketches and watercolours. Over the years his output increased, as though he had a premonition that he would not live long, and therefore had much to accomplish. Towards the end of his life, he sometimes produced a painting a day. His will to work was by no means inhibited by the lack of interest of the art world, art dealers and art critics. It was only just before his death that a critic published a review which praised his work.

A vocation and a mission

Van Gogh had a vocation and a mission to be a painter, although events constantly seemed to conspire against this. Why did he receive so little recognition in his own lifetime, when he was to become so famous after his death? In 1888 he had written prophetically: 'A lot of money is paid for a painter's work once he's dead.' In Van Gogh's case, the explanation is possibly that he was too far ahead of his time.

Van Gogh's work was based on a deep and passionate need to express his observations and experiences in paintings and drawings. It is a visual expression of his emotions; in fact, he was a precursor of Expressionism, and even of Fauvism. He did not fit into a particular school; he cannot simply be classified under the heading 'Post-Impressionist'. He never made any attempt to make his work fashionable and saleable. He simply wanted to be completely honest and sincere, to paint and draw what he saw and how he saw it, but his contemporaries often failed to understand this.

At the art dealer's

Van Gogh started his career as an art dealer's apprentice at the early age of sixteen, but after seven years he decided to change direction. He envisaged becoming an evangelist, following in the footsteps of his father and

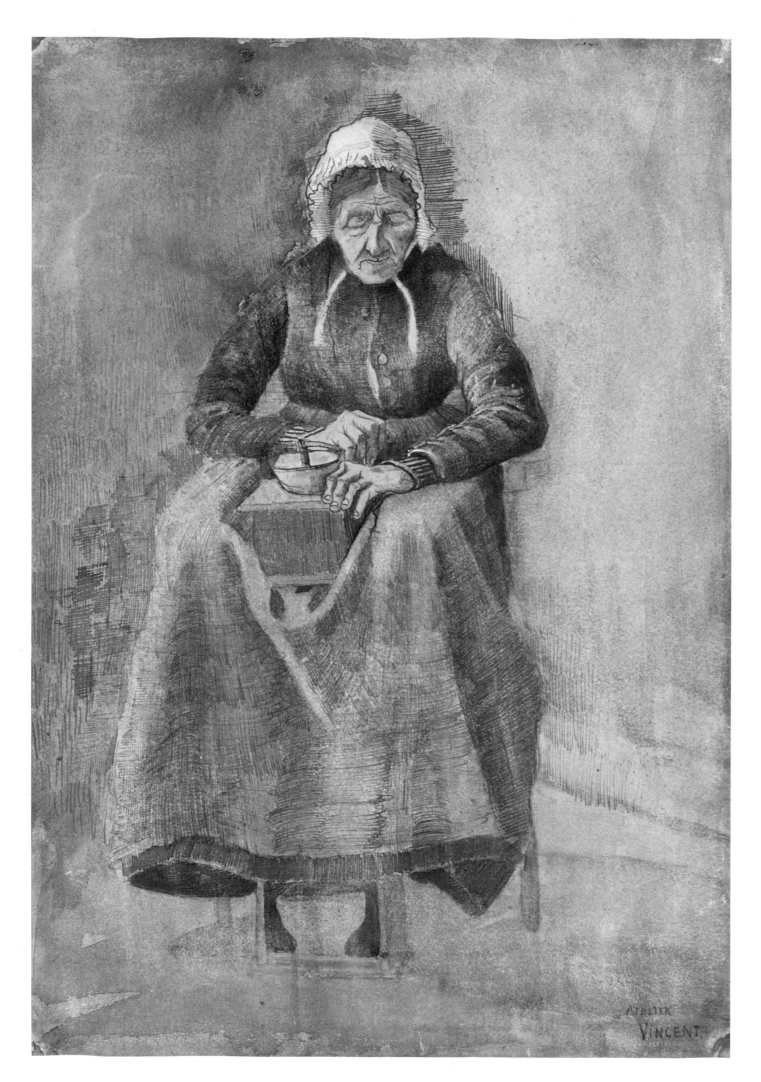

10

his grandfather. But his missionary work amongst the impoverished workers of the Borinage, a coal-mining district of Belgium, came to grief because of his own fanatical zeal. From that point, he knew that only by expressing his vision in pictures could he give meaning to his life, and bring consolation to humanity.

Having found his true means of self-expression, a period of rapid development and fulfillment as an artist followed, interrupted by frequent bouts of mental illness. In 1890 he committed suicide in despair at his sense of personal failure. Yet his last paintings radiate enormous vitality, a colossal life force. This is the great paradox of a life that came to such a sad and premature end.

In this book attention has been focussed on the last years of Van Gogh's life, spent in France. His early years as an artist in Holland - Etten, The Hague, Drenthe, and perhaps more importantly Nuenen - are dealt with only briefly. For it was in France that Van Gogh discovered the new art forms of Impressionism and Pointillism. In France - in Paris, Provence and Auvers - Van Gogh created an innovative idiom and personal style: a twentieth-century painter living and working at the end of the nineteenth century. Edvard Munch, Maurice de Vlaminck, Henri Matisse, the German Expressionists of the artistic community Die Brücke, including Ernst Ludwig Kirchner, and later on, Francis Bacon, continued this tradition. At the end of the twentieth century the influence of Vincent Van Gogh is still prevalent, and he is generally recognized and respected as the greatest Dutch artist after Rembrandt.

Literary legacy

Van Gogh is remembered not only as an artist. He has also left an important literary oeuvre of approximately 800 letters, mostly to his brother Theo. These letters, which were certainly not intended to be published, provide an illuminating understanding of Van Gogh's life as an artist. In the whole of the history of art, no painter has ever explained his own work in so much detail and in such descriptive language.

This story of Van Gogh as an artist begins when, profoundly disillusioned, he returned to the Netherlands from Belgium, where he had started to study drawing at the Brussels Academy.

Woman Grinding Coffee
Etten, November 1881
F889 JH75
Pen, pencil, watercolour,
heightened with white, 56 x 39 cm
Otterlo, Rijksmuseum
Kröller-Müller

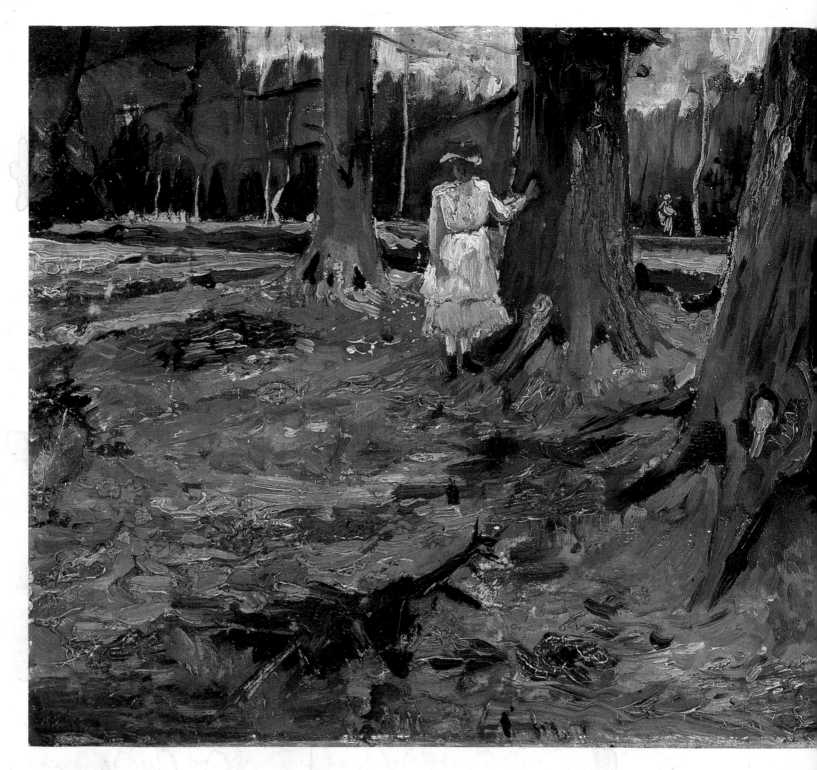

A Girl in a Wood
The Hague, August 1882
F8 JH182
Canvas, 39 x 59 cm
Otterlo, Rijksmuseum
Kröller-Müller

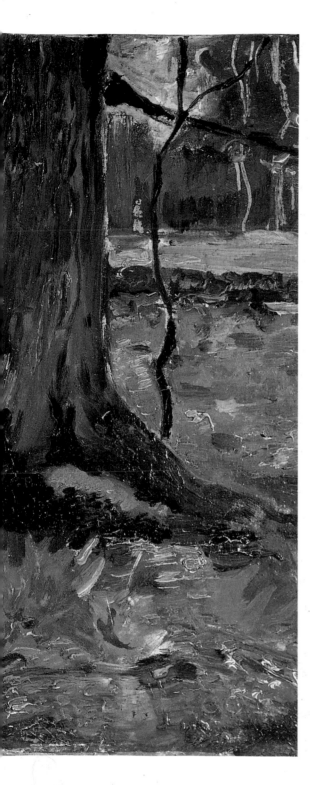

Chapter II
A painter of peasants

At the end of April 1881, Van Gogh, aged twenty-eight, left Brussels for Etten, where he lived at his parents' parsonage. He wrote to Theo (144): 'I'm so glad that things have turned out so that I can work here quietly for some time.' His stay in Etten was the beginning of his career as an artist. Initially he worked in pen, pencil, black chalk and charcoal, sometimes highlighted in white and given a wash of watercolour. He also produced two still lifes in Etten, which were not altogether successful.

The *Woman Grinding Coffee* (JH 75; see p. 10), of November 1881, highlighted in white, is a very fine drawing. It is executed in pen and pencil, with a wash of watercolour. The peasant woman is wearing a Brabant cap and holds the coffee grinder between her knees while she rotates the handle with her right hand. As it is a chilly autumn day, she rests her feet on a foot warmer. It is a very realistic scene from Brabant life over a century ago.

During this period in Etten, Van Gogh was especially stirred by peasant life. He drew peasants working in the fields, farmers sowing and digging, women peeling potatoes, or engaged in needlework. He was particularly inspired by the work of the French painter, Jean-François Millet (1814-1875), whose paintings of rural life made a significant impression on him. His drawings of a sower and a reaper are in the style of Millet, and eight years later he used them as studies for paintings executed in Saint-Rémy. The ideology of peasant life was central to his artistic career, and during the last years of his life in Auvers, he often drew on his early memories of the Brabant countryside.

At Christmas 1881, Van Gogh had a terrible quarrel with his father, which was sparked off by his refusal to go to church: 'At Christmas I had rather a bad row with Father', Vincent wrote to Theo (166), 'and things went so far that Father said it would be better if I left home. Well, he was so adamant that I left the very same day.' But the root of the conflict between father and son was Vincent's obstinate and passionate love for his niece, Kee Vos, who had unequivocally rejected him. This infatuation immediately incurred the displeasure of the pastor.

With Mauve in The Hague

In 1881, Van Gogh left Etten for The Hague, where he was taught to paint in watercolours by the artist Anton Mauve (1838-1888). Until now, Van Gogh had virtually restricted himself to drawing. However, this apprenticeship did not last long as the teacher had no faith in his pupil's skill, and Van Gogh's Hague paintings were not altogether successful. *The Farm in Loosduinen* is not very impressive, but the *Girl in a Wood* (JH 182), which can be seen in the Kröller-Müller Museum in Otterlo, is a beautiful and moving work. He painted this in the woods near The Hague in August 1882. In a letter to Theo (227), he refers to a study of a beech wood with

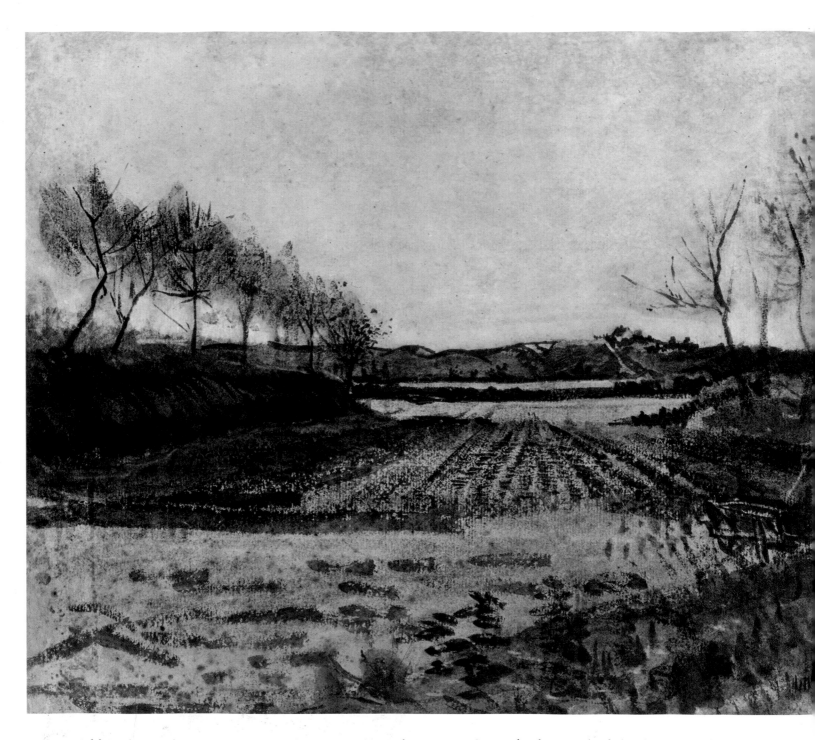

Potato Field in the Dunes
The Hague, August 1883
F1037 JH390
Brush, ink, heightened with white,
27.5 x 42 cm
Otterlo, Rijksmuseum
Kröller-Müller

statuesque green trunks seen against a background of dry leaves, and a figure of a girl in white. Van Gogh's aim had been to re-create the sensation of place, so that 'you could breathe and walk round the wood, and smell it.' He achieved his aim in this composition. Even though this is one of his earliest paintings, it is already a masterpiece.

The painting *Potato Field in the Dunes* (JH 390; see p. 14) is an equally fine work, but the intimate homely scene executed in black chalk and pencil, *Girl in Front of a Cradle* (JH 336), is even more successful. Who are the children in this drawing? The answer to this question is to be found in events which occurred in Van Gogh's personal life.

Sien Hoornik

At the beginning of 1882, Van Gogh met a prostitute in The Hague, the 32-year-old Sien Hoornik, an unmarried mother of a five-year-old

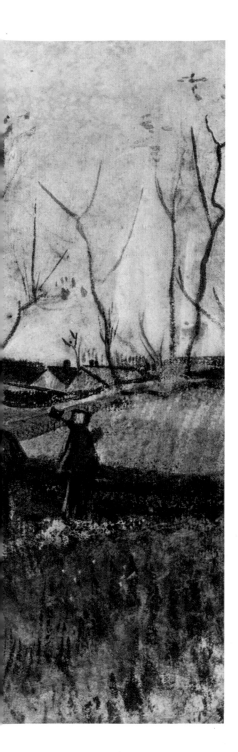

daughter, Maria. Sien was expecting her second child. She moved in with Van Gogh, and he planned to marry her. At first he did not mention the affair to Theo, but at the beginning of May 1882, he wrote to his brother (192): 'This winter I met a pregnant woman who was abandoned by the man whose baby she is expecting. A pregnant woman wandering the streets in winter, who had to earn her bread - you can imagine how. I took the woman for a model and worked with her all winter. I could not pay her the full wages of a model, but that did not prevent me from paying her rent, and so far, thank God, I have been able to protect her and her child from hunger and cold by sharing my own bread with her.'

By the time Van Gogh had completed the drawing of *Girl in Front of a Cradle* in March 1883, the baby had been born. It shows the daughter Maria, with her baby brother Willem, about eight months old, lying in 'a small iron cradle with a green coverlet'.

At this time Van Gogh, Sien and her children were living close to the railway station –Rijnspoor– at 138 Schenkweg, which also formed a subject for his drawings.

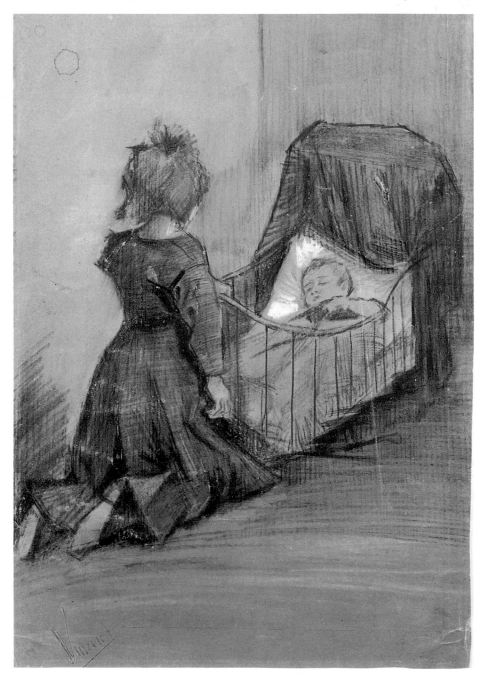

Girl in Front of a Cradle
The Hague, March 1883
F1024 JH336
Black chalk, pencil, heightened in white, 48 x 62 cm
Amsterdam, Rijksmuseum
Vincent van Gogh

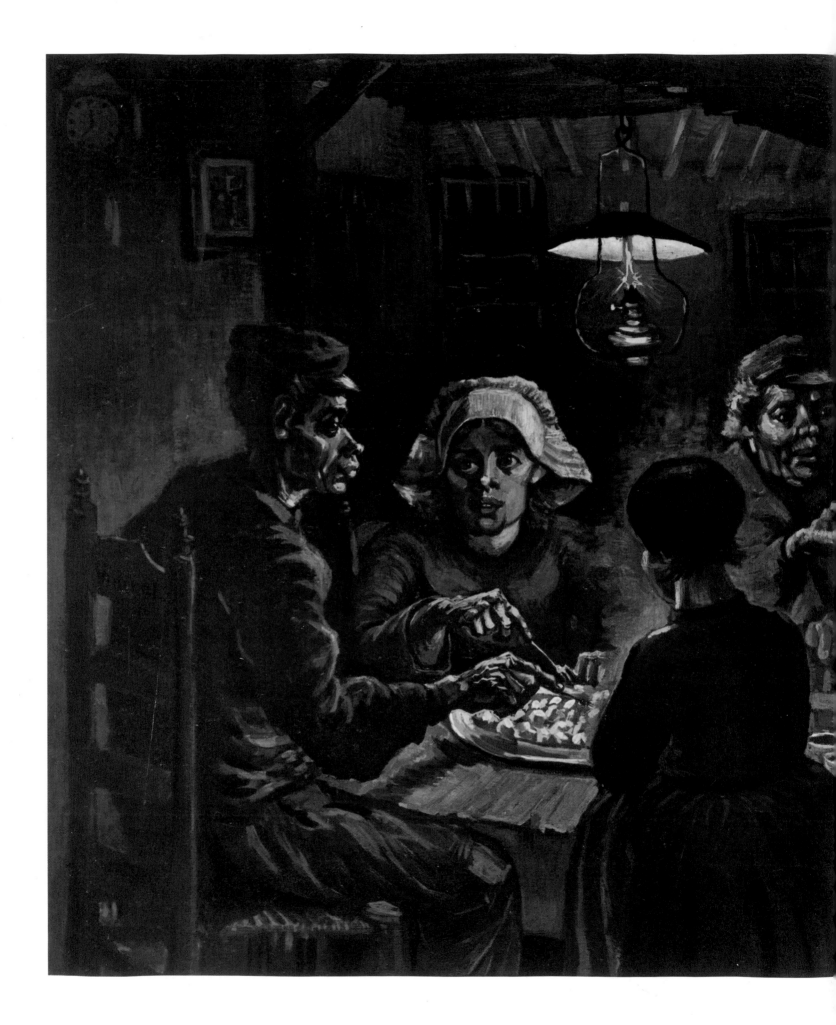

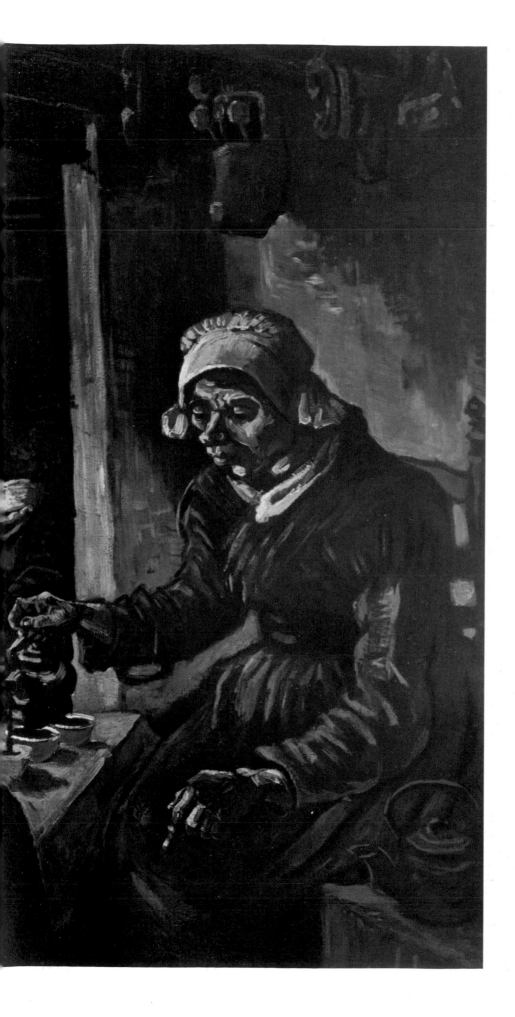

The Potato Eaters
Nuenen, April 1885
F82 JH764
Canvas, 82 x 114 cm
Amsterdam, Rijksmuseum
Vincent van Gogh

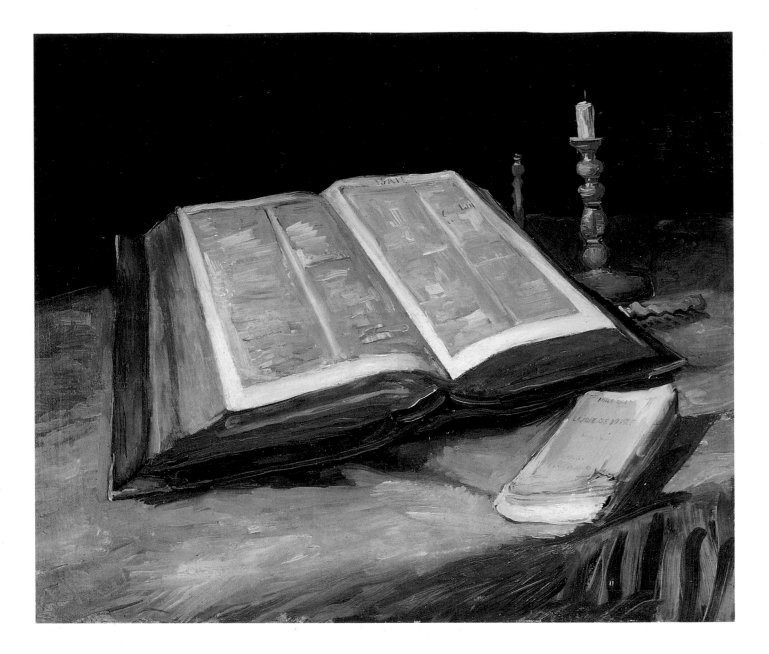

*Still Life with Open Bible,
Candlestick and Novel*
Nuenen, October 1885
F117 JH946
Canvas, 65 x 78 cm
Amsterdam, Rijksmuseum
Vincent van Gogh

The move to Drenthe

Van Gogh's relationship with Sien became increasingly strained, and by the summer of 1883, he had decided to leave her and the children. On 11 September he took the train to Hoogeveen in Drenthe. He had lived in The Hague for twenty months, and during this period had become proficient at drawing, producing some truly sublime works.

His stay in Drenthe was brief, for he was there for less than three months, living first at Hoogeveen and then Nieuw-Amsterdam. Some good drawings have survived from these autumn months, in particular one splendid watercolour of the drawbridge at Nieuw-Amsterdam (now in the Groninger Museum in Groningen).

From Drenthe, Van Gogh returned on 3 or 4 December 1883 to his parents, now living in Nuenen, where his father was pastor. This was a long trip. Van Gogh made the first part of the journey on foot, carrying his bags and artist's materials through a storm from Nieuw-Amsterdam to Hoogeveen - a six-hour walk. From Hoogeveen he travelled by train to Nuenen.

Nuenen

Van Gogh had not intended to stay long in Nuenen, but events did not turn out as he expected. In fact, he was to live there for almost two years.

Van Gogh was tremendously involved with the subject of peasant life during the spring of 1885. He did a series of heads of peasant men and women, both painted studies and drawings, as well as sketches of a hand holding a coffee cup or a bowl, a hand with a fork, a spoon rack on the wall, and a wall clock.

He first painted group views from life in a peasants' living room and then completed the final version of the painting in his studio from memory. He said that in the preliminary studies he fed his imagination from reality during the creative process. Perhaps one would consider a painting painted *in situ* to be more realistic than a version which had been painted in the studio without a model, but Van Gogh thought otherwise.

It was at this time that he produced what he considered to be one of his best works: *The Potato Eaters*. To begin with, in March 1885, he painted a study of four peasants eating potatoes (JH 686). This was followed in April by a second version with five figures (JH 734), and finally in May by the definitive *The Potato Eaters* shown here (JH 764; see p. 16/17), with five peasants having a meal. This work was then sent to Theo in Paris.

What gave Van Gogh the inspiration to paint this scene? A friend of the artist described how this came about (435e): 'One evening, after painting outside all day, he passed the cottage of the De Groot family, where he often worked, and he stepped inside to have a rest. The family was just gathered under the lamp and starting their meal. Spontaneously Vincent grabbed his canvas, paintbrushes and palette and started to paint the group.' (The cottage of the peasant family was situated on the present Gerwenseweg in Nuenen, near the windmill De Roosdonck; the original cottage was burnt down in the Second World War and a new cottage was built in its place.)

We do not know the name of the girl, who is shown from the back, but the other figures in this work are from left to right: the mother, Cornelia de Groot-van Rooij, who is pouring the coffee; her brother, This van Rooij, holding a cup of coffee in his hand; her daughter, Cordina de Groot; and her younger brother, Sis van Rooij.

It is interesting to note Van Gogh's own views on *The Potato Eaters* in his letters. On 30 April 1885 he wrote to Theo (404): 'I certainly wanted to evoke the feeling in my work that these people are eating their potatoes by the light of the lamp with the very hands which they used to dig the earth, so that there is a sense of hard work and the feeling that they have earned their food honestly. I wanted it to evoke a completely different style of life from our life - that of cultured people. Thus I certainly wouldn't want everybody to simply think it was just good or beautiful.'

He described *The Potato Eaters* as 'a true peasant painting'. He added: 'But anyone who prefers to view the peasant sentimentally - let him. As far as I'm concerned, I am convinced that in the long term the results are better when they are painted as crude as they are than with conventional prettiness... A peasant wearing his fustian suit in the field is more beautiful than when he goes to church on Sunday wearing his Sunday best.'

For Van Gogh, a peasant painting had to smell of 'bacon, smoke and potato steam', a characteristic remark which mirrors the realism in his work.

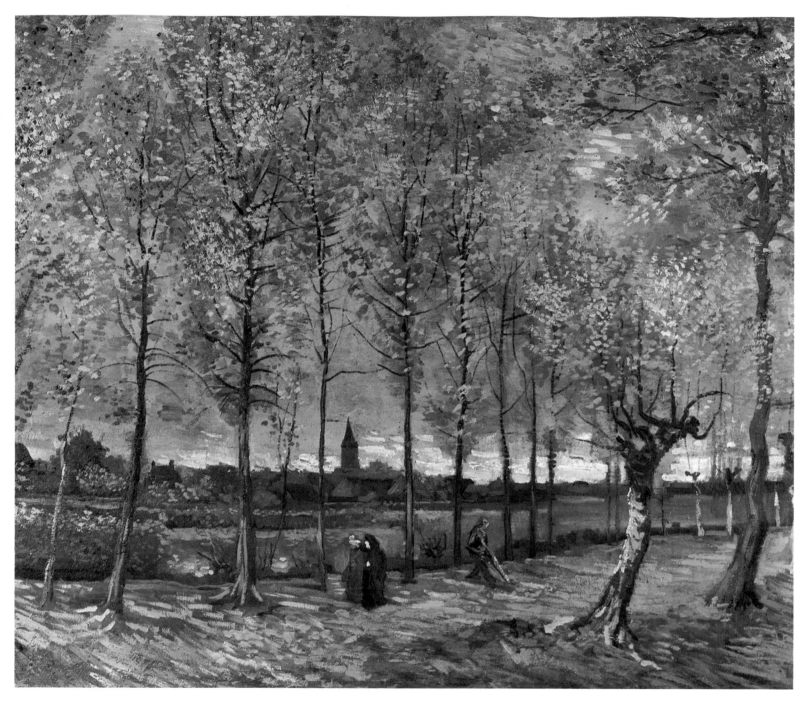

Lane with Poplars
Nuenen, November 1885
F45 JH959
Canvas, 78 x 97.5 cm
Rotterdam, Museum Boymans-van
Beuningen

The theme of peasants and peasant life pervaded Van Gogh's work throughout his life. Even three months before his death on 29 April 1890, he wrote to Theo from Saint-Rémy (629): 'Could you send me some of my old drawings which have figures in them? I'm thinking of doing another version of the painting with the peasants with the effect of the lamplight.' He wrongly imagined that by then the canvas would have become 'quite black', and he wanted to paint it all over again from memory. He never did this, but in the spring of 1890 in Saint-Rémy he did complete a number of striking drawings or studies of peasants having their meal.

Artistic influences

The influence of other painters on Van Gogh's work can be seen in *The Potato Eaters*. He himself mentioned the French peasant painter L. A. Lhermitte (1844-1925), an artist eight years older than Van Gogh, but he also greatly admired the work of Jozef Israëls (1824-1911), one of The

Hague School artists. At the beginning of March 1882 Van Gogh had seen Israëls' *The Frugal Meal*, which was painted in 1876 and has a similar subject. Israëls had taught Van Gogh how to express light by contrasting it with dark, and in *The Potato Eaters* Van Gogh used the Rembrandt technique of chiaroscuro to great effect. As regards his use of colour, he had a preference for tertiary colours or earth colours for these paintings of peasants. In a letter to Theo he wrote: 'The colour in which they are painted is more or less the colour of a really dusty potato, unpeeled of course.' Van Gogh also knew how he wanted his work to be framed (405): 'As regards the *Potato Eaters*, it is a painting which would look good framed in gold, I'm sure.' In fact, the painting in the Van Gogh Museum in Amsterdam has a dull gold frame.

Symbolism

One painting from the Nuenen period which is full of symbolism is *Still Life with Open Bible, Candlestick and Novel* (JH 946; see p. 18). Van Gogh wrote to Theo on its completion at the end of 1885: 'I am sending you a still life of an open - i.e., a broken white - bible, bound in leather, against a black background and a yellowish-brown foreground, with a touch of lemon yellow. I painted it in one go on a single day.' It is a fascinating composition in the style of a seventeenth-century *vanitas* painting. The heavy bible represents Van Gogh's father, who had died six months earlier on 27 March 1885. The book is open at Isaiah, chapter 53, verse 6: 'All we like sheep have gone astray; and we have turned everyone to his own way; and the Lord hath laid on him the iniquity of us all.' Next to the Bible there is a candlestick with an extinguished candle, symbolizing death. In the foreground lies a modern Parisian novel, *La Joie de Vivre* by Emile Zola, a book that had been published a year earlier in 1884. Van Gogh was familiar with contemporary French naturalist literature. The book stands for Van Gogh himself, the artist who has bade farewell to the church. It is a worldly, anti-religious work which his father would have deplored, in contrast to the Holy Book, the Word of God, the book of the pastor.

Autumn scenes

In November 1885 Van Gogh painted his *Lane with Poplars* (JH 959; see p. 20). He described the painting as follows: 'The horizon is a dark line against a light line of white and blue air. In this dark line there are flecks of red, bluish green or brown, forming the outline of the roofs and orchards, and the field is greenish. The air higher up is grey, with the black tree trunks and yellow leaves contrasting with this. The foreground is completely covered with fallen, yellow leaves, with two black and one blue figure. To the right there is a white and black trunk of a birch tree, and a green trunk with reddish brown leaves.'

In the background stands the Roman Catholic church of St. Clemens (built by the Roermond architect C. Weber), which had been consecrated thirteen years earlier in 1872. Next to the church is the house of the sacristan, J. Schafrat, where Van Gogh had a studio from May 1884 to November 1885, while he continued to live at the parsonage of the Reformed Church with his parents.

This painting has a splendid sunny, autumn feeling. The fungus on the

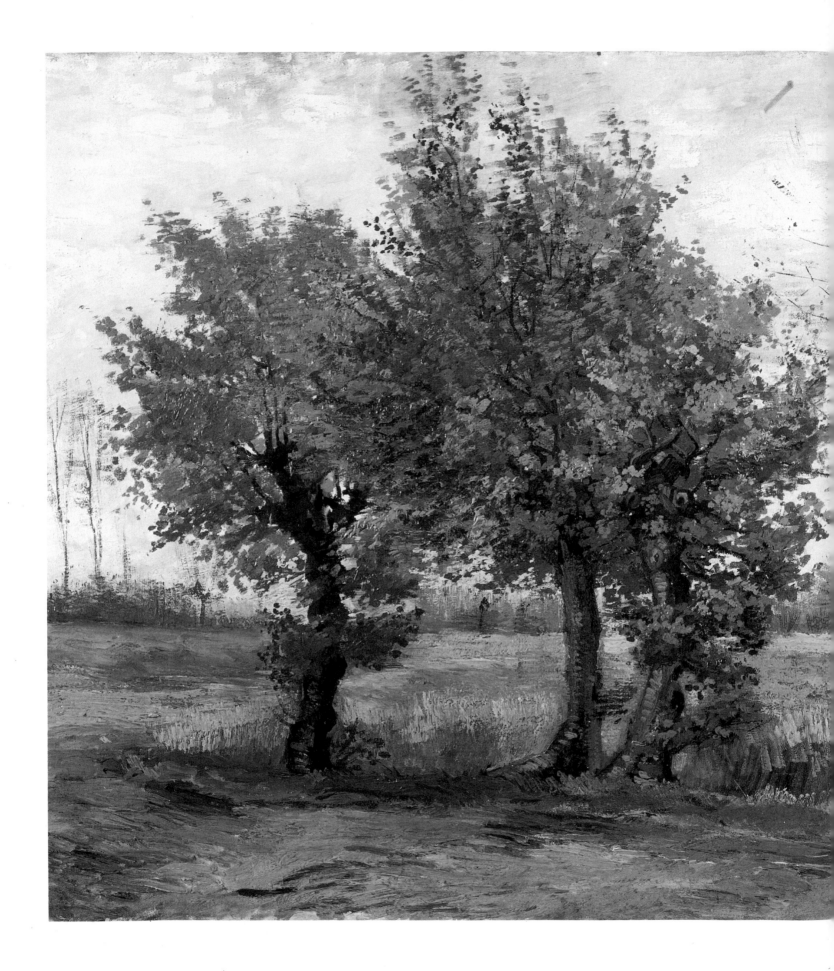

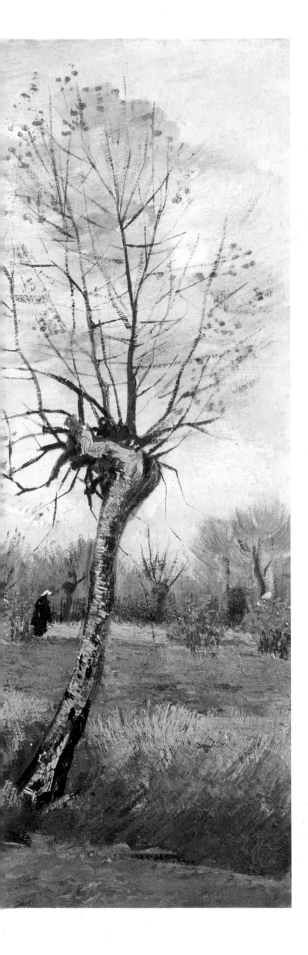

Autumn Landscape with Four Trees
Nuenen, November 1885
F44 JH962
Canvas, 64 x 89 cm
Otterlo, Rijksmuseum
Kröller-Müller

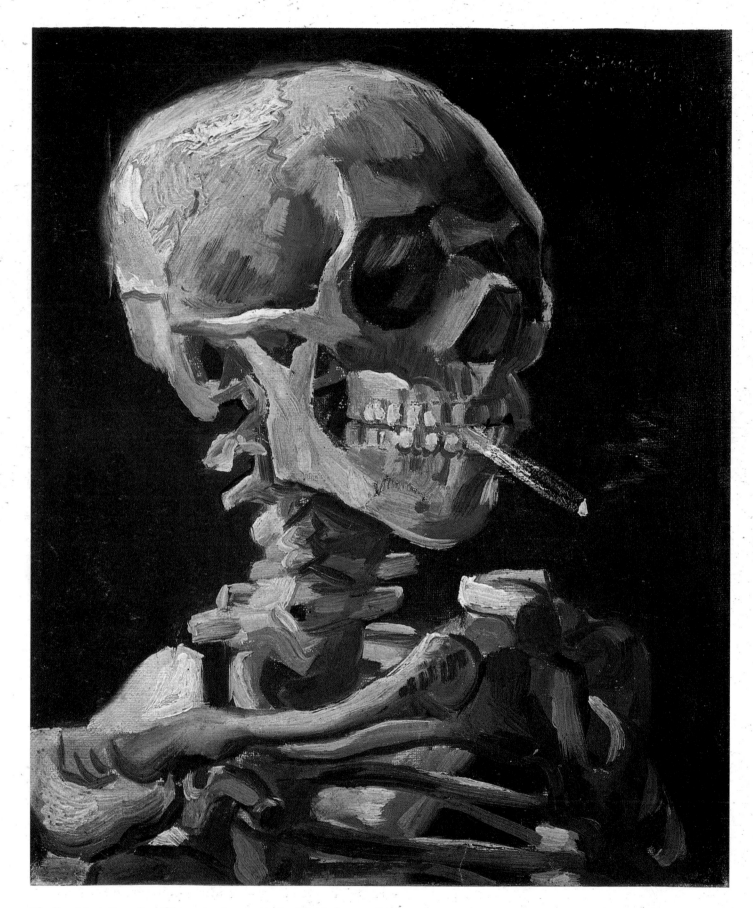

Skull with a Burning Cigarette between the Teeth
Antwerp, February 1886
F212 JH999
Canvas, 32.5 x 24 cm
Amsterdam, Rijksmuseum Vincent van Gogh

tree in the foreground on the right catches the light, which also flickers through the golden foliage of the poplars.

A very similar Nuenen autumn scene is depicted in *Autumn Landscape with Four Trees* (JH 962; see p. 22/3). Painted in the style of the Barbizon School, it shows the parsonage garden. In the foreground there are three gnarled oak trees which are still in full leaf, and to the right of them stands a pollarded birch. Between them in the background there is a woman wearing a white cap.

One evening in November 1885 Van Gogh took this painting to an acquaintance, Anton Kerssemackers, who lived opposite the station in Eindhoven. 'He's a tanner who has time and money and is about forty years old.' The painting was hung in 'a rather grand room', where it looked good against the grey wallpaper and black and gold furniture. Van Gogh wrote what happened next: 'Although the man has money, and although he wanted it very much, I felt such a glow of satisfaction when I saw that it was pleasing, that it created an atmosphere hanging there because of the soft melancholy peace of that combination of colours, that I *could not sell it*. But because he was moved by it, I gave it to him, and he accepted it in the spirit in which I intended it, without many words, in fact, little more than "the thing's damn good".' Van Gogh, who at that time was living on an allowance of 75 guilders per month from his brother, was finally able to make money with his work. However, in his unimaginable naivety, or disinterested idealism, he let this opportunity go.

To Antwerp

On 21 November 1885, Van Gogh left Nuenen for Antwerp, intending to go back after a few months, but he never returned. He left most of his paintings behind, stored above the weaver's house of Louis Begemann, now 65 Berg. In May 1886, Van Gogh's mother moved from Nuenen to Leyden. All his work was packed into crates and left in storage with a carpenter, Mr. Schrauer, in Breda, where they were forgotten. Eventually the carpenter gave everything to the second-hand dealers, M. and J.C. Couvreur. The Couvreur brothers tore up and threw away a hundred chalk drawings by Van Gogh, which they considered to be of no value, gave some of the large canvasses to a rag and bone man, and then sold a number of drawings for five or ten cents.

Van Gogh spent some three months in Antwerp before leaving for France. Once again he took classes at the Academy of Fine Arts. However, the teachers did not understand his talent, and he was sent back to the first year because he could not draw! Knowing the beautiful drawings which he did in particular in The Hague and Nuenen, this seems quite incomprehensible. *The Potato Eaters*, too, went unnoticed in Antwerp. He did a number of very beautiful portraits of women, such as *The Woman with a Red Ribbon in her Hair* (JH 979) and the *Woman with Loose Hair* (JH 972), in which he reveals himself as a late-nineteenth-century Rubens. But he also mocked academic and anatomical painting with his *Skull with a Burning Cigarette between the Teeth* (JH 999; see p. 24). No other satirical works are known to have been painted by Van Gogh.

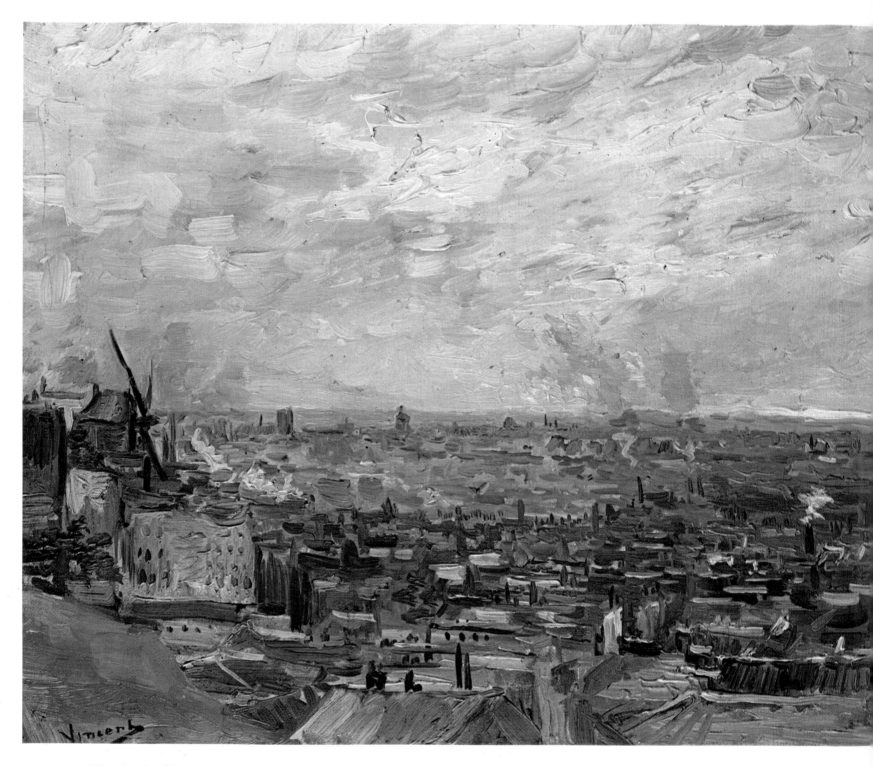

The Roofs of Paris
Paris, April-June 1886
F262 JH1102
Canvas, 38.5 x 61.5 cm
Basel, Öffentliche Kunstsammlung,
Kunstmuseum

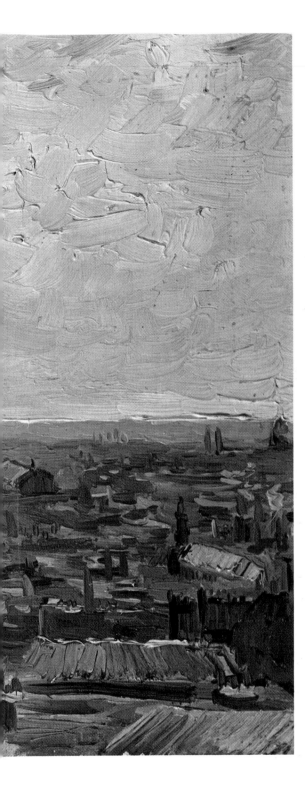

Chapter III
A light palette
Paris

At the beginning of March 1886, Van Gogh took the night train from Antwerp to Paris, where he arrived in the morning at the Gare du Nord. It is typical of his impulsive character that he did not warn Theo in advance of his arrival. At the railway station in Paris he wrote his brother a brief note in black chalk on a scrap of paper (459): 'My dear Theo: Don't be angry at my turning up so unexpectedly. I've been thinking about it for a long time, and I believe that we'll gain time like this. I'll be in the Louvre just after midday, or earlier if you like. Please reply and let me know what time you can come to the Salle Carrée. As far as money is concerned, I'll say again it doesn't make much difference. Anyway, I obviously still have some money - and I want to talk to you before I spend anything. We'll come to an arrangement, you'll see. So come as early as you can.'

Van Gogh had the message delivered to Theo by a porter at his place of work, 19 boulevard Montmartre, the branch of the art dealer, Goupil, of which Theo was the director. It was characteristic of Van Gogh to choose the Louvre as a meeting place. He was an enthusiastic visitor of museums, and he was familiar with the Louvre from his earlier stay in Paris.

At that time Theo was still living in a small apartment at 25 rue de Laval (now the rue Victor Massé) in the 9th *arrondissement*, close to the place Pigalle. Van Gogh moved in with him, but he did not have his own studio. The situation improved considerably in June, when Theo moved to a larger apartment close by at 54 rue Lepic, where Van Gogh had his own work room. The house can still be seen, situated at the bottom of the Butte or hill of Montmartre, to the west of the place du Tertre and the Sacré-Coeur, which was still being built in 1886. There is a commemorative plaque on the front of the house which tells us that Theo and his brother lived there between 1886 and 1888. Van Gogh painted a view of Paris from his window (now in the Van Gogh Museum in Amsterdam), as well as *The Roofs of Paris* (JH 1102; see p. 26/7), which is in the Art Museum in Basel.

During his stay in Paris, Van Gogh painted no fewer than twenty-eight self-portraits, including the *Self-portrait* illustrated here (JH 1249; see p. 29). He wrote that the reason he painted himself so often was because he had no money to pay models, but it remains a mystery why he never painted his brother Theo when they were living together.

He also painted a few nudes in Paris. *Reclining Nude* (JH 1212; see p. 30), reproduced here, is a beautiful image, but the three other nudes reflect more closely Van Gogh's preoccupation with realism. It is fascinating to compare these works with the numerous portraits of young girls that Renoir was painting at that period.

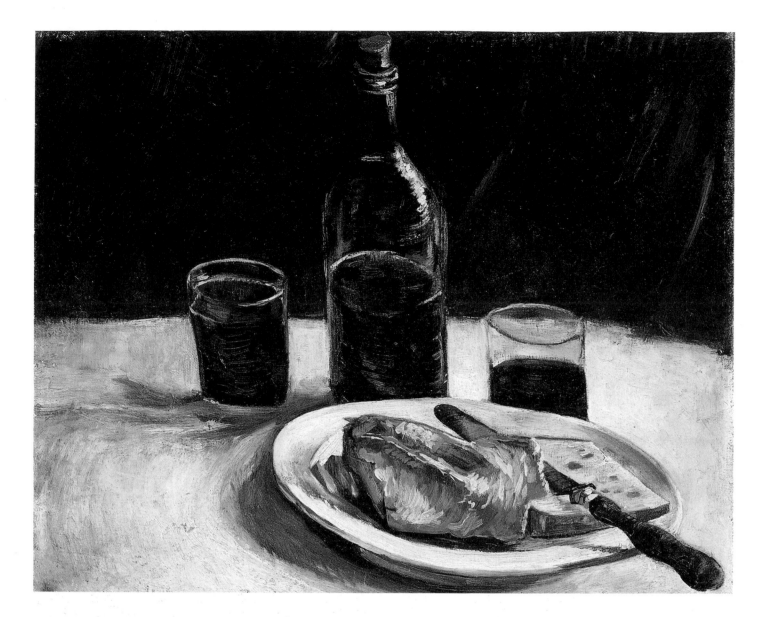

Still Life with Wine Bottle and Two Glasses
Paris, July-September 1886
F253 JH1121
Canvas, 37.5 x 46 cm
Amsterdam, Rijksmuseum
Vincent van Gogh

Van Gogh lived a very unhealthy life in Paris, drinking too much wine and absinthe. The *Still Life with Wine Bottle and Two Glasses* (JH 1121; see p. 28), like many of his still lifes, has a deeper symbolic meaning; it is a kind of self-portrait. This still life of an extremely frugal meal of bread and cheese can be seen as a counterpart to the seventeenth-century Dutch still lifes of food, a genre popularized by the work of the Haarlem painters, Willem Claesz Heda and Pieter Claesz.

A dream come true

Initially Van Gogh was very happy in Paris. In Antwerp he had dreamt of being able to work in this city, where he could meet other avant-garde painters, and where he could continue schooling himself in life drawing at the 'atelier libre' of Fernand Cormon at 4 boulevard de Clichy. Now this dream had come true. He had visited Paris three times before his arrival in March 1886: very briefly in May 1873, on his way to London; then in the autumn of 1874, when he was working at the Parisian branch of the art dealer, Goupil; and finally, a further ten months, again employed by Goupil, from 15 May 1875 to 1 April 1876. During this time he learned to speak French well, just as he had mastered the English language in the months he spent in England. It is surprising that Van

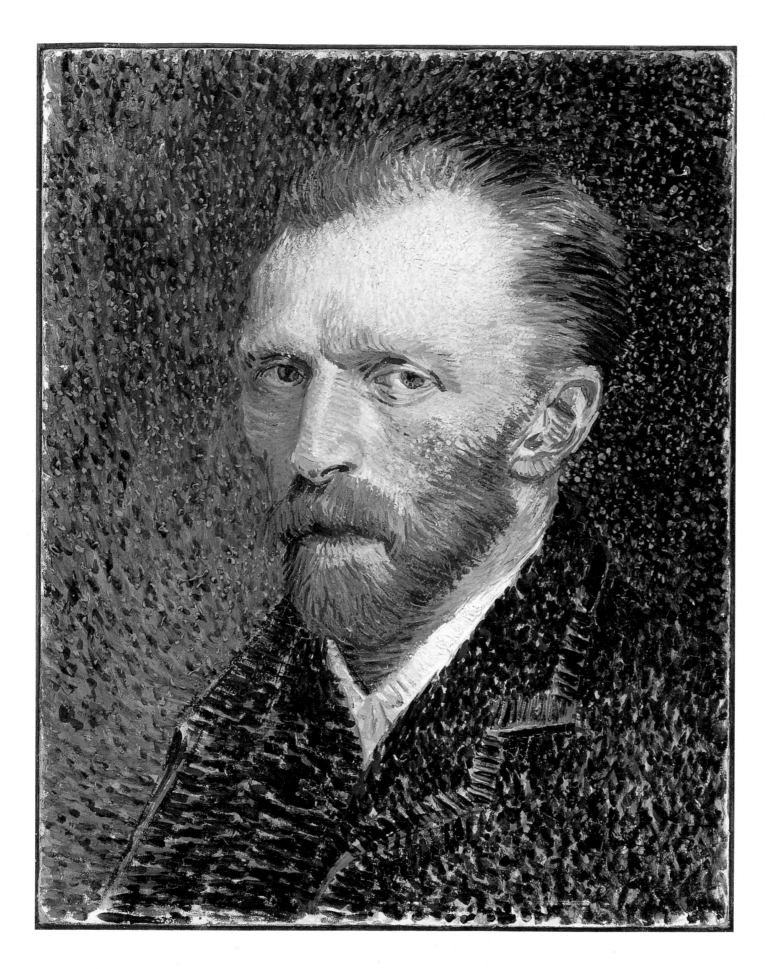

Self-portrait, Paris, April-June 1887
F345 JH1249 - Cardboard mounted on panel, 41 x 32.5 cm
Chicago, The Art Institute, The Joseph Winterbotham Collection

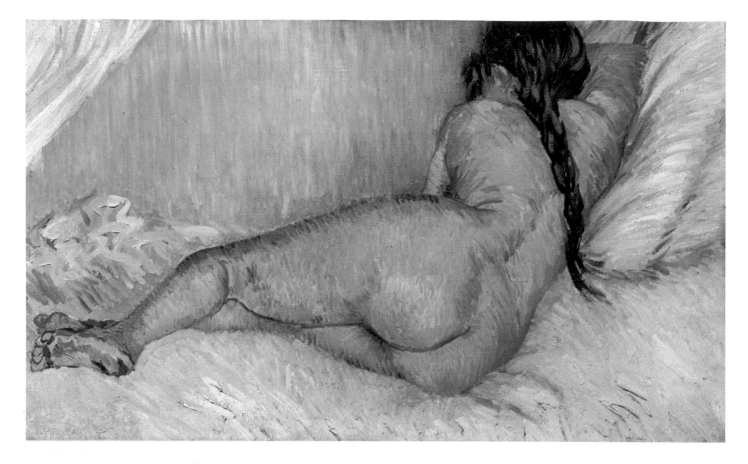

Reclining Nude, seen from the Back
Paris, January-March 1887
F328 JH1212
Canvas, 38 x 61 cm
Paris, private collection

Gogh was so good at languages after only a few years of secondary schooling; moreover, his many French letters bear witness to a great talent for expression, so not only are they of enormous documentary value to art history, but they also form a significant literary contribution.

Van Gogh's wanderings around Paris as a painter and sketcher were mainly restricted to the north-western parts of the city: Montmartre, Clichy and Asnières. He was not interested in the tourist sights, or the great monuments. He liked to visit museums such as the Louvre and the Luxembourg, which he also painted. He was fascinated by views of the city, especially the banks of the Seine, as revealed by the painting of *Fishing in Spring, Two Boats near a Bridge across the Seine* (JH 1270; see p. 32/3). An Impressionist work in green and blue with sudden touches of pink and red, it bears a resemblance to a painting by Claude Monet of fishermen on the Seine at Poissy.

He was also fascinated by the thirty-mile-long city walls around Paris, which had been built in about 1843 for defence, but which had failed in the Franco-Prussian War of 1870, when the city was bombarded. About seventeen years later, at the time when Van Gogh was painting there, many people wished to pull down these walls with their bastions and forts, especially as they stood in the way of the expansion of the city. Van Gogh painted a watercolour of the city walls: *The Ramparts of Paris near Port de Clichy* (JH 1281; see p. 34). Under a bright blue sky a block of houses sticks up just above the city ramparts; a lady is going for a walk carrying a parasol. He also did a drawing of a couple walking in front of the city walls which he did not complete as a watercolour. (The Metro station, Porte de Clichy, on the boulevard Berthier, is now roughly at this point.)

Agostina Segatori, the 'beautiful Italian' who owned the café Le Tambourin at 62 boulevard de Clichy, was a good friend of Van Gogh's, and was possibly his mistress during this Parisian period. He often ate at the café, and would pay his bills with paintings, sometimes two or three a week, especially still lifes of flowers. In this painting of her, *Agostina Segatori in her Café du Tambourin* (JH 1208; see p. 36), the Japanese prints from his own collection can be seen in the background. Agostina, who had sat in the past for famous painters such as Corot and Gérome, is shown here in a pensive mood, sitting at a tambourine-shaped table, with a glass of beer and a cigarette in her right hand. The red edge of the table is the complementary colour to the surrounding green, a typical Van Gogh effect. This theme of a woman sitting at a table in a café was also a favourite subject of the Impressionists, Manet and Degas, and later Toulouse-Lautrec.

Another striking portrait of a woman, *Lady, Sitting by a Cradle* (JH 1206; see p. 37), dates from the same period as the painting of La Segatori, the spring of 1887. This is reminiscent of *The Cradle* (Musée d'Orsay, Paris), a beautiful painting which had been completed fifteen years earlier by the Impressionist painter Berthe Morisot, Manet's sister-in-law.

Van Gogh's portrait of the young mother and her son - there is a blue ribbon hanging on the cradle - shows Léonie Rose Davy-Charbuy, the niece of an art dealer who was one of Van Gogh's friends. He felt attracted to this subject because he hoped to be a father himself one day, a blessing which was to come Theo's way in 1890.

What did Van Gogh look like in those days ? The answer to this question can be seen in the *Self-portrait with Grey Felt Hat* (JH 1353; see p. 39), or at least this is how he saw himself, for a better likeness was probably painted in 1886 by John P. Russell, an Australian friend, a portrait which can be seen in Amsterdam. The *Self-portrait with Grey Felt Hat* was painted in the Pointillist style, though Van Gogh used dashes rather than dots. Like several of his self-portraits, this work was executed in the complementary colours of blue (for the background) and orange (for his reddish beard). In this work he reveals himself as an extremely self-conscious character with a penetrating gaze. For its time it was a very daring painting in a style which must have been shocking to many art lovers.

Parisian life

Near his home in Montmartre, Van Gogh painted *The Moulin de la Galette* (JH 1170; see p. 38). The name is shown indistinctly on the mill under the roof. It is also shown over the door of the café which was actually called Le Radet. For the mill no longer worked as such, but was a place to relax and dance. This was quite clear from the famous painting with the same title which Renoir had painted ten years earlier in 1876 (Musée d'Orsay, Paris), and also from a painting by Toulouse-Lautrec of 1889, *Au Bal du Moulin de la Galette* (Art Institute of Chicago).

In painting this subject, Van Gogh restricted himself to the outside of the building, which he saw as a picturesque element, while Renoir showed the festivities inside. In Van Gogh's time, Montmartre still had the atmosphere of a village on the edge of Paris. This Montmartre, where Clemenceau, who later became prime minister, had been the mayor for a short while in 1870, was a hillside of mills and kitchen gardens, which Van Gogh painted a number of times as rural landscapes.

The Moulin de la Galette is a realistic painting, which is evident from a comparison with a photograph dating from that time. It was painted with

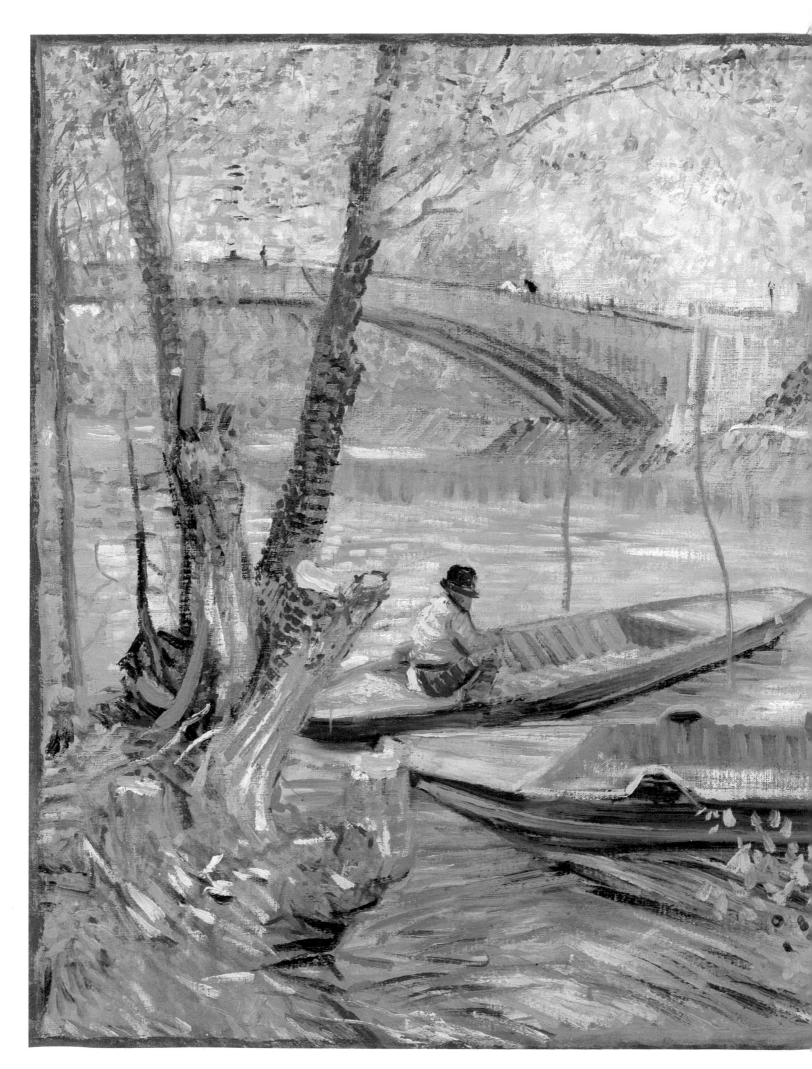

*Fishing in Spring, Two Boats near a
Bridge across the Seine*
Paris, April-June 1887
F354 JH1270
Canvas, 50.5 x 60 cm
Chicago, The Art Institute,
Gift of Charles Deering
McCormick, Brooks McCormick
and Roger McCormick

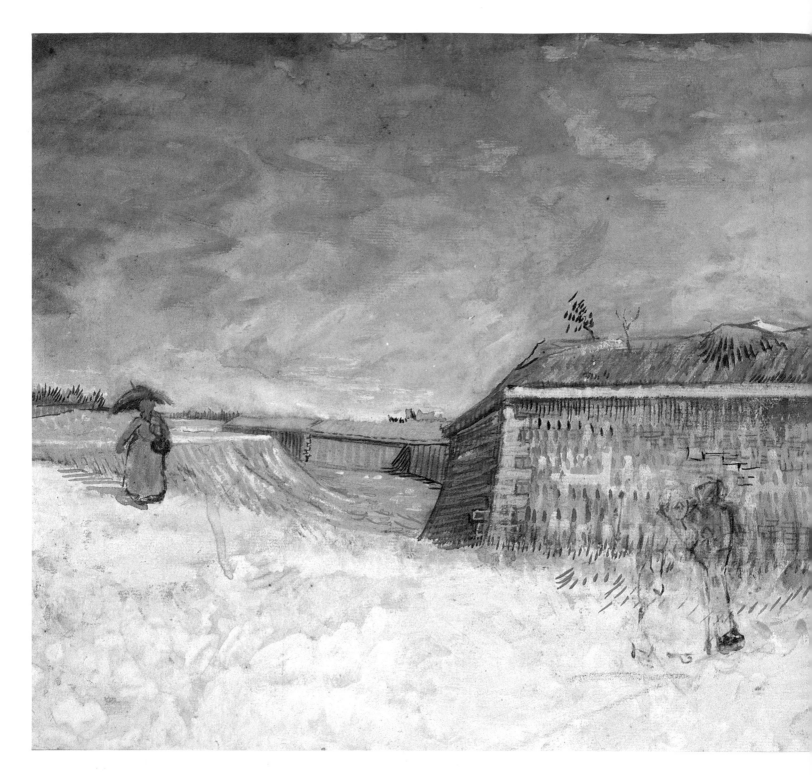

The Ramparts of Paris near Porte de
Clichy
Paris, July-September 1887
F1402 JH1281
Watercolour, 39.5 x 53.5 cm
Manchester, Whitworth Art
Gallery, University of Manchester

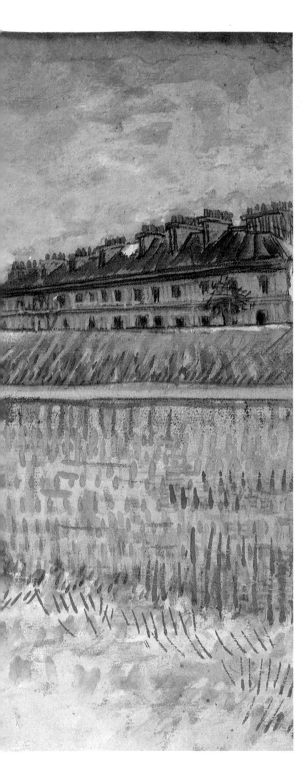

a fairly dark palette, like his work from the Nuenen period, with strong brush strokes in reddish and yellowish brown. In contrast, another painting of a mill on Montmartre, *Le Blute-fin* (JH 1221; Carnegie Museum of Art, Pittsburgh), is predominantly green and blue, in the style of Corot and other Barbizon painters.

Although he depicted social life in a different way from his Impressionist friends, Renoir, Degas, Monet and Toulouse-Lautrec, Van Gogh did experiment with Impressionism in the *Restaurant de la Siréne at Asnières* (JH 1251, see p. 40/41) in the summer of 1887. The restaurant was situated at 7 boulevard de la Seine, near the Pont d'Asnières. The owner was Louis Paté, who specialized in wedding banquets, according to an inscription in the painting. It is strange that Van Gogh only came across Impressionism when he arrived in Paris in 1886, although the movement was in full swing when he visited the city in 1875 and 1876. The important series of annual Impressionist exhibitions, which had started in 1874 with Monet, Pissarro, Sisley, Renoir, Cézanne and Degas, had just ended in 1886 with an exhibition to which Monet, Sisley and Renoir refused to contribute. By this time a new school had developed - Neo-Impressionism, with protagonists such as Seurat and Signac.

What is Impressionism?

A good description of Impressionism is given in a letter written by Camille Pissarro (1830-1903):

'You must paint with small brush strokes, and directly put down what is observed. The eye should not concentrate on a particular point, but should be able to survey everything, and at the same time observe the reflection of the colours on the surrounding area. It is a matter of working simultaneously on the sky, water, the branches of a tree and the ground ... and returning to these constantly so that it is captured ... The first time the whole canvas should be covered and then go on until there is nothing to add. In doing this, aim for a perfect atmosphere both in the foreground and in the horizon, and the reflection of the sky and leaves ... Never be afraid of colour, and elaborate the painting slowly: do not follow rules and principles, but paint what you see or feel. Paint generously, without hesitation, the first impression should never be lost ... Nature is our teacher.' (Horst Keller, *The Art of the Impressionists*, 1975)

Van Gogh was an admirer of Camille Corot (1796-1875), like Pissarro, who had actually taken lessons from this important painter of the Barbizon School. Later Pissarro was one of the teachers of Paul Cézanne, who in turn influenced Pablo Picasso. In this way a line can be drawn between nineteenth- and twentieth-century art.

Lighter colours

Soon after his arrival in Paris, Van Gogh put away his sombre Nuenen palette and started painting in much lighter colours, influenced by typical Impressionists such as Monet. But, even during the Nuenen period he had explored the techniques of colour, and now he started experimenting with them. Following the example of some of the Impressionists, he used the three primary colours - red, blue and yellow - with the three secondary colours, which are created by mixing two primary colours - purple (a mixture of red and blue), green (blue and yellow), and orange (red and

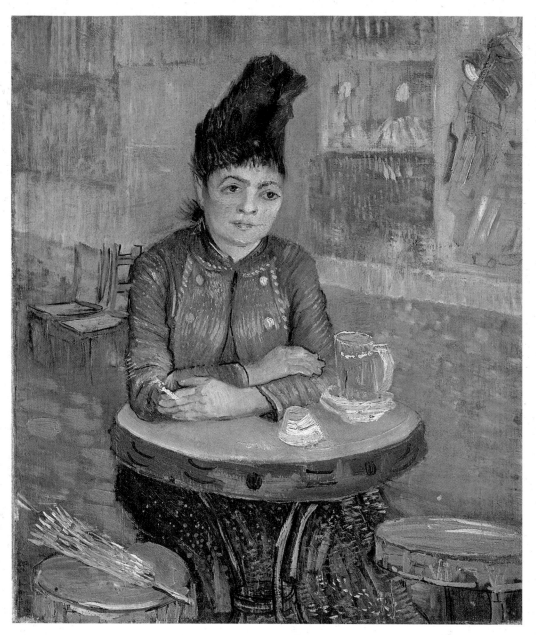

Lady, Sitting by a Cradle
Paris, January-March 1887
F369 JH1206
Canvas, 61 x 46 cm
Amsterdam, Rijksmuseum
Vincent van Gogh

Agostina Segatori in her Café du Tambourin
Paris, January-March 1887
F370 JH1208
Canvas, 55.5 x 46.5 cm
Amsterdam, Rijksmuseum
Vincent van Gogh

yellow). He used these six colours in a pure unmixed form, where possible. In addition, he heightened the effect of these colours by juxtaposing them with their complementary colours: red and green, blue and orange, yellow and purple. Under the influence of Signac, Van Gogh used these pure colours in his Pointillist paintings.

The painting *Restaurant de la Sirène at Asnières* is a good example of the use of these pure colours in complementary contrast. The red of the wall to the far right contrasts strongly with the green of the ivy next to it, a colour combination used elsewhere. A combination of blue and orange tones is used on the gallery of the first floor. Van Gogh matched vibrancy of colour with a compositional energy created by his use of vertical and horizontal lines. The effect of the whole is festive and lively.

Van Gogh painted this work in the bright summer light of 1887. In the summer of the previous year he had already started playing with pure and complementary colours, placing flowers in vases in such a way that the pure colours produced striking contrasts (459a): 'As I was painting, I have done a series of colour studies of simple flowers, red poppies, blue cornflowers and forget-me-nots, white and red roses, yellow chrysanthemums, and in doing so I was looking for the contrast between blue and orange,

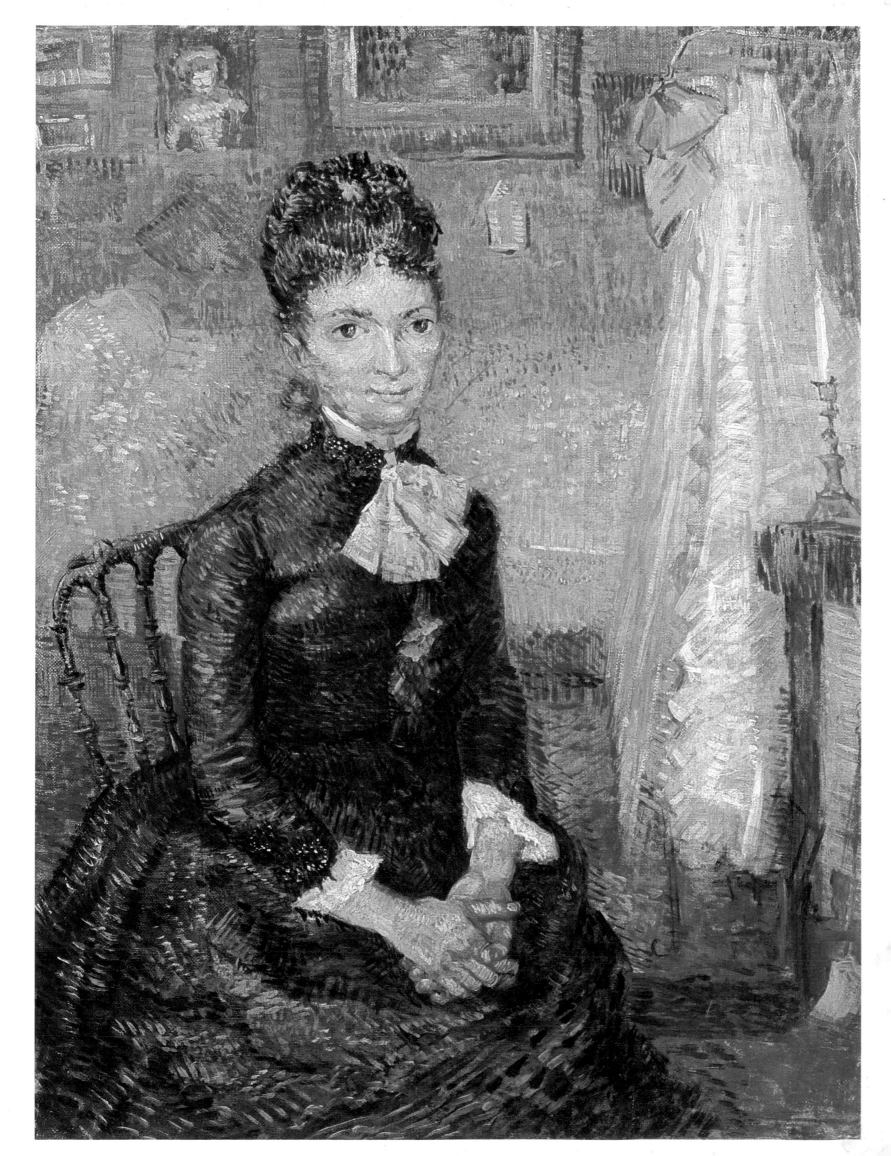

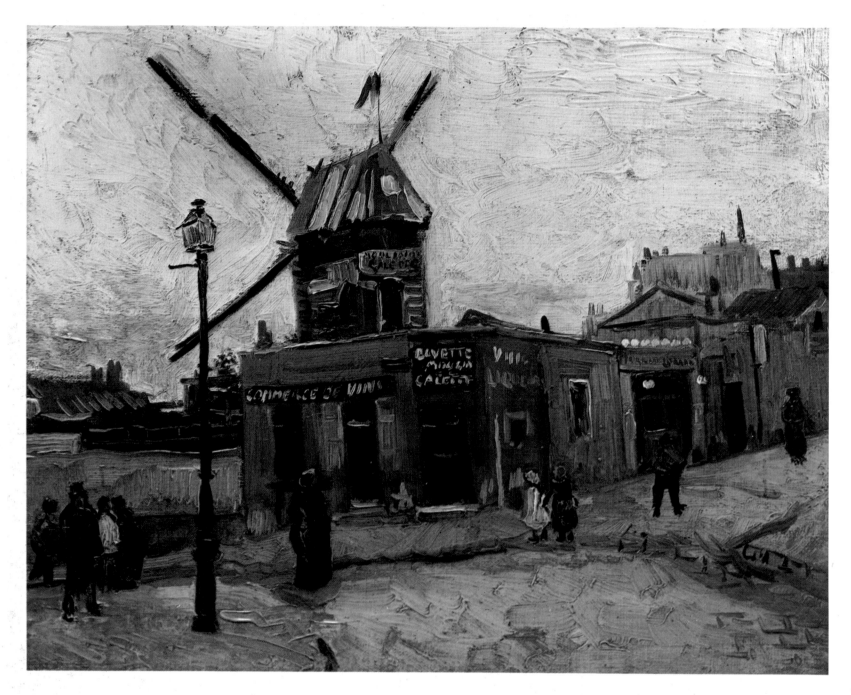

The Moulin de la Galette
Paris, October-December 1886
F227 JH1170
Canvas, 38.5 x 46 cm
Otterlo, Rijksmuseum
Kröller-Müller

Self-portrait with Grey Felt Hat
Paris, winter 1887-1888
F344 JH1353
Canvas, 44 x 37.5 cm
Amsterdam, Rijksmuseum
Vincent van Gogh

red and green, yellow and violet. I was looking for broken colours and neutral tones to create a harmony between the most striking extremes. I wanted to produce powerful colours rather than a greyish harmony.' Then he added: 'In this way I am battling for life and for progress in art.'

This is an excerpt from a letter, written in English, to his friend, the painter H.M. Livens. He also expressed his admiration for Delacroix's exuberant use of colour, and also for the work of Degas and Monet - 'Even though I don't belong to that club.'

Painter of flowers

Renoir and Fantin-Latour were painting still lifes of flowers during this period, but Van Gogh chose to follow the example of the shiny, thickly painted works of Adolphe Monticelli (1824-1886), who was greatly admired both by Van Gogh and his brother, Theo. (Sometimes it is difficult to understand Van Gogh's admiration for certain minor masters, such as the romantic French-Dutchman, Ary Scheffer.)

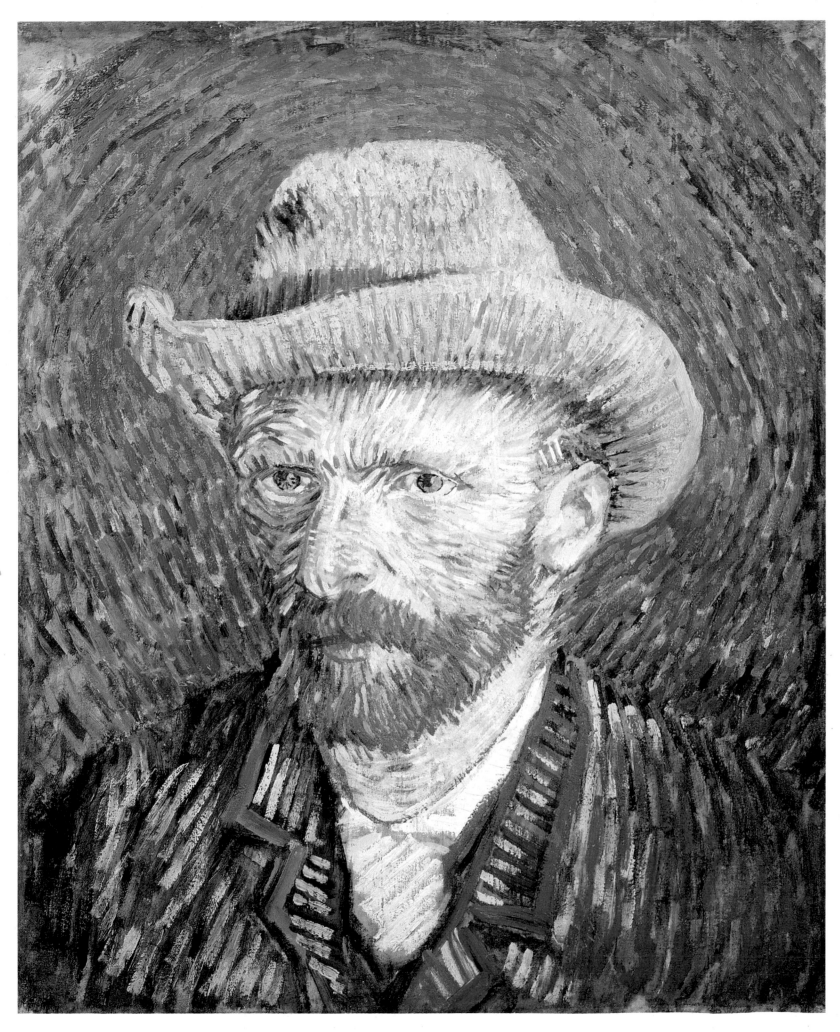

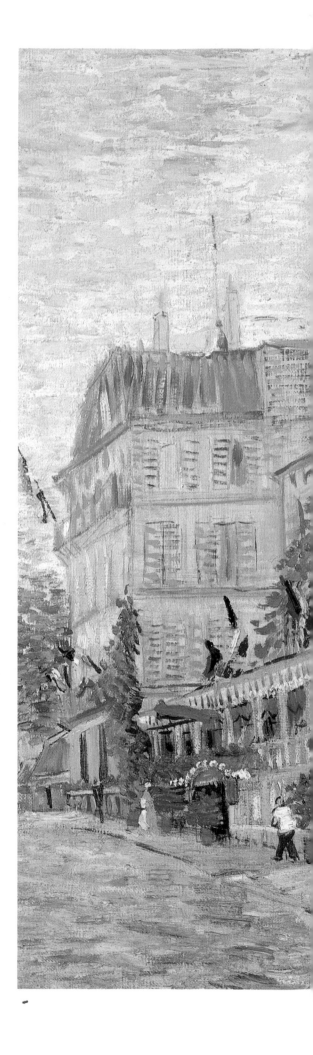

Restaurant de la Sirène at Asnières
Paris, April-June 1887
F313 JH1251
Canvas, 57 x 68 cm
Paris, Musée d'Orsay

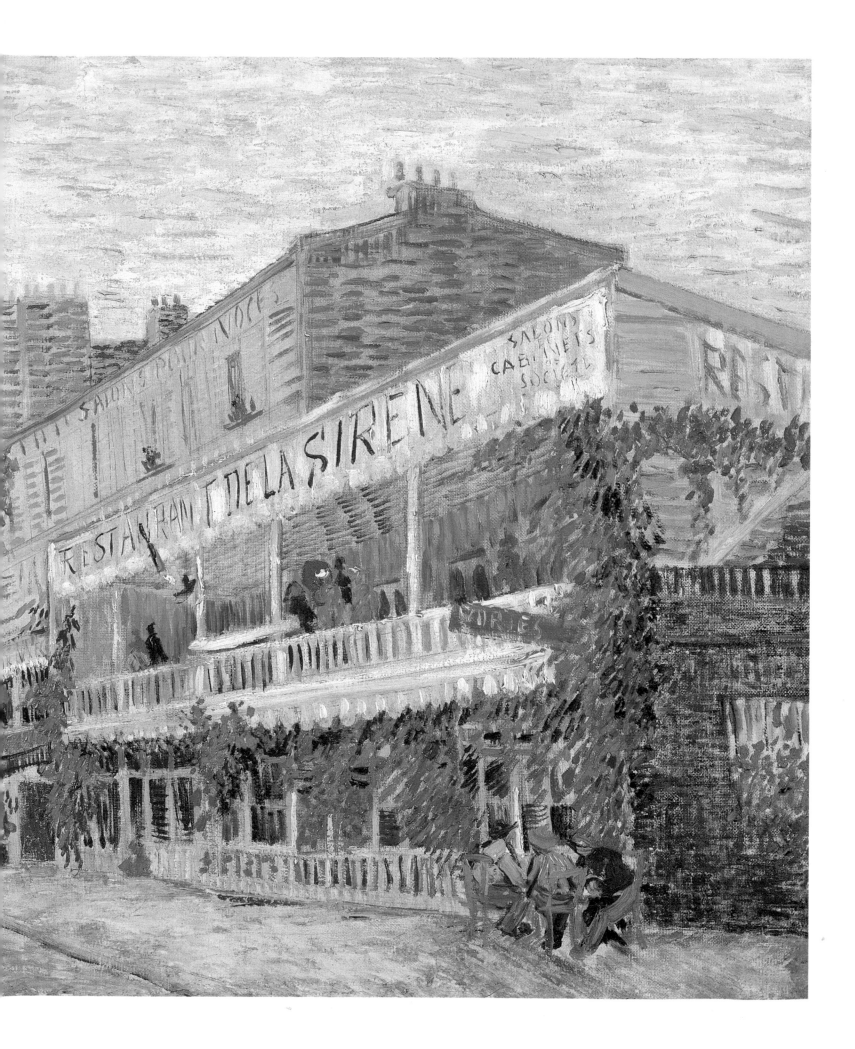

41

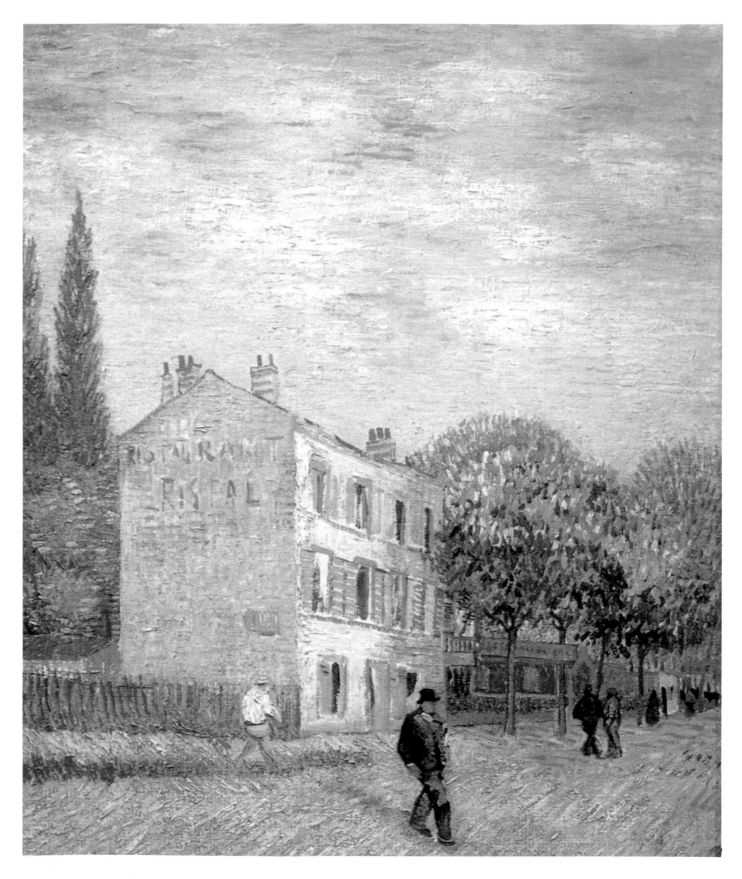

Restaurant Rispal at Asnières
Paris, April-June 1887
F355 JH1266
Canvas, 72 x 60 cm
Private collection

Another Impressionist painting of 1887 is the *Restaurant Rispal* (JH 1266; see p. 42), painted in Asnières. This work shows a restaurant which was situated at 117 boulevard de la Seine (now the Quai Aulagnier), near the Pont de Clichy, not far from the place where he painted *The Ramparts of Paris*. The name of the restaurant is shown in blue capital letters on the blind side wall of the restaurant. It is not exactly a picturesque scene, but Van Gogh succeeded in making an attractive painting of it.

Camille Pissarro, the Impressionist painter who became a friend of Van Gogh's at that time, met him once on the way to Asnières. Van Gogh laid out on the road all the canvasses that he was carrying with him for Pissarro's comments. He took no notice of the astonishment or irritation of passers-by, who were obliged to walk around the paintings exhibited in this way. Paul Signac described how he and Van Gogh had gone to Asnières together to paint. Van Gogh had argued for the entire duration of the walk, gesticulating with the still-wet canvasses so that he covered his own clothes and those of passers-by with paint.

In fact, Van Gogh was so passionate about his art that he neglected everything else, which often caused Theo a great deal of distress. 'He is so dirty and untidy that the household looks anything but attractive.' But no matter how much difficulty Theo had living with his brother, who seemed

Interior of a Restaurant
Paris, April-June 1887
F342 JH1256
Canvas, 45.5 x 56.5 cm
Otterlo, Rijksmuseum
Kröller-Müller

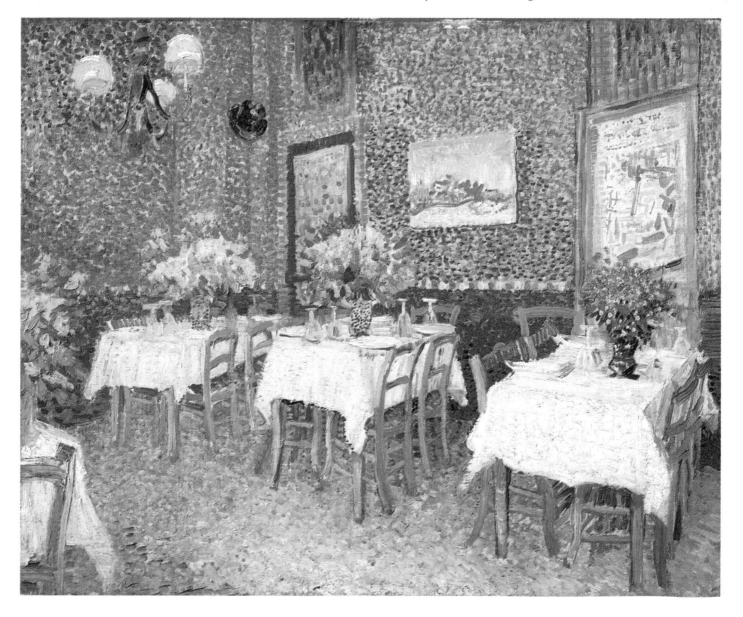

to be two people in one -'One marvellously cultured, fine and gentle; the other selfish and unfeeling' - Theo always believed in the talent of this socially impossible man. 'There is no doubt', he wrote to his sister Wil, 'that he is an artist. What he is doing now may not always be beautiful, but it will certainly stand him in good stead later on, and then it may well be sublime.'

A festive canvas

Van Gogh had painted the outside of the two restaurants in Asnières, La Sirène and Rispal, but in that summer of 1887 he also painted *Interior of a Restaurant* (JH 1256; see p. 43), possibly a room in one of these eating places. A careful examination of this light, charming and festive work, warmly inviting us to a convivial meal, reveals that it is an Impressionist work with a strongly Pointillist slant. It complements the two other paintings of restaurants, but in this work he combines the technique of colourful complementary dots of red and green, particularly in the wallpaper of the dining-room, with a more traditional style for the yellow tables and chairs. Yet, typical of Van Gogh, the room is empty, without any guests,

Edge of a Wheat Field with Poppies and a Lark
Paris, April-June 1887
F310 JH1274
Canvas, 54 x 64.5 cm
Amsterdam, Rijksmuseum
Vincent van Gogh

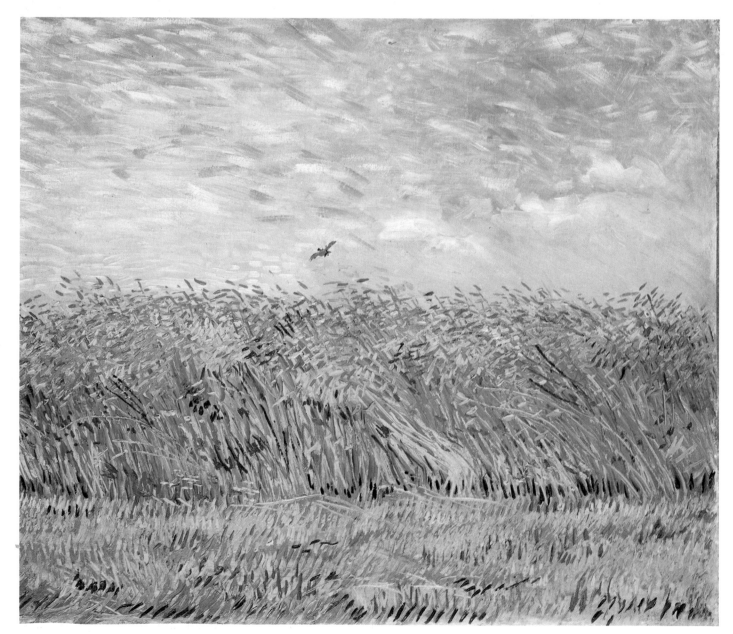

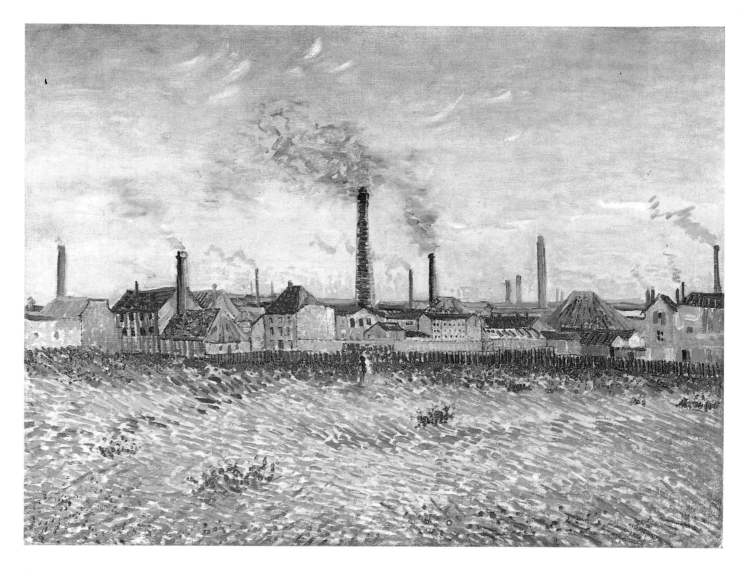

Factories at Asnières
Paris, July-September 1887
F317 JH1287
Canvas, 54 x 72 cm
St.Louis, The Art Museum,
Gift of Mrs Mark Steinberg

while paintings of restaurants by Edouard Manet, for example, are full of cheerful people dining well and chatting amicably. Later, in Arles, Van Gogh did paint a room with people, but the scene was a night café, the atmosphere melancholy.

Painter of town views

In Nuenen Van Gogh had been a painter of landscapes and peasant scenes, following the great example of the Barbizon artist François Millet, *le peintre paysan*. He now became a painter of towns, with an eye for modern industry. Just as his paintings in Nuenen smelled of 'bacon and steaming potatoes', this time his paintings were to smell of 'gas and coal', as Van Gogh's friend Emile Bernard remarked. *Factories at Asnières* (JH 1287; see p. 45) was one of the big surprises of the Van Gogh exhibition in the Musée d'Orsay, Paris, in 1988. The bright red roofs of the factory buildings, set against a greenish-blue sky sullied by dirty plumes of smoke from the tall chimneys, are very impressive. The image of intense environmental pollution is reinforced by the contrasting yellowish-green area of untouched ground in the foreground of the painting. However, Van Gogh's concerns were not with pollution. For him, this was an image of modern technology, industrial development, enterprise and employment, a painting reminiscent of his drawings from The Hague of a washhouse with gasometers.

Like Claude Monet, with his stations and trains, Van Gogh too was

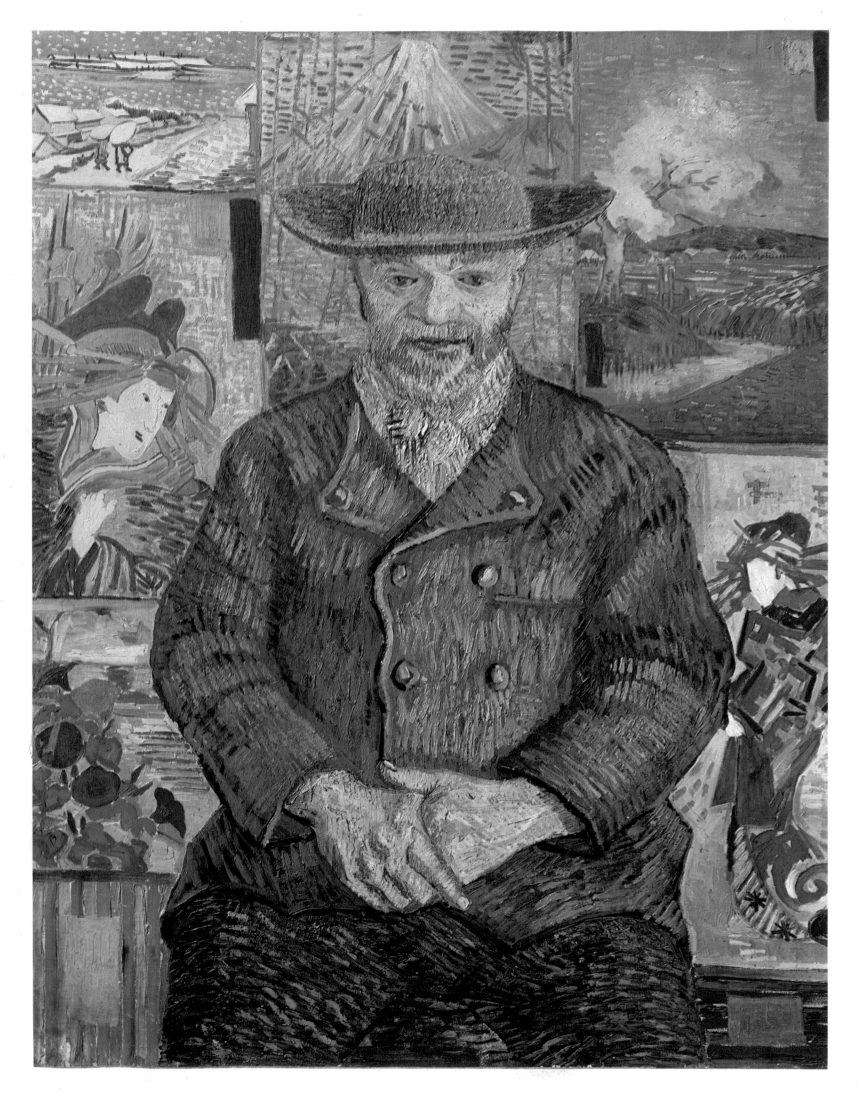

fascinated by the new technological inventions of his age, and he also had trains running through his paintings. However, in the same summer of 1887 in which he painted *Factories at Asnières*, he produced a surprising, purely pastoral canvas: *Edge of a Wheat Field with Poppies and a Lark* (JH 1274; see p. 44), a subject he was to paint later whilst travelling around Arles and Auvers. This cheerful, fresh and lively work contrasts sharply with one of his last paintings, *Wheat Field under Threatening Skies with Crows* (JH 2117; see p. 194/195), which is so sombre, threatening and ominous that it seems to anticipate Van Gogh's imminent suicide attempt.

This canvas by Van Gogh dates from the summer of 1887, but a year earlier, in the summer of 1886, Charles Angrand (1854-1926) had painted similar views to this wheat field, and to the factories in Clichy with the empty fields in the foreground. Van Gogh must have seen these paintings at the Salon des Indépendents in Paris in the autumn of 1886. During this period he also met Angrand - they both bought their artists' materials from Père Tanguy, a shopkeeper who was a good friend to many avant-garde painters. Occasionally Van Gogh paid him with a painting. In this way Tanguy acquired the *Irises* (sold by Sotheby's, New York, in November 1987 for the record sum of $ 53.9 million).

Père Tanguy

The *Portrait of Père Tanguy* (JH 1351; see p. 46) was owned by the sculptor, Auguste Rodin, who bought it from the Tanguy heirs. Van Gogh painted it in pure colours: unmixed paints, straight from the tube. At the bottom of the work he used the complementary colours of orange and blue, which he also used in his self-portraits, while in the top half red and green are used to reinforce each other. Traditionally, portrait photographs use a neutral, quiet background with little depth. Van Gogh did quite the opposite - he used a very colourful background with bright colours and sharp images. Tanguy is shown against a wall covered with Japanese prints, which undoubtedly came from Van Gogh's collection. The picture of a Japanese woman (bottom right) is taken from a print by Kesai Eisen: *The Courtesan*. He had already done a separate painting of this subject in the summer of 1887, *Japonaiserie: Oiron* (JH 1298), which is now in the Van Gogh Museum in Amsterdam.

Tanguy was very pleased with his portrait. When anyone asked him what he would sell it for, he replied: 'Five hundred francs'. When told that this was rather an exorbitant sum, he would answer: 'I really don't want to sell my portrait at all.'

This is not Van Gogh's only portrait of Tanguy. A second bears a great resemblance to that now in the Musée Rodin in Paris, and shows the same background of Japanese prints. There is also a portrait of Tanguy drawn in pencil on the back of a menu from the Restaurant du Chalet on the avenue de Clichy, which Van Gogh called the 'Petit Boulevard'. At the end of 1887 he exhibited his work in this restaurant, together with the work of other painters of the Petit Boulevard, a group which included his 'copains': Emile Bernard, Paul Gauguin, Paul Signac, Louis Anquetin and Henri de Toulouse-Lautrec. (Van Gogh considered the painters of the Grand Boulevard - the boulevard Montmartre - to be Monet, Sisley, Renoir and Degas. These are the painters whose works were exhibited by Theo. During the period 1886-1888 alone, Theo sold twenty paintings by Monet, and seven by Sisley, but not one by his brother, Vincent.)

Portrait of Père Tanguy
Paris, winter 1887-1888
F363 JH1351
Canvas, 92 x 75 cm
Paris, Musée Rodin

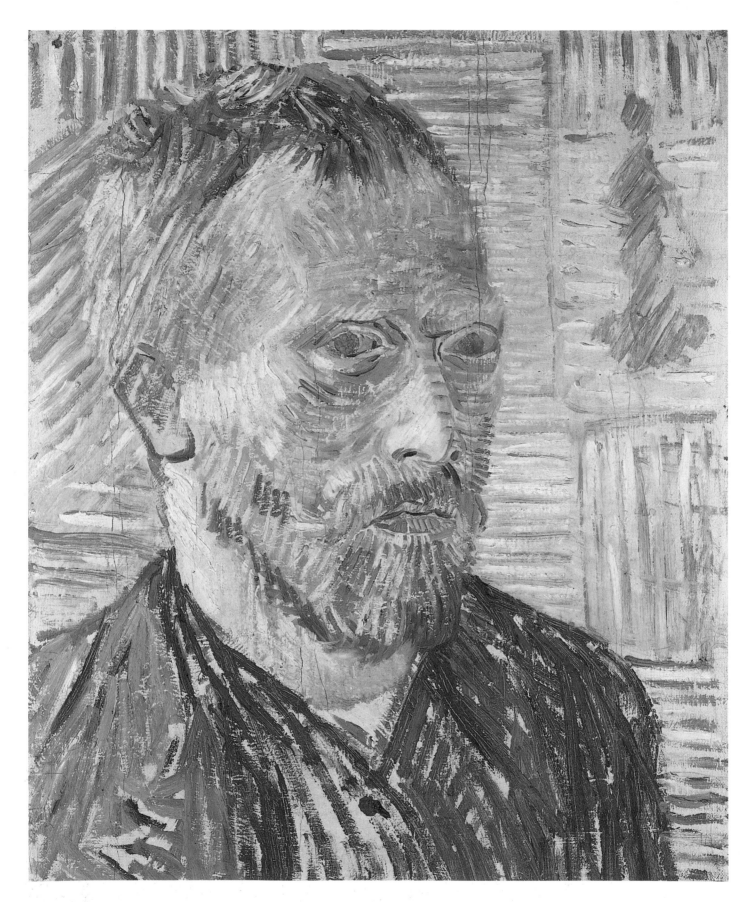

Self-portrait
Paris, October-December 1887
F319 JH1333
Canvas, 44 x 35 cm
Basel, Kunstmuseum,
Dr Emile Dreyfus Foundation

Japonaiserie: Bridge in the Rain
(after Hiroshige)
Paris, July-September 1887
F372 JH1297 - Canvas, 73 x 54 cm
Amsterdam, Rijksmuseum
Vincent van Gogh

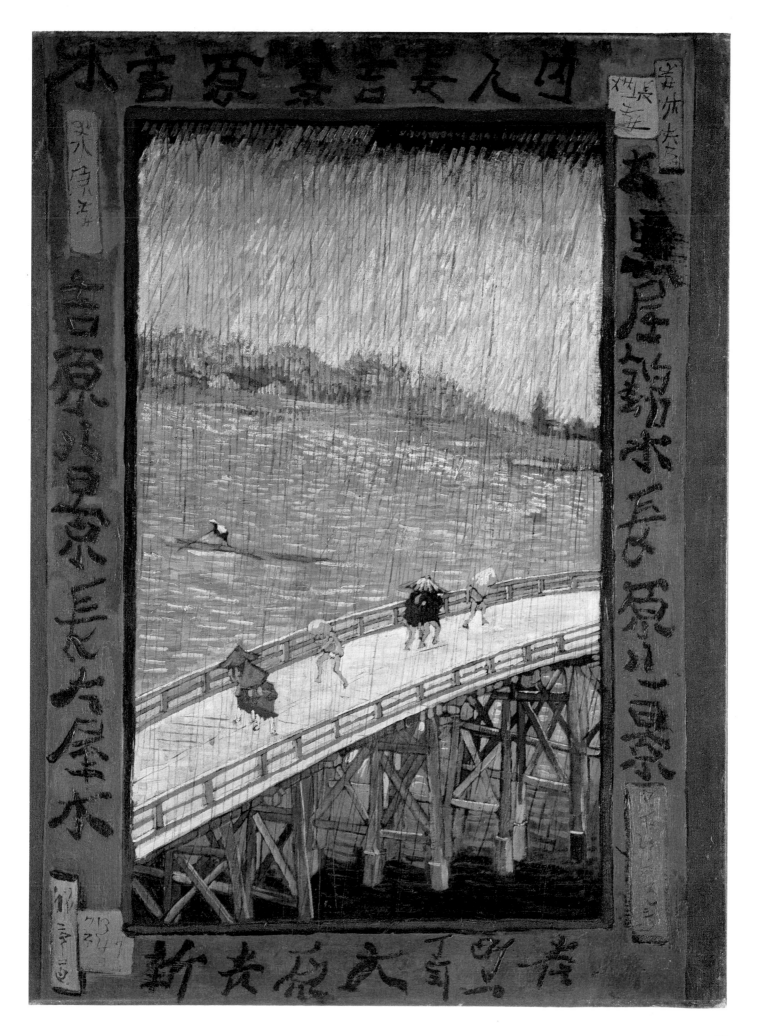

49

Japonaiserie

Van Gogh started collecting Japanese prints when in Antwerp, and he went on collecting them in Paris. (The collection of about 400 prints is now in the Vincent Van Gogh Museum in Amsterdam.) Like Monet and other painters, he was strongly attracted by this art form, often buying prints from the Parisian dealer in Japanese art, Siegfried Bing, for less than fifteen centimes each. Japanese prints can be seen in paintings by Edouard Manet, dating from as early as the 1860s and 1870s. The interest in this linear style, with its plain blocks of colour and strongly contrasting colours, had been stimulated by the authors Jules and Edmond de Goncourt.

At the end of 1887 Van Gogh painted a *Self-portrait* (JH 1333; see p. 48) in the style of a Japanese print. In this work he anticipated the Fauvist movement, which included such artists as Henry Matisse, Raoul Dufy and Maurice de Vlaminck. Van Gogh's painting is composed entirely of lines in complementary colours: orange for the beard, moustache and sideburns; blue for the jacket. The background of horizontal, vertical and diagonal rectangles creates a more measured atmosphere than the restless, colourful background in the portrait of Tanguy. However, the most striking feature of this painting is that of the artist's empty green eyes, like those of a blind man; his other self-portraits, in contrast, always reveal a penetrating gaze, the eyes of an artist critically observing his surroundings.

The *Bridge in the Rain* (JH 1297; see p. 49) after the nineteenth-century Japanese artist Hiroshige, is a genuine work of Japonaiserie. It is an accurate copy of a coloured woodcut or *crépon*, which Van Gogh owned. He wanted to copy the original exactly so he traced the outlines on transparent paper. Then he divided the drawing into squares to enlarge the picture to approximately 75 x 50 cm. It is strange that he took such pains over an imitation. Clearly he was so fascinated by the two-dimensional style of contrasting pure colours that he wished to master it for himself.

The painting in the Van Gogh Museum in Amsterdam is framed by complementary colours of green and red, and decorated with Japanese characters. The yellow of the bridge looks splendid against the green of the sea, and the deliberate lack of perspective brings out the blue background of the rain clouds even more strongly. The painting may be compared with the original print which is also in the Van Gogh Museum in Amsterdam. The lively figures either walking quickly to escape the rain, or sheltering under an umbrella, have a humorous quality.

Still slightly influenced by the Japanese style is a portrait of *The Italian Woman* (JH 1355; see p. 51), which Van Gogh also painted at the end of 1887. It is similar to the portrait of Père Tanguy from the same period, but this time a plain reddish-yellow background was used, and the painting is almost two-dimensional, without any depth. The portrait is outlined halfway round only, at the top and on the right-hand side, with vertical and horizontal lines in complementary colours of red and green, alternating with yellow. Some people have recognized La Segatori in this portrait, but by the time the painting was completed, Van Gogh had already broken off his relationship with Agostina.

Sunflowers

The sunflower was one of Van Gogh's favourite flowers. In fact, it has become a symbol of his art. This painting of *Four Cut Sunflowers* (JH 1330;

The Italian Woman: La Segatori(?)
Paris, winter 1887-1888
F381 JH1355
Canvas, 81 x 60 cm
Paris, Musée d'Orsay

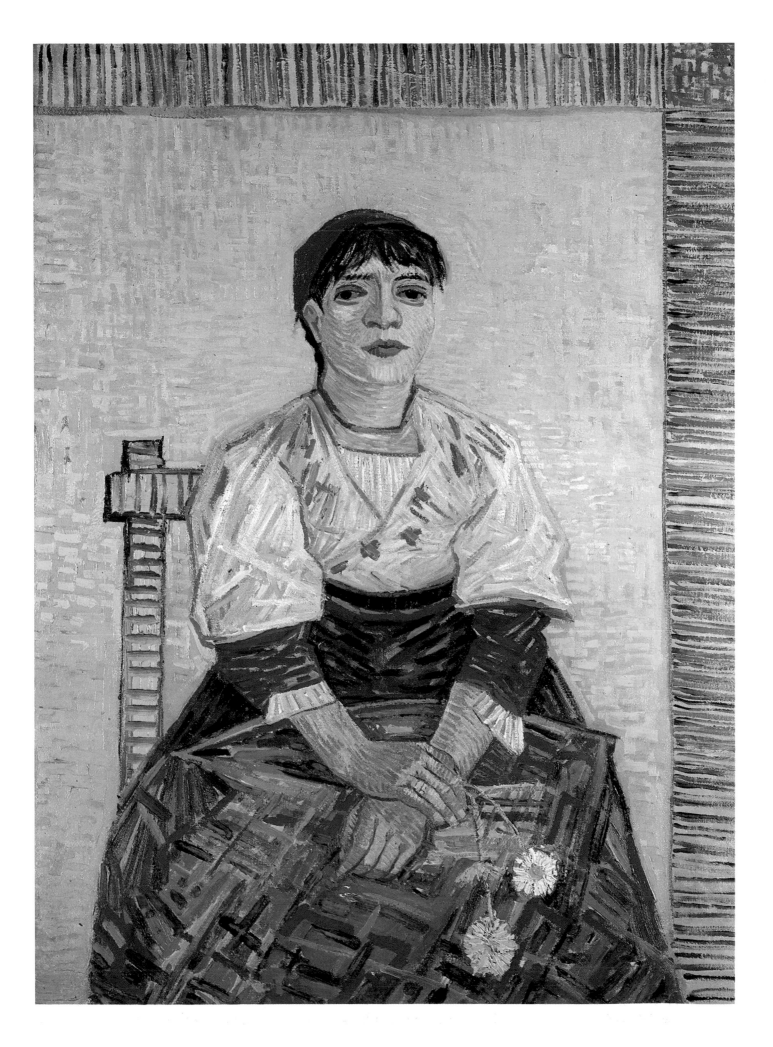

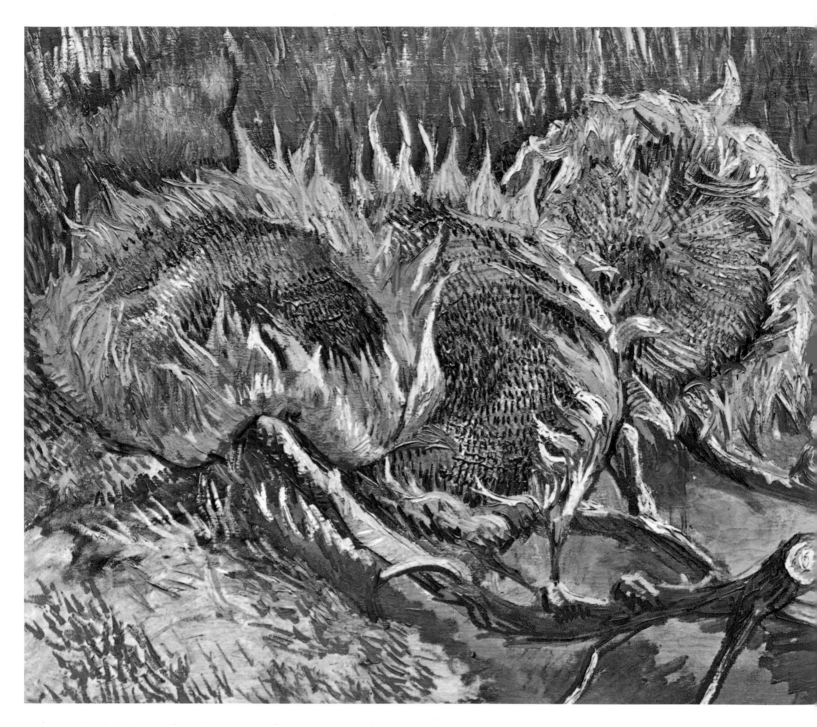

Four Cut Sunflowers
Paris, July-September 1887
F452 JH1330
Canvas, 60 x 100 cm
Otterlo, Rijksmuseum
Kröller-Müller

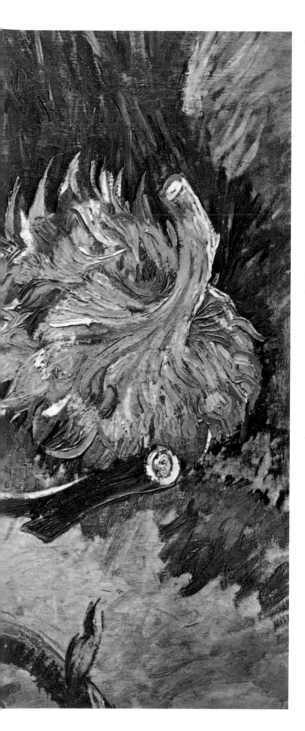

see p. 52/3), which he painted in Paris, anticipates a theme which was to play a dominant role in Arles a year later. Powerful use is made of the three complementary colour combinations: blue and orange; red and green; and yellow and purple. It is no longer an Impressionist painting, but has moved on to Symbolism. This will be discussed in more detail in the description of the sunflower paintings from Arles (see p. 121).

Van Gogh's four paintings of cut sunflowers were done at a time when he was also working on a large number of landscapes and still lifes of fruit, as well as self-portraits. The last self-portrait from the Paris period is *Self-portrait in Front of the Easel* (JH 1356; see p. 55), which shows Van Gogh at work in February 1888, just before he left for Arles. The colours on the palette and in the paint brushes are the ones shown in the portrait. He shows us not only what he looked like, but also how this likeness was achieved: with lines of pure, unmixed colour, and the contrasting tones of orange and blue - used for his artist's smock, coat and beard - that are so characteristic of his self-portraits. In painting his hair, mouth and eyes, as well as the actual palette, he used red contrasting with green.

Vincent

It is exceptional that he noted the year in which the painting was made: '88', underneath his signature. This provocative signature, orange on a yellow background, states simply 'Vincent', for in Paris, as afterwards, he only signed his work with his Christian name. There could be at least two reasons for this. For Frenchmen the name 'Van Gogh' is unpronounceable and sounds very foreign, but there are no problems with 'Vincent'. Then there could also be a psychological reason, as Vincent did not feel very much like a Van Gogh. He had often been a problem to his father - though his father cared a great deal about him - and in addition, his uncle, the art dealer Cor Van Gogh, had not been very friendly towards him. He sometimes felt too dependent on his brother Theo, who was so infinitely patient with him, although he was particularly fond of his youngest sister Willemien, to whom he wrote twenty-two long letters in the last four years of his life.

Self-portraits

It was to Wil that he wrote of his self-portraits: 'In my view, one person can provide material for extremely diverse portraits'. He then wrote to his 'dear sister' about 'a portrait which I painted from a mirror, and which Theo has ... a pinky grey face with green eyes, ash-grey hair, a wrinkled forehead, and with a bright red beard surrounding the stiff wooden mouth, rather unkempt and sad, but with full lips, a blue coarse linen smock, and a palette of lemon yellow, vermilion, Veronese green, cobalt blue, in fact all the colours on the palette except the orange beard, the only pure colours. The figure is shown against a dirty white wall.' For the unhealthy expression of the face in this self-portrait, he referred to 'the face of death in the book by V. Eden' (*De Kleine Johannes* by Frederik Van Eeden), which had just been published.

This last *Self-portrait* from Paris is similar to one of the first from the spring of 1886 (JH 1090), which was still in the sombre Nuenen style, 'in green soapy colours'. Between these two works there is a whole series of self-portraits revealing a remarkable development towards a lighter and

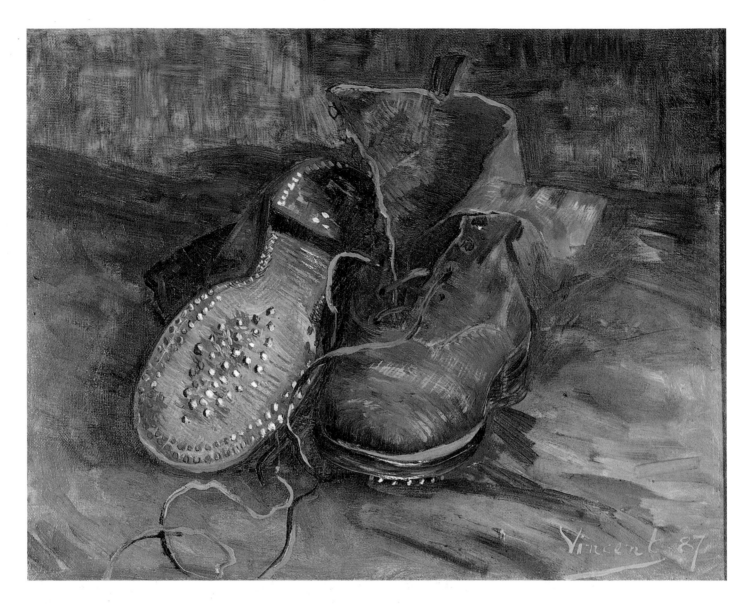

A Pair of Shoes
Paris, early 1887
F333 JH1236
Canvas, 34 x 41.5 cm
Baltimore, Museum of Art,
The Cone Collection

Self-portrait in Front of the Easel
Paris, February 1887-1888
F522 JH1356
Canvas, 65 x 50.5 cm
Amsterdam, Rijksmuseum
Vincent van Gogh

more expressive use of colour and other techniques. This painting has been compared to a self-portrait with a palette by Cézanne, painted a few years earlier - Van Gogh had met Cézanne in Tanguy's shop - but it particularly lends itself to a comparison with Rembrandt's *Self-portrait at an Easel* (1660; Louvre, Paris) which Van Gogh had seen at an exhibition in The Louvre of *One hundred and four artists' portraits*.

The painting of *A Pair of Shoes* (JH 1236), finished a year earlier, can also be viewed as a sort of self-portrait from the Paris period. Van Gogh often trudged through Montmartre to Clichy and Asnières, seven miles there and back, wearing these heavy high hobnail boots which he was to paint a number of times. This work is striking because of the challenging and fierce 'self-portrait combination' of the complementary colours, orange and blue.

After two years Van Gogh was tired of city life, and longed to look at nature under a brighter sky - that of Provence. On his last day in Paris, after hearing a concert of music by Wagner, 'which was performed by a large orchestra, but was no less intimate for all that', he went with his brother Theo to the studio of the Pointillist painter, Seurat. On Sunday 19 February 1888, Van Gogh left for Arles by train, and Theo saw him off from the Gare du Midi.

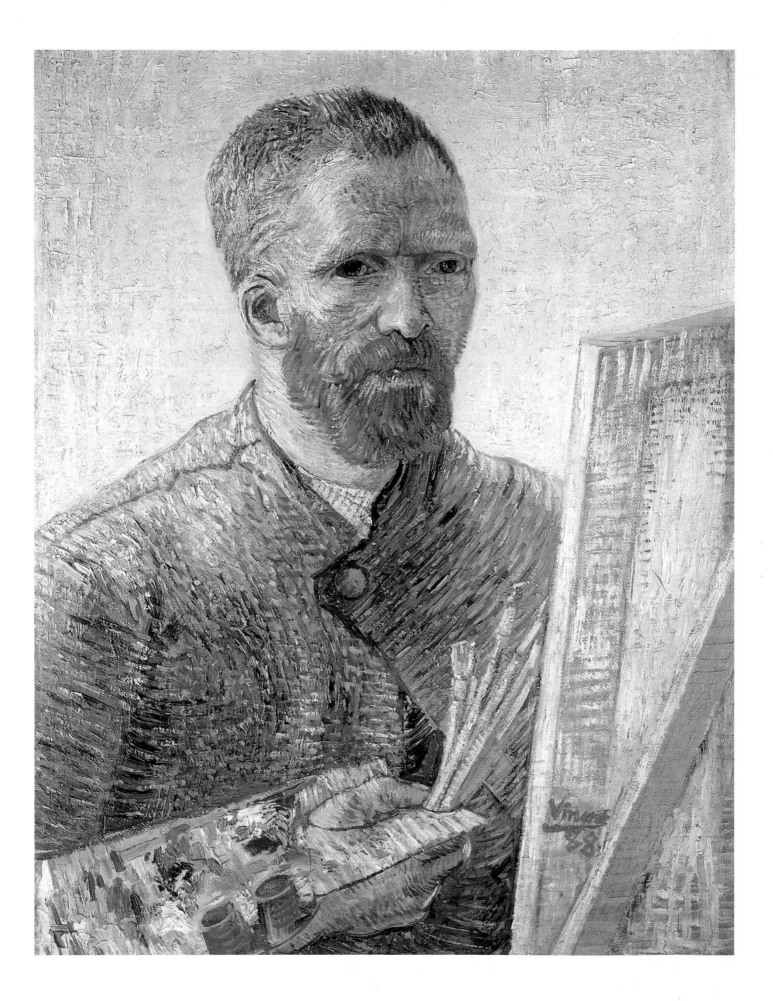

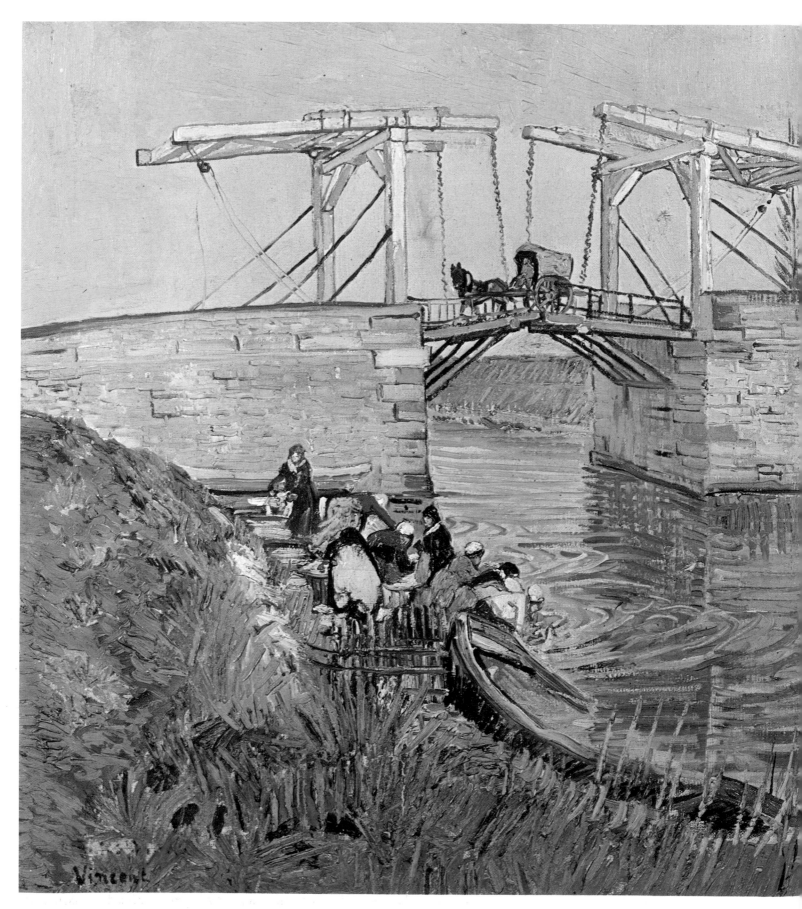

Pont de Langlois, a Drawbridge
Arles, March 1888 F397 JH1368
Canvas, 54 x 65 cm
Otterlo, Rijksmuseum
Kröller-Müller

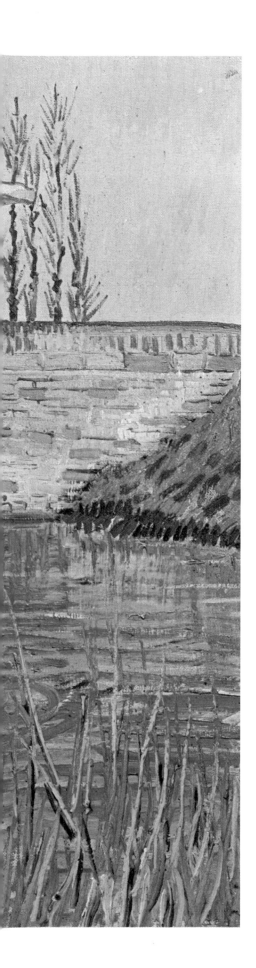

Chapter IV

The sun of Provence

Arles

Van Gogh arrived in Arles the following day after a journey of sixteen hours. He went to Provence to enjoy the sun, but to his great surprise he found a thick layer of snow and a hard frost, which he captured in a group of winter landscapes.

He moved into a cheap hotel at 30 rue Cavalerie, near the station, for five francs a day. In Arles he again showed virtually no interest in ancient monuments such as the Arena and the Theatre. He thought the magnificent twelfth-century gateway of the St Trophime was 'admirable', but the Romanesque sculpted figures seemed to him to come 'from another world.'

On Saturday 10 March, he received a letter from Theo, together with a hundred franc note, and that very day he bought fifty francs' worth of paint and canvasses. One subject that particularly appealed to him was the *Pont de Langlois* (JH 1368; see p. 56/57), a drawbridge over the canal to Bouc. It reminded him of Dutch drawbridges, like the one at Nieuw-Amsterdam, Drenthe, of which he had painted a watercolour in October 1883. The Pont de Langlois, which was named after a former bridgekeeper, was demolished in 1935 to make way for the construction of a new road, but in 1962 a copy of this historic bridge was built three kilometres further up the canal. On 17 March, Van Gogh wrote to Theo about this canvas 'of a drawbridge with a coach driving over it, outlined against a blue sky - the river is also blue, the banks are an orange colour with green vegetation, and there is a group of washerwomen wearing smocks with bonnets on their heads.'

A closer look at this beautiful painting in the Kröller-Müller Museum in Otterlo draws attention to the colourful group of washerwomen on the left, busily going about their work and chatting happily amongst themselves. You can almost hear the splashing of the washing in the water, which was then still clear and clean. The yellow two-wheeled wagon, drawn by a horse and driven by a self-assured farmer, completes a very lively scene, a more successful rendition than a later painting of 1888 of the same bridge (JH 1371, now in Amsterdam) in which no activity takes place on the bank or on the bridge.

In addition, there is a faithful copy of the Otterlo work, which he made for Theo (JH 1392) and another version (JH 1421) in the Wallraf-Richartz Museum in Cologne. This painting depicts a woman dressed in black with a dark parasol, walking over the drawbridge. There are cypresses instead of poplars at the side of the road. Lastly, there are also two drawings in pen and ink, and a watercolour of this bridge, as well as a sketch in a letter. The number of variations on this theme reveal the extent to which this subject appealed to Van Gogh. The bridge may have acted subcon-

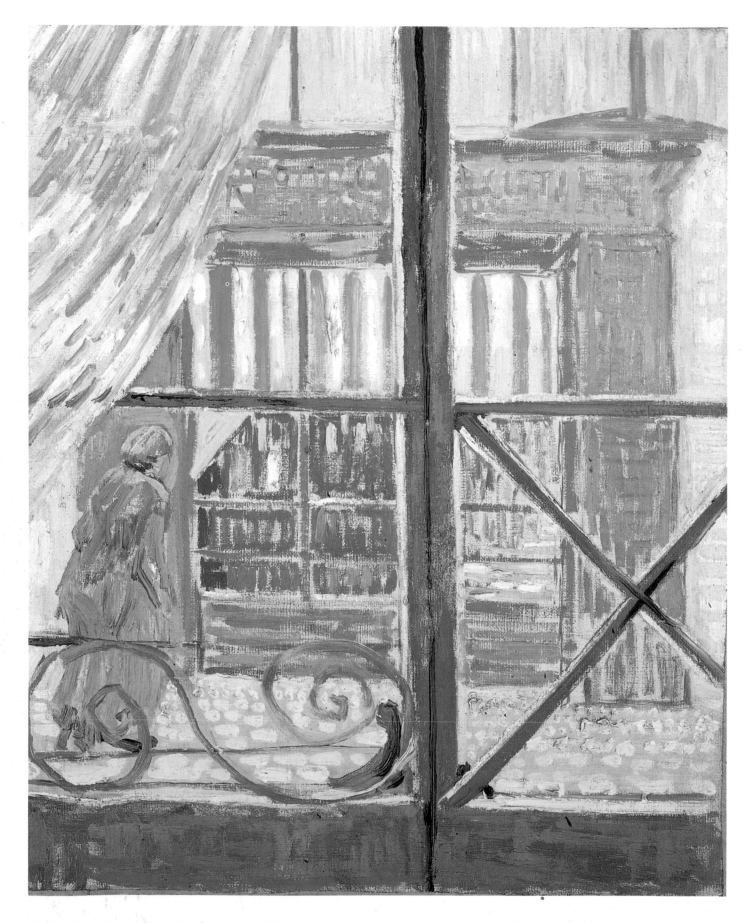

A Pork Butcher's Shop seen from a Window
Arles, February 1888 F389 JH1359
Canvas on cardboard, 39.5 x 32.5 cm
Amsterdam, Rijksmuseum
Vincent van Gogh

Blossoming Almond Branch in a Glass
Arles, March 1888 F392 JH1361
Canvas, 24 x 19 cm
Amsterdam, Rijksmuseum
Vincent van Gogh

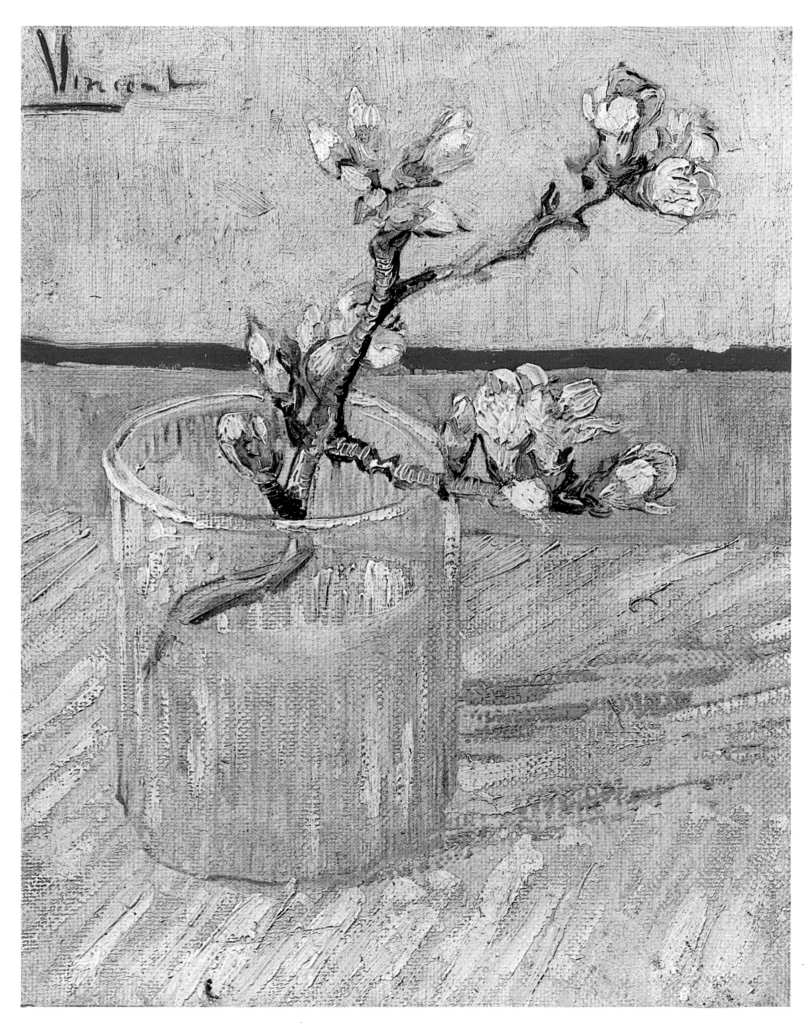

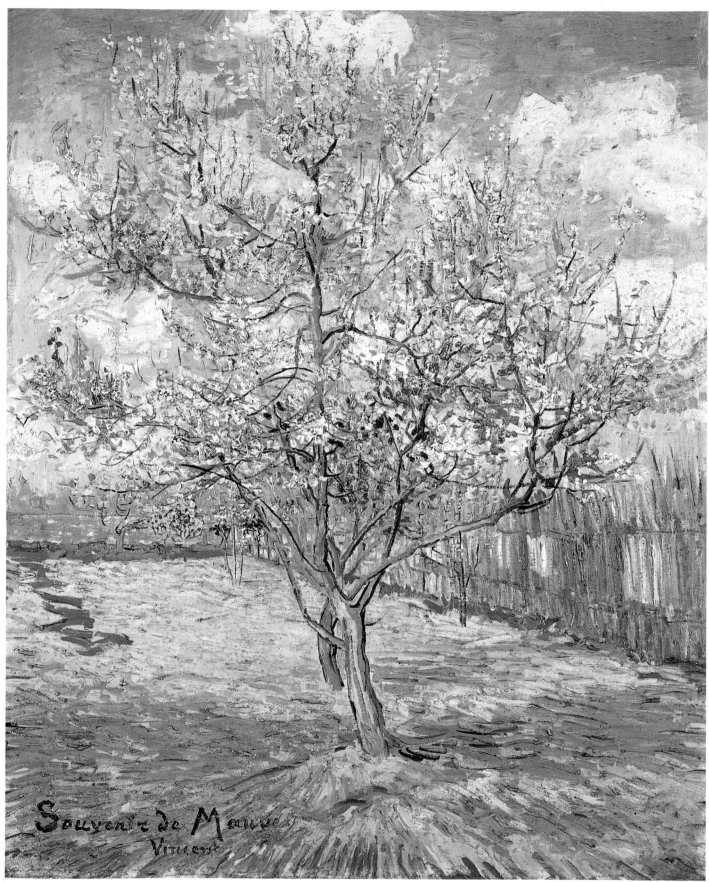

Souvenir de Mauve
Arles, March 1888
F394 JH1379
Canvas, 73 x 59.5 cm
Otterlo, Rijksmuseum
Kröller-Müller

sciously as a symbol of connection and separation: his physical separation from Theo bridged by the close bond of his letters.

Harbinger of spring

In February 1888 Van Gogh painted *A Pork Butcher's Shop seen from a Window* (JH 1359; see p. 58), as seen from his pension at 30 rue de la Cavalerie in wintry weather. This was the shop of Charcutier Reboul, whose name appears above the shop window. It was situated at 61 rue de la Cavalerie. A warmly clad woman from Arles glances quickly at the shop window as she walks past.

Despite the cold weather, Van Gogh found an almond branch which he brought indoors to flower. He painted it in anticipation of the spring: *Blossoming Almond Branch in a Glass* (JH 1361; see p. 59). A thick horizontal red line, two-thirds of the way up the canvas, creates a strong dynamic effect, without which the painting would be very static, as it is divided into two halves by the yellow table and greyish-blue background. He painted the glass with a branch twice, the second time adding a book. This version was a birthday present for his sister Wil: 'As I would like to give you some of my work that you might like, I will keep a small study for you of a book and a flower.' Theo took the present back to Holland.

Meanwhile, by the end of March 1888, spring had come to Provence, which was by then full of flowering fruit trees. This subject kept Van Gogh busy for several weeks. On about 1 April 1888 he wrote a letter to Wil from Arles: 'At the moment I have six paintings of blossoming fruit trees. And the one I have brought home today would certainly please you - it is a patch of dug earth in an orchard, a cane fence, and two peach trees in full blossom. Pink against a sparkling blue sky, with white clouds in the sunshine. You may see it yet, as I have decided to give it to Jet Mauve, and have written on it "*Souvenir de Mauve, Van Gogh & Theo*"'.

Anton Mauve, who had been Van Gogh's teacher during his time in The Hague, had died on 8 February. Wil had sent him the text of an obituary. He also wrote to Theo about this painting: 'For Mrs. Mauve. I have purposely chosen the best study I have done. I don't know what they'll say about it in Holland, but we don't care. I wanted to use a tender and gay subject to remember Mauve by, and not a study in a more serious style.'

This painting (JH 1379; see p. 60) was sent to Holland on 10 May, but Van Gogh probably removed the words '& Theo' at his brother's request, as it was really a present from him alone. In a letter to Theo, he wrote of this painting: 'Probably the best landscape I've done.'

Open-air painter

In the early spring of 1888 it was very windy in Provence. Van Gogh wrote: 'Painting is hard work in this wind, but I secure my easel with poles which I have put in the ground, and in this way I still manage to work - it's quite beautiful.' Obviously he painted in the open air, but this method of working had only been introduced some ten years earlier by the painters of the Barbizon School and by the first Impressionists. Before that time painters sketched outside, but completed their landscape paintings in their studios. This is how all the famous seventeenth-century Dutch landscape painters had worked. But during the nineteenth century the invention of tubes of paint made it possible to paint in the open air.

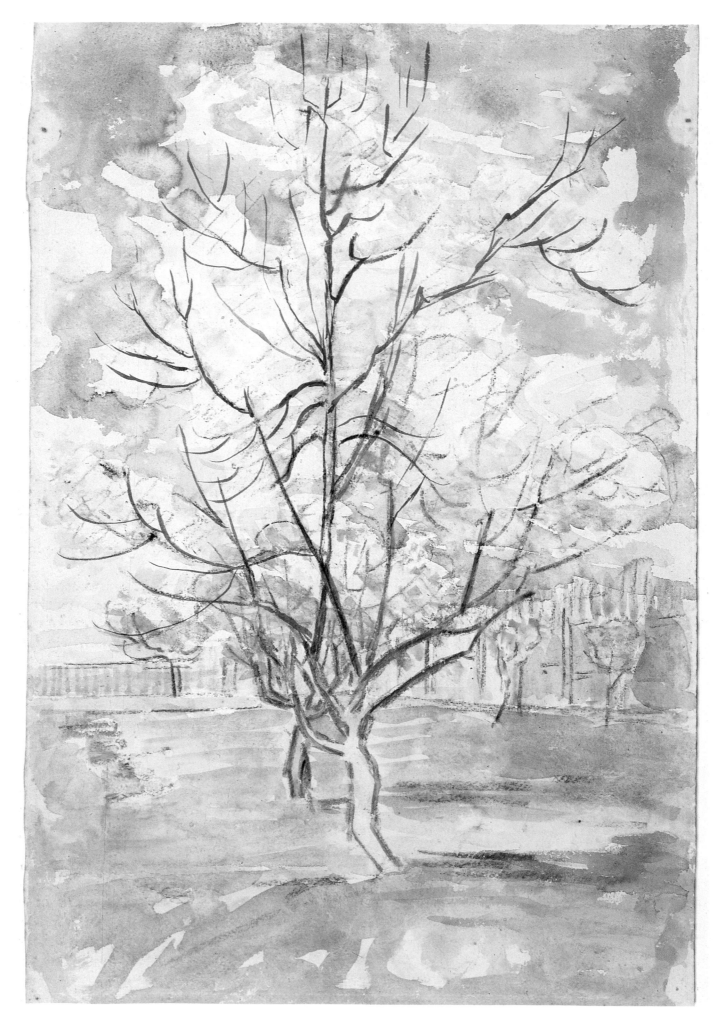

With regard to the new technique of painting, he wrote in a letter to his friend Emile Bernard (B3):

'At the moment I am completely preoccupied with flowering fruit trees: pink peach trees, yellowish white pear trees. There is no system in my efforts. I dab the canvas with irregular strokes and leave the result as it is. Sometimes I apply thick layers of paint; sometimes I leave parts of the canvas unpainted, and there are corners which I do not finish. I repeat myself, and sometimes I do very daring things. I believe the final result is quite disquieting and challenging, so that people with fixed ideas about painting techniques will not be happy with it ...

'I am working like a madman because the trees are flowering and I want to make an orchard of exceptional gaiety in Provence.'

Meanwhile, he needed a great deal of canvas, and a great deal of paint. At the beginning of April, Theo sent him fifty francs, which he spent immediately on artists' materials, leaving him once again penniless. On 9 April he received another hundred franc note, while Theo also paid his brother's order for more than a hundred tubes of paint, which were sent from either Tasset or L'Hôte, the main Paris manufacturers. The order gives us an idea of the colours that he used: silver-white, Veronese green, chromium yellow, vermilion, carmine, Prussian blue, emerald green and zinc white.

Theo's patience

Theo continued to support his brother, sending money and paying for his painting materials, though he himself certainly did not have an enormous salary. Vincent demanded extreme patience from Theo, who simply had to trust that one day his work would sell. The letters from Vincent to Theo - as regards money matters - reveal a great naivety and complete lack of any business sense.

At one point Van Gogh sent his brother a chest of canvasses and drawings, asking him to pay the freight costs. He wrote that Theo could keep the best paintings for himself to pay off his debt: 'Take three for your own collection, and do not sell them, for later they will be worth five hundred francs each.' This was all very well, but for the time being they were worthless in the art market. (The paintings included *The Drawbridge*, now worth some two to three million francs.)

Flowering orchards

Van Gogh repeatedly concentrated on a single subject, with which he became intensely involved. For example, during his time in The Hague, there were the trustees of an orphanage; during the Nuenen period, portraits of peasant men and women; during the years in Paris, there were flowers in vases, the mills of Montmartre, and finally self-portraits.

In the spring of 1888 Van Gogh painted at least fifteen orchards, or single flowering fruit trees, together with watercolours and drawings of this subject. *Pink Peach Trees* (JH 1384; see p. 62), in charcoal and water-colours, is now in Amsterdam, but can only be exhibited occasionally as watercolours are very sensitive to light and damp. In this fine sketch, the branches of the tree are sharply outlined against the cloudy sky.

The peaceful orchards which he painted during this period in Arles are in great contrast to the capricious, tormented and wild style of the pine

Pink Peach Trees
Arles, April 1888
F1469 JH1384
Charcoal, watercolour,
45.5 x 30.5 cm
Amsterdam, Rijksmuseum
Kröller-Müller

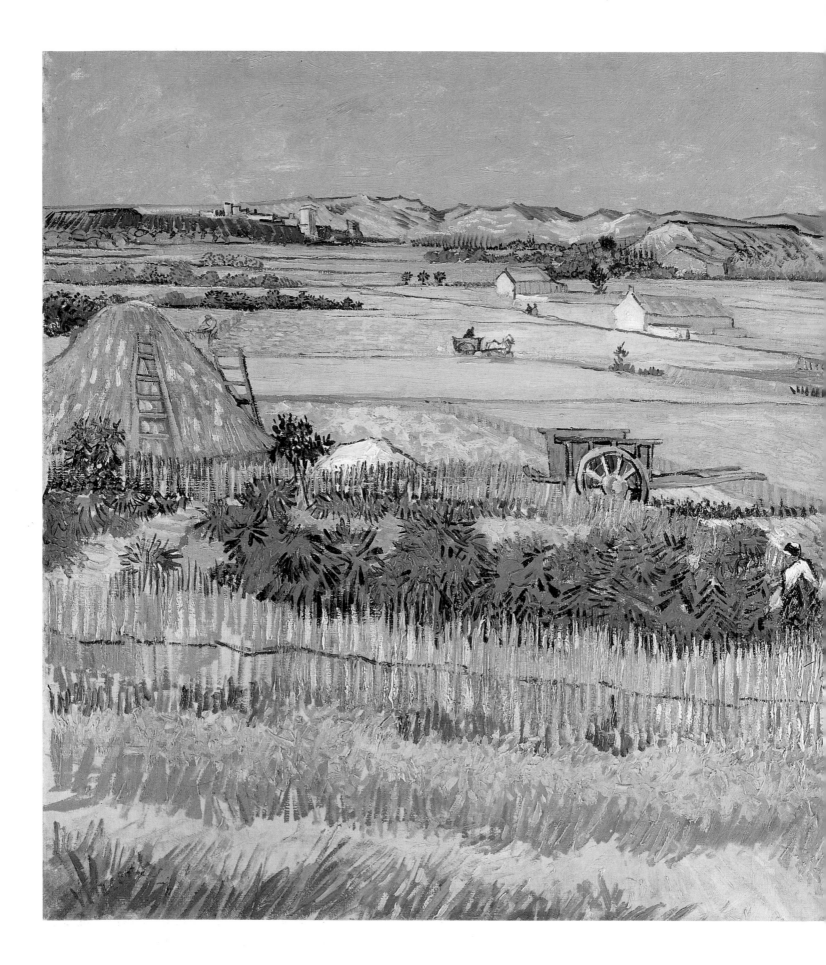

Harvest Landscape, Arles, June 1888
F412 JH1440 - Canvas, 72.5 x 92 cm
Amsterdam, Rijksmuseum Vincent van Gogh

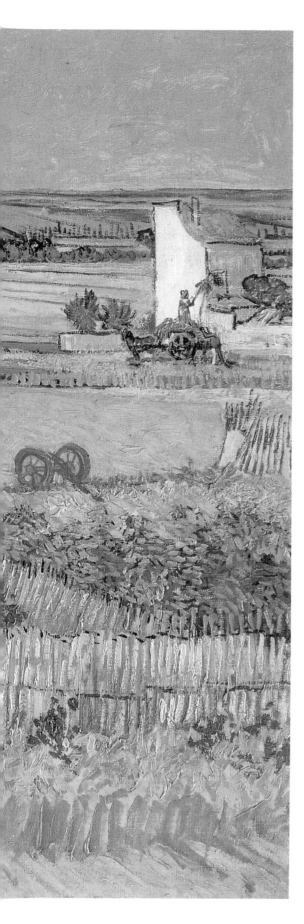

trees and olive groves he was to paint later in Saint-Rémy. Van Gogh's studies of trees, which continued throughout his artistic career from Nuenen and Arles to Saint-Rémy and Auvers, reveal an increasing restlessness, reflecting a change in his character, an increase in inner tensions. His perception of nature changed too, and his landscapes are imbued with a more dynamic energy. He confronts us with the potent life force in nature which was matched by his own enormous production of paintings and drawings at this time, as well as a quantity of long emotional letters to Theo and others.

Autumn harvest

One of the justifiably famous paintings from the Arles period is *Harvest Landscape* (JH 1440; see p. 64/5), which is one of the best works in the Amsterdam collection. There is a great deal of activity in this cheerful, sunny and warm painting of June 1888, which shows peasants hard at work. There is a fine sense of depth in the painting, enhanced by the receding effect of cool colours - blue and yellowish green - which are used for the mountains and the air, and the advancing sensation of the warm yellow in the foreground. To the left, in front of the mountains painted at the top of the painting to give the impression of depth, are the ruins of Montmajour, which Van Gogh visited many times, and of which he also did some drawings. The remains of this medieval Benedictine abbey, five kilometres north-east of Arles, can still be seen; its monks have drained the marshes and cultivated this area on the banks of the Rhône since the eleventh century. Exactly in the middle of the harvest landscape is a two-wheeled wagon, the centre of activity. The yellow wheat fields are enlivened by a series of three diagonal red roofs which draw the eye to the ruined abbey. Van Gogh completed this rich painting in one single day.

The painting *Haystacks near a Farm* (JH 1442; see p. 66/7) can be considered as a counterpart to *Harvest Landscape*. For this work Van Gogh first did a preliminary study in pen and ink with watercolours. In the final painting he changed this sketch slightly. The haystacks are all too dominant, but there is a beautiful colour contrast between the yellowish-gold haystacks and the azure-blue sky, as well as between the yellow house and its reddish purple roof. However, this second painting has a less harmonious composition, and there is less activity depicted in it.

The painting of the haystacks was also completed in a single day, but Van Gogh admitted that this had been too taxing for him. His reaction was to start drinking excessively and smoking too much, which was even more damaging to his health than the tremendous effort of working continuously on a painting in which he invested all his skill and all his soul. He wrote to Theo that it was not only his paintings which were rather wild, but that he also felt confused himself. He compared himself to the fifteenth-century Flemish primitive painter Hugo van der Goes, who actually became insane. In July 1888 Van Gogh noted that he felt on the border of insanity at times, but it was another six months before he was in such a state of crisis that he had to go into an asylum.

Idiosyncratic style

A trip which Van Gogh made to the fishing village of Les-Saintes-Maries-de-La-Mer, between 30 May and 3 June 1888, was to be of great impor-

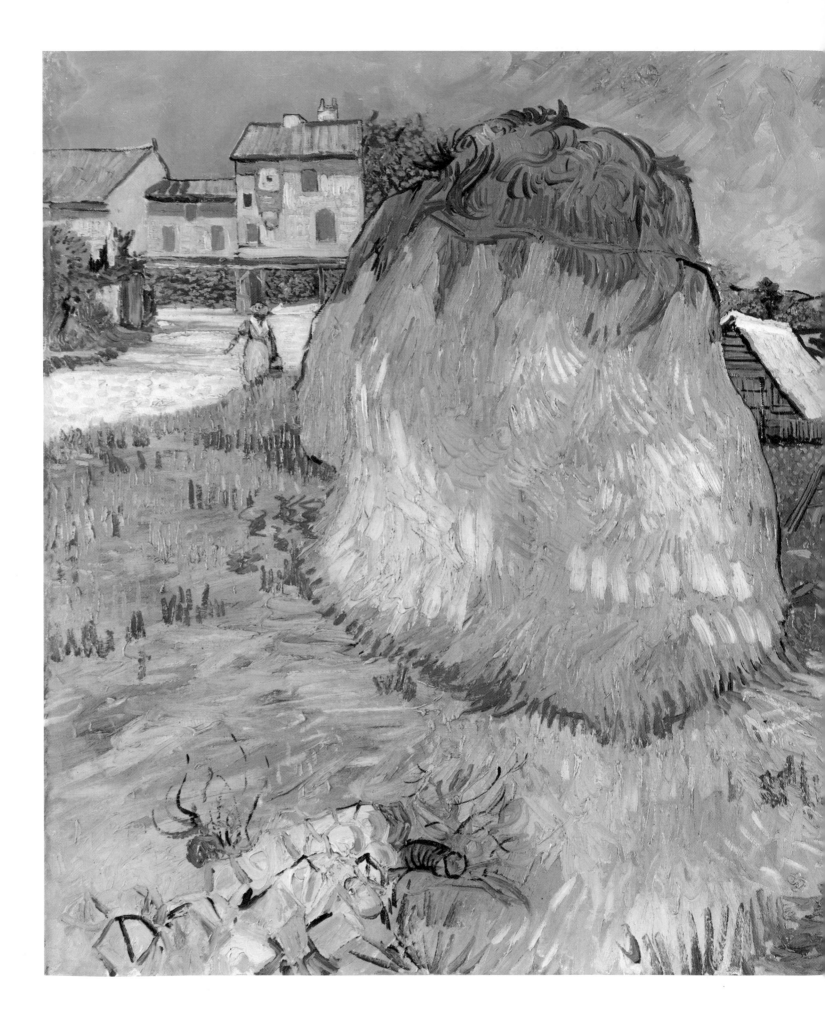

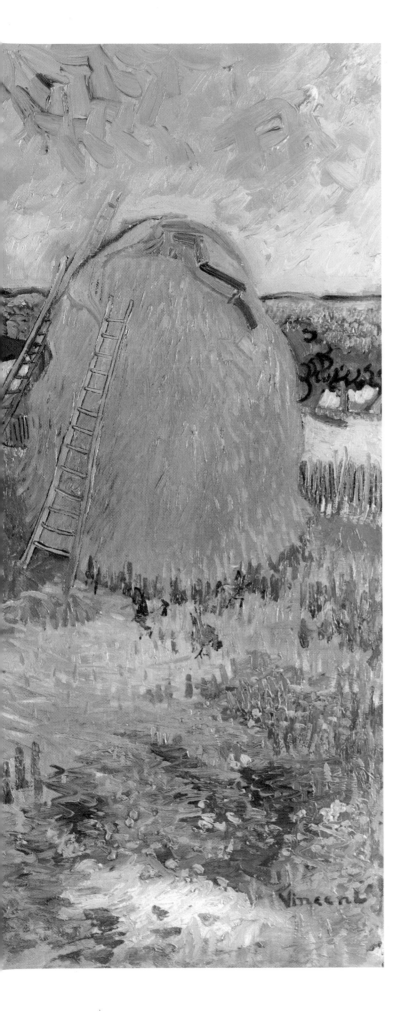

Haystacks near a Farm
Arles, June 1888
F425 JH1442
Canvas, 73 x 92.5 cm
Otterlo, Rijksmuseum
Kröller-Müller

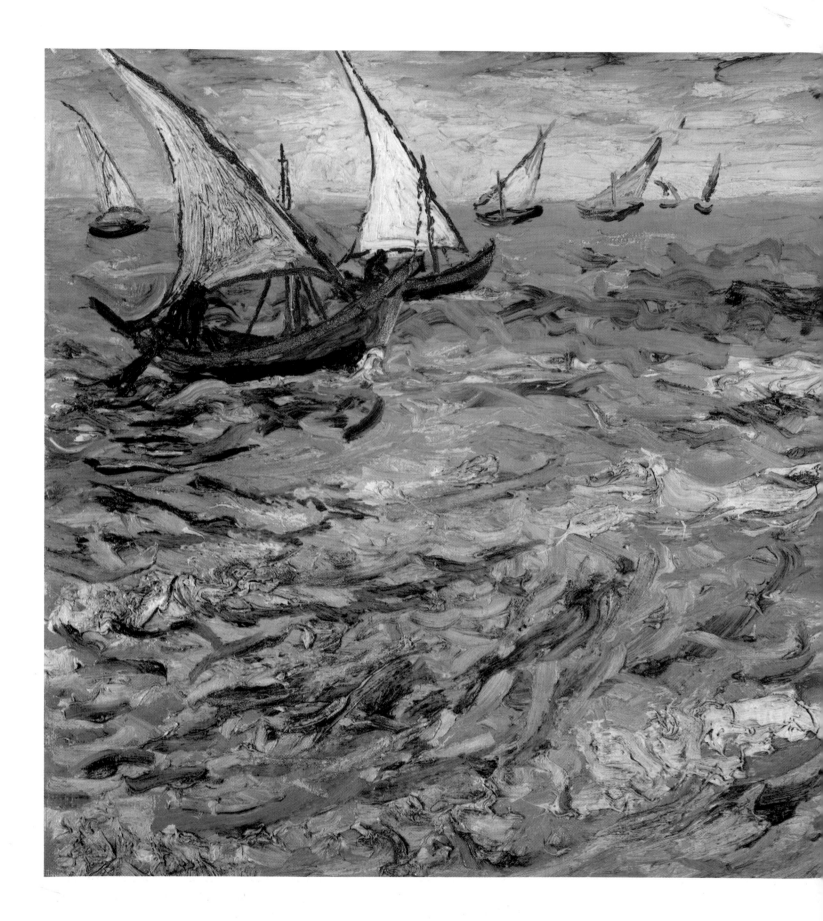

Fishing Boats at Sea
Saintes-Maries/Arles, June 1888
F417 JH1453
Canvas, 44 x 53 cm
Moscow, Pushkin Museum.

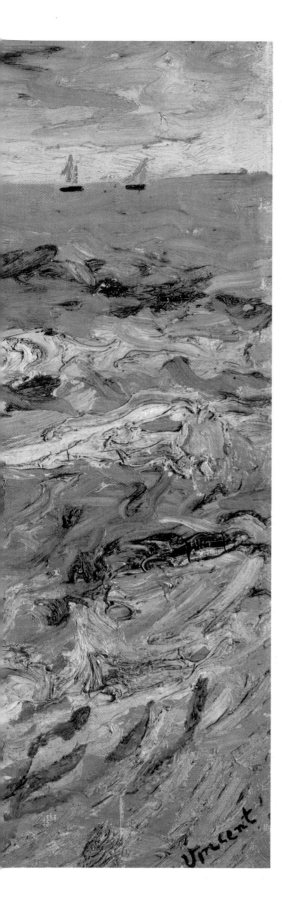

tance to his artistic development. During these few days he did a series of beautiful and extremely important paintings. He wrote to Theo on 29 May (495): 'Tomorrow morning early I'm leaving for Saintes-Maries on the Mediterranean coast. I'll be staying there until Saturday evening. I'm taking two canvasses, but I'm afraid it'll be too windy to paint. I'm going there by coach - it's fifty kilometres away. You cross the Camargue, a grassy plain where you see herds of bulls and small semi-wild white horses, which are very beautiful. I'm taking everything so that I can draw ... Things here have so much style. And I want to develop an idiosyncratic, more extravagant style of drawing.'

The colour of mackerel

While Van Gogh was working in the fishing village, he wrote to Theo on 2 June (499):

'I'm finally writing to you from Saintes-Maries, from the coast of the Mediterranean Sea. The sea is the colour of mackerel, which means it keeps changing. You don't always know whether it is green or violet or blue, because a second later the changing reflections assume a pink or grey hue ... I often think of our uncle the sailor [Vice Admiral Johannes Van Gogh], who has undoubtedly seen the sea like this many times. I took my canvasses with me and I have finished them. Two seascapes, one view of the village, and also some drawings, which I will post to you, for tomorrow I will be back in Arles. I have full board here for four francs a day, although they first asked me for six francs.' (During this period Theo gave him fifty francs per week, and sometimes fifty francs extra.)

'There is a sandy beach here, no cliffs or rocks - it's like a Dutch beach without dunes, and with a blue sky ... I think there must be less than a hundred houses in this village or town. After the old church, an ancient fortress, the main building is the barracks. Then there are a few houses - it's rather like the peat moors of Drenthe. You'll see examples of it in the drawings.'

One of the two seascapes which he referred to in this letter is *Fishing Boats at Sea* (JH 1453, see p. 68/9); the other is *Fishing Boats on the Beach* (JH 1460; see p. 70/71). The play of green, violet or blue tones, known as 'changeant' in the world of fashion, has been used in a fascinating way in the former seascape. The fishermen are struggling with their small single-sailed boats on the stormy waves, hugging the coast for safety. Van Gogh wrote to Emile Bernard (B6): 'On the flat beach there are small boats, green, red and blue, such pleasant shapes and colours that they remind you of flowers. They are sailed by one man and must not go into the open sea. They go out to sea when there's no wind, and come back to the beach when there's too much.'

Fishing Boats on the Beach illustrates this description, with its red, green and blue boats. In the letter to Bernard, he sketched the boats in the same way, indicating the colours 'rouge' and 'jaune' in front of the mast. On the third blue boat is the word 'Amitié', or Friendship.

The rich harvest from this three-day trip to the sea comprised a total of three paintings of the sea and of boats, and one watercolour and three drawings of the same subject.

In addition, Van Gogh painted *View of Saintes-Maries* (JH 1447; see p. 72) which shows the village church and houses, a view of which there are a total of four paintings and eight drawings. In fact, three of the paintings

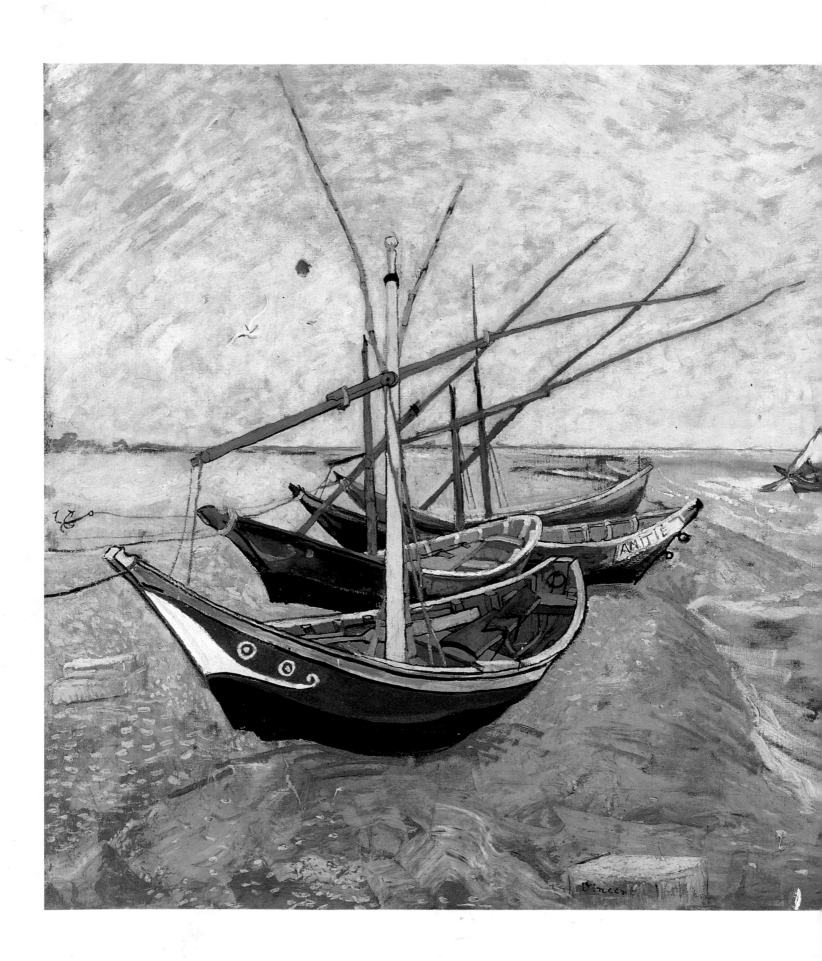

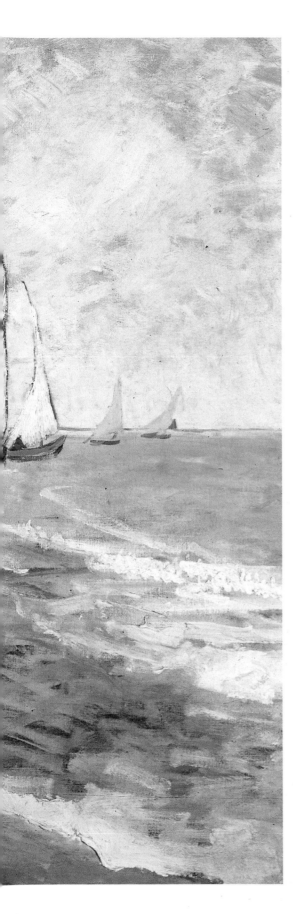

Fishing Boats on the Beach
Saintes-Maries/Arles, June 1888
F413 JH1460
Canvas, 64.5 x 81 cm
Amsterdam, Rijksmuseum
Vincent van Gogh

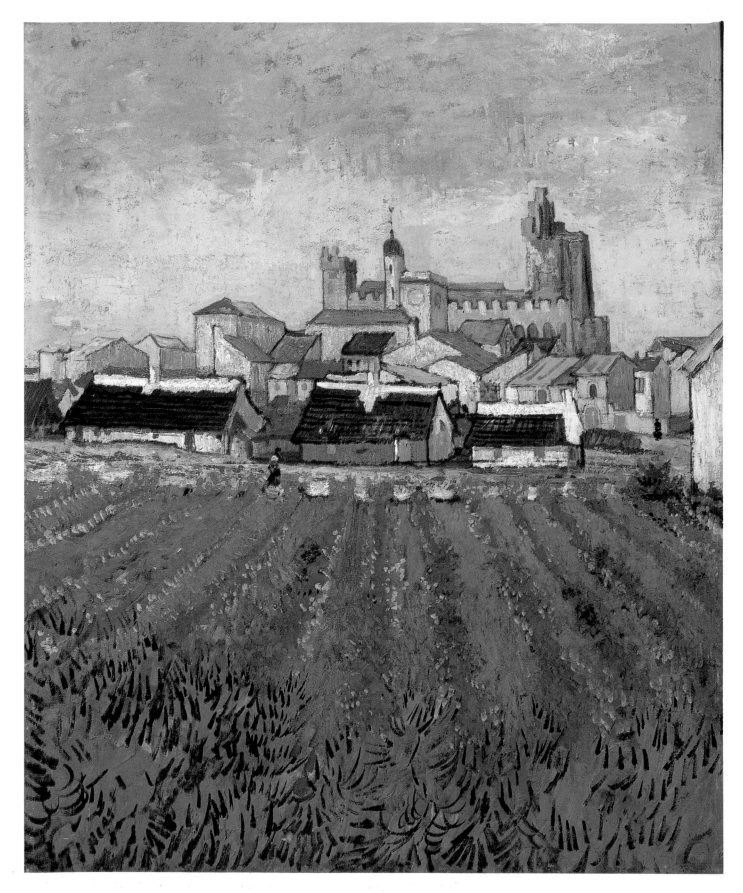

View of Saintes-Maries
Arles, June 1888
F416 JH1447
Canvas, 64 x 53 cm
Otterlo, Rijksmuseum
Kröller-Müller

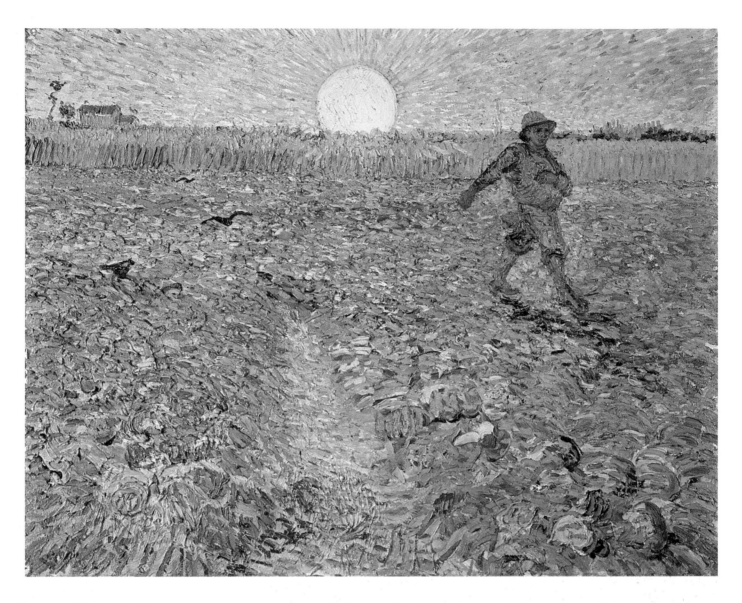

Sower with Setting Sun
Arles, June 1888
F422 JH1470
Canvas, 64 x 80.5 cm
Otterlo, Rijksmuseum
Kröller-Muller

were done in his studio after Van Gogh had returned home, and were based on the sketches he had done. These works are amongst his most important masterpieces; not only is there an overwhelming wealth of colour but one can also see the interplay of sea and clouds, hear the waves break and smell the seawater. In places the paint was applied very thickly to emphasize the breaking waves. On one of these seascapes Van Gogh signed his name, 'Vincent', in large red letters against a greenish blue sea, almost as a challenge.

The sower as a symbol

In that same month, June 1888, Van Gogh painted the *Sower with Setting Sun* (JH 1470; see p. 73) in complementary colours of yellow (used for the background of wheat fields and for the sun) and purple (used for the field being sown in the foreground).

On about 18 June he wrote to Emile Bernard from Arles (B7):

'Here is a sketch of a sower: a stretch of land with clods of ploughed earth, mostly purple all over. A ripe field of wheat in ochre yellow with a little bit of carmine. The chrome yellow sky is almost as bright as the sun, which is chrome yellow 1, with a little bit of white, while the rest of the sky is a mixture of chrome yellow 1 and 2. So it's very yellow. The sower is wearing a blue smock and white trousers. There's quite a lot of

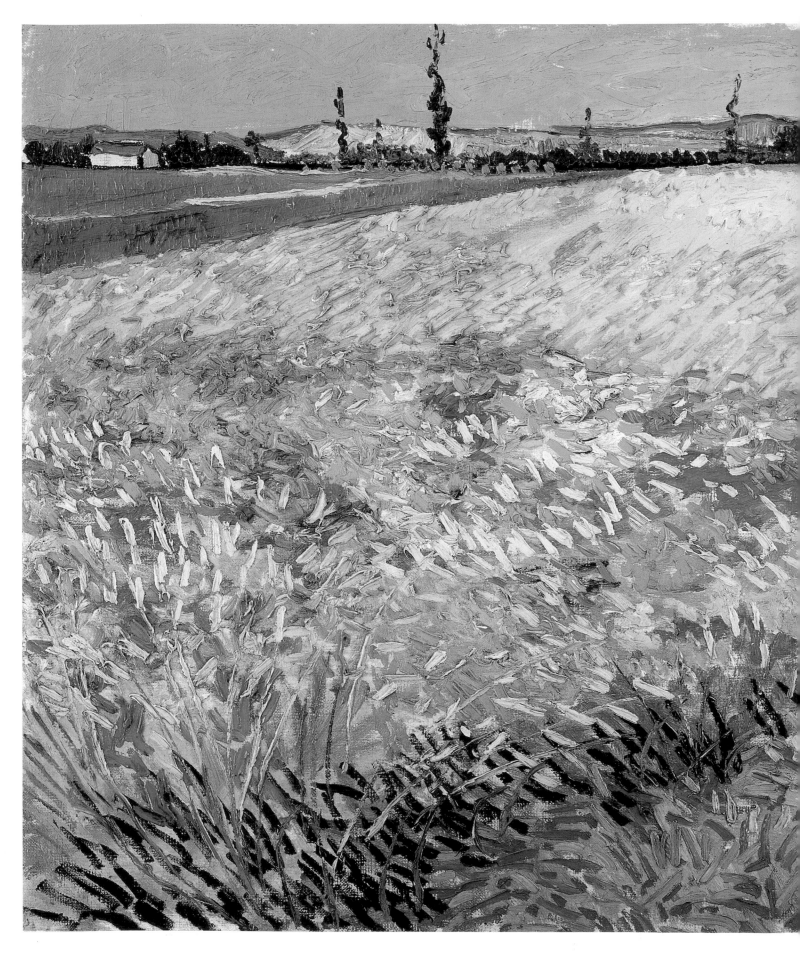

Wheat Field, Arles, June 1888
F411 JH1476
Canvas on cardboard, 54 x 65 cm

Amsterdam, Rijksmuseum
Vincent van Gogh

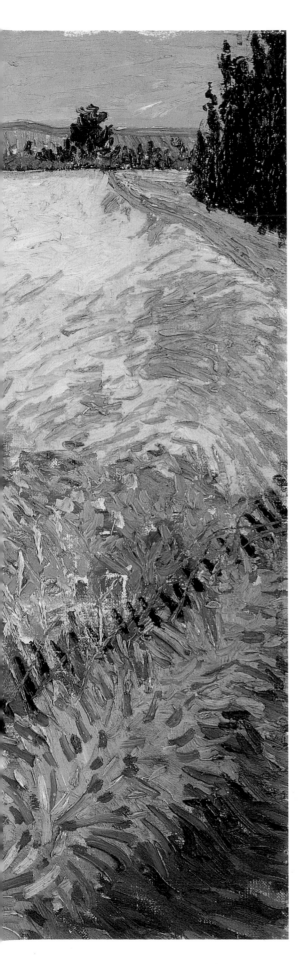

yellow in the earth, neutral shades which are the result of the mixture of purple and yellow ... I took great pains to get the right colours.'

In April 1881, more than seven years earlier, Van Gogh had completed a pen and ink wash of a sower while he was still living with his parents in Etten. His inspiration was a woodcut based on a painting by Millet of 1850. This drawing marks the beginning of his career as an artist, and of the sower as a theme in his work: he was to complete another thirty views of sowers after Millet.

Van Gogh was fascinated by this image, which plays a symbolic role in his work. It was clear that he was not destined to be a sower of the message of salvation and in his personal life he sowed the seeds of friendship for his fellow man in vain. Moreover, he failed to establish a permanent relationship: his love affairs were unhappy, he never married, nor did he have children - he was not a sower for posterity.

However, as a prophetic artist he did sow the message of his close relationship and empathy with working men and with nature in his paintings and drawings. Again, his work seemed to fall on infertile ground; he did not live to see it spring up and bear fruit. It was only after his lifetime that his work received due recognition.

Wheat field

Van Gogh returned to Arles in June 1888 and painted *Wheat Field* (JH 1476; see p. 74/75), which bears a resemblance to *Harvest Landscape* with its green wheat with poppies in the foreground, and a golden yellow field of wheat behind it. To the left there is a green field and in it a white house with a red roof. It is an exuberant painting bursting with colour, but in the absence of working peasants, it looks more static. Nothing is happening, although we can almost see Van Gogh himself working passionately to capture this still scene with strong brush strokes.

Barge labourers

The *Quay with Men Unloading Sand Barges* (JH 1558; see p. 76/7) is much more anecdotal. Two sand barges are moored next to each other on the Quay Saint-Martin on the Rhône. Is it significant that the French flag on one is at half mast? In a letter to Theo, Van Gogh wrote about this work (524): 'At the moment I am working on a study of boats which I can see from the top of the quay, the two boats are a purplish pink, the water is very green, there is no sky and a tricolor is hanging from the mast. A labourer with a wheelbarrow is unloading sand. I have also made a drawing of it.'

This drawing was included in the letter. In the sketch the flag is at the top of the mast. The labourers on the boat to the right are omitted, and the small rowing boat in the painting is not shown either. Thus it is clear that after doing this sketch, he went on to elaborate the composition in oils by adding elements to it which make the whole painting more lively. A comparison of the sketch in the letter with the completed painting gives us some idea of the way in which he worked.

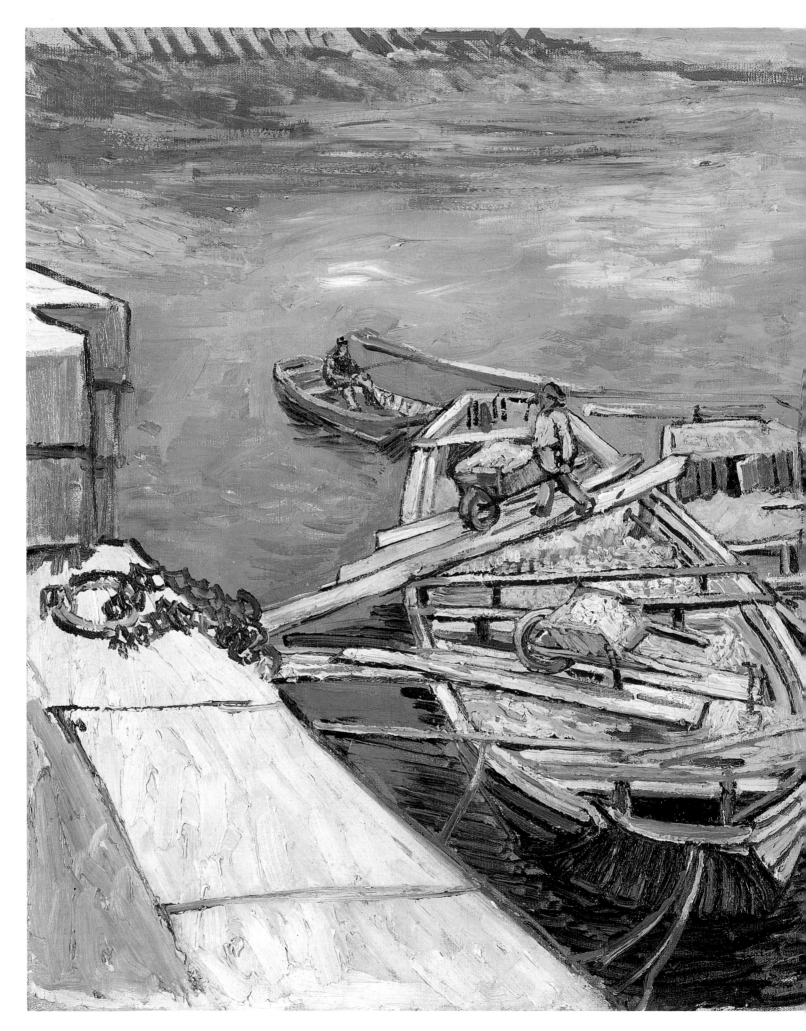

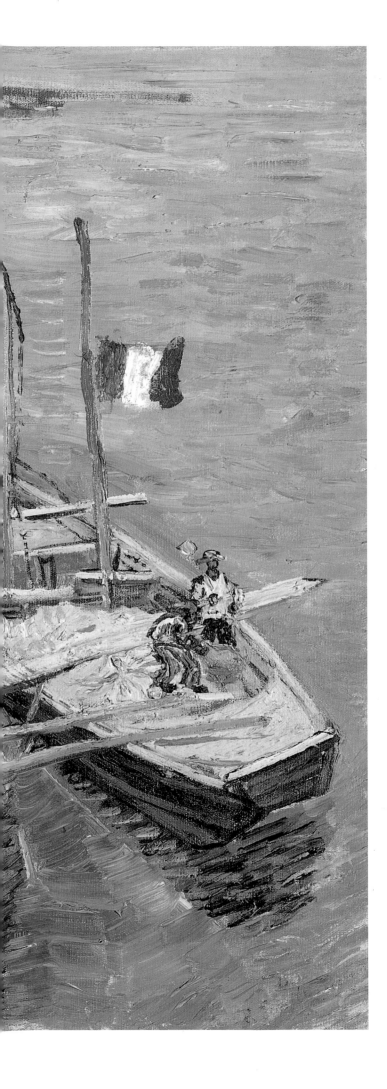

Quay with Men Unloading Sand Barges
Arles, August 1888
F449 JH1558
Canvas, 55 x 66 cm
Essen, Folkwang Museum

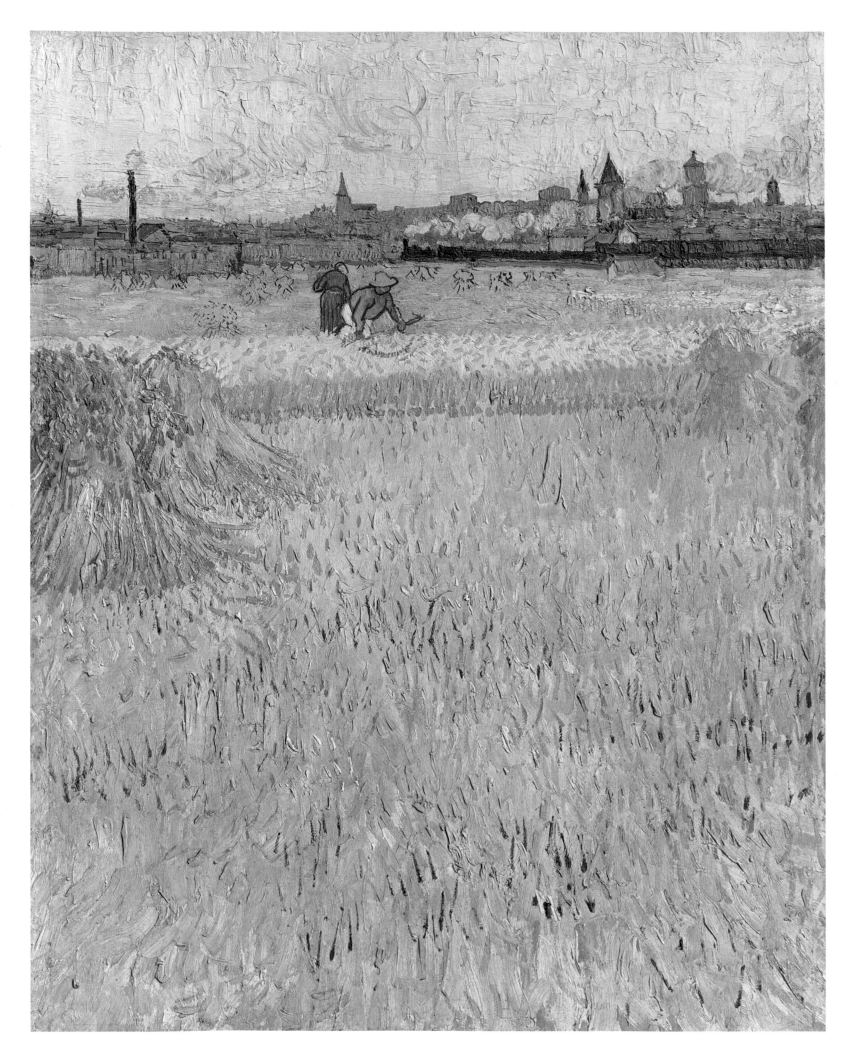

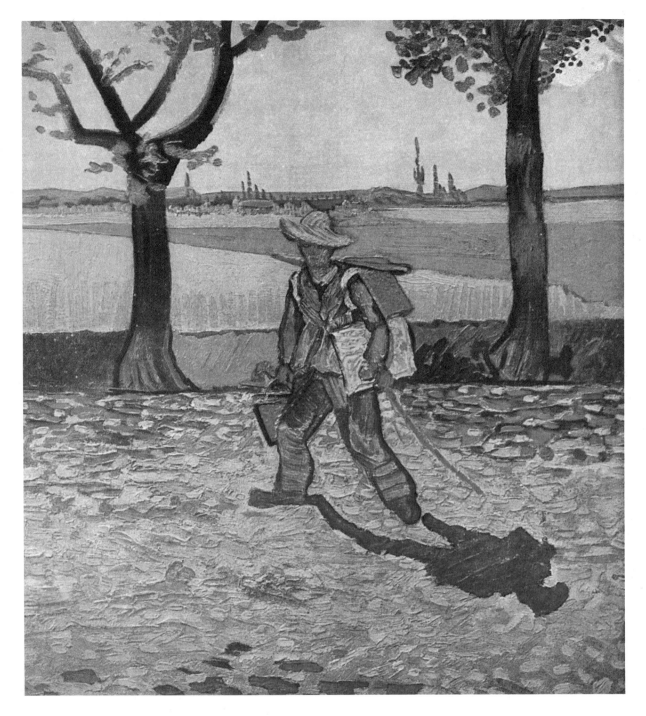

The Painter on the Road to Tarascon
Arles, July 1888
F448 JH1491
Canvas, 48 x 44 cm
Lost in the Second World War: formerly Magdeburg, Kaiser Friedrich Museum

Wheat Field with Sheaves and Arles in the Background
Arles, June 1888
F545 JH1477
Canvas, 73 x 54 cm
Paris, Musée Rodin

Towns and countryside together

The *Wheat Field with Sheaves and Arles in the Background* (JH 1477; p. 78) shows the arena, a number of church spires and the town hall in the background. To the left we see industrial Arles with the tall towers of the railway yards and the gas works. A long train passes by behind the wheat field and the locomotive leaves a ribbon of smoke behind it. However, by far the greatest part of the painting is taken up by the wheat field, most of which has been cut, with the sheaves already gathered. The scene is all the more lively because of the central position of the toiling peasants, figures on which the attention focusses first of all. In this work the town and the country have been brought together.

In June and July 1888 Van Gogh did a series of paintings on this theme of golden fields of wheat, partly cut and with gathered wheat sheaves. In addition, in July and August he made a sketch and a drawing in chalk of this pastoral scene, as well as a number of pen and ink drawings.

When the artist is dead

During the second half of June, or at the beginning of July 1888, when Van Gogh was painting his wheat fields, he wrote about himself in a letter to his sister Wil (W4):

'We are now living in an artist's world where it is unspeakably awful and miserable. Exhibitions, shops selling paintings, everything, everything is run by people who intercept all the money. You mustn't think that this is my imagination. *A lot of money is paid for his work when the artist himself is dead*, and the living artists are always held back by the work of those who are no longer alive.

'I know that we can't do anything about this to change it. Thus you have to protect or console yourself either by finding a rich woman or something else, otherwise it is impossible to work. All the independence you hope to gain by your work, or the influence you hope to have on others, comes to absolutely nothing.

'And yet it is certainly a pleasure to make a painting and there are actually about twenty painters here all with more debts than money etc., all with a lifestyle more or less like that of a street dog, who could possibly be more significant than the whole official exhibition insofar as the way of working in the future is concerned. I imagine that the main characteristic of a painter is that he can paint. Those who can paint, those who are best, are the seeds of something that will exist for a long time; as long as there are eyes to enjoy something that is extraordinarily beautiful. Meanwhile I constantly regret that one does not become richer by working - on the contrary.'

How prophetic these words are, and how significant his prediction: 'A lot of money is paid for his work when the artist himself is dead.' In fact, 53.9 million dollars was paid for the *Irises* and 39.9 million dollars was paid for the *Sunflowers* ninety-seven years after Van Gogh's death. But how happy he would have been with the 32,000 francs which Mrs. Kröller paid for the *Drawbridge in Arles* at an auction in Amsterdam in 1912. For in 1888 he was living and working on 200 francs a month.

Like a porcupine

Let us return to Van Gogh's time in Arles in the summer of 1888. In July, a month spent exploring the outskirts of the town looking for a good subject, he painted a self-portrait: *The Painter on the Road to Tarascon* (JH 1491; see p. 79). Unfortunately this painting no longer exists, having been destroyed by fire in 1945. But we know what it looked like from photographs and reproductions of the painting.

In the same letter to his sister Wil (W4), Van Gogh described his appearance as he captured it in this self-portrait:

'Nowadays I look different, in that I no longer have any hair or a beard, and these have both been shaved smooth. Quite unlike the greenish grey pink, my face has assumed a greyish orange colour, and I am wearing a white suit instead of a blue one. I'm always dusty and increasingly loaded up like a porcupine with sticks, an easel, canvasses and other articles. Only the green eyes have remained the same. But another colour in the portrait is naturally a yellow straw hat, like a "hannekemaaier" (a farm labourer in the old days who came to Holland from Westphalia for the haymaking).'

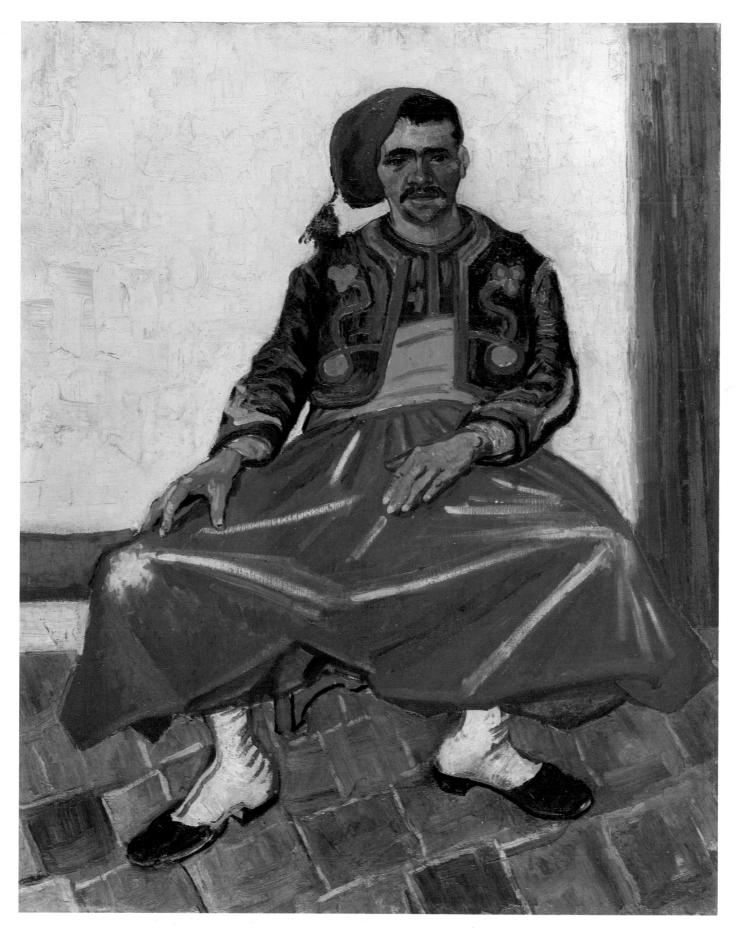

The Zouave, Arles, June 1888
F424 JH1488
Canvas, 81 x 65 cm
Private collection

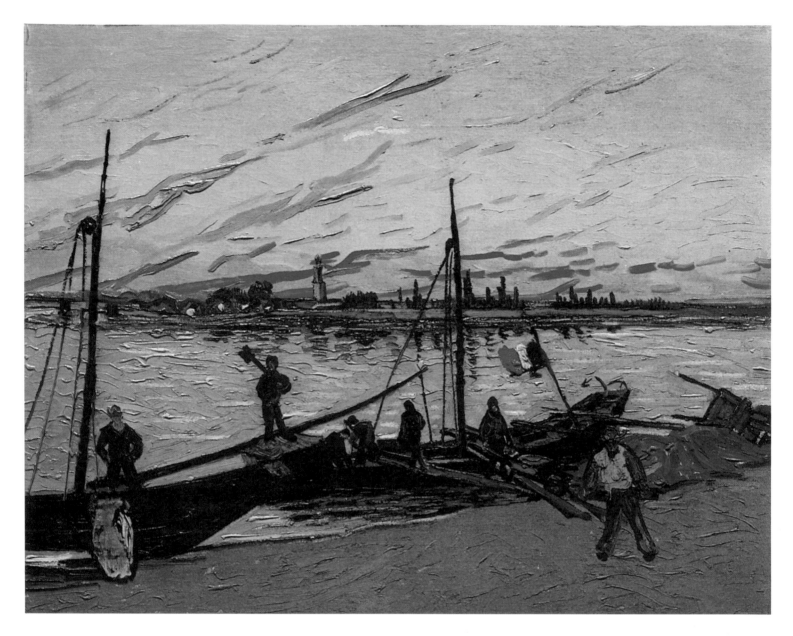

Coal Barges
Arles, August 1888
F437 JH1570
Canvas, 71 x 95 cm
Annapolis, private collection

In addition to this painting he did a single rough sketch or *pochade*. In this work he again showed himself 'loaded up with crates, poles and a canvas, on the way to Tarascon', as he wrote to Theo. The position of the deep black shadow shows the direction of the sun's rays, while the sun itself is left out of the picture: at other times, for example in his landscapes or paintings of sowers, the sun is often shown as a bright golden disc.

Homage to Vincent

The sculptor Ossip Zadkine made a lively and dynamic statue of Van Gogh carting all his bits and pieces - undoubtedly he was quite a sight as he walked along. This statue is now in a park in Auvers-sur-Oise, the last place where Van Gogh lived.

In 1957 the English painter, Francis Bacon, who was born nineteen years after Van Gogh's death, painted a *Study for Portrait of Van Gogh* with several variations, as well as *Van Gogh in a Landscape*; two paintings which were clearly inspired by the self-portrait on the way to Tarascon. Just as Van Gogh painted with Millet as his inspiration, Bacon was inspired by Van Gogh. Bacon's work was exhibited in early 1985 at the exhibition *La Grande Parade* in the Stedelijk Museum in Amsterdam.

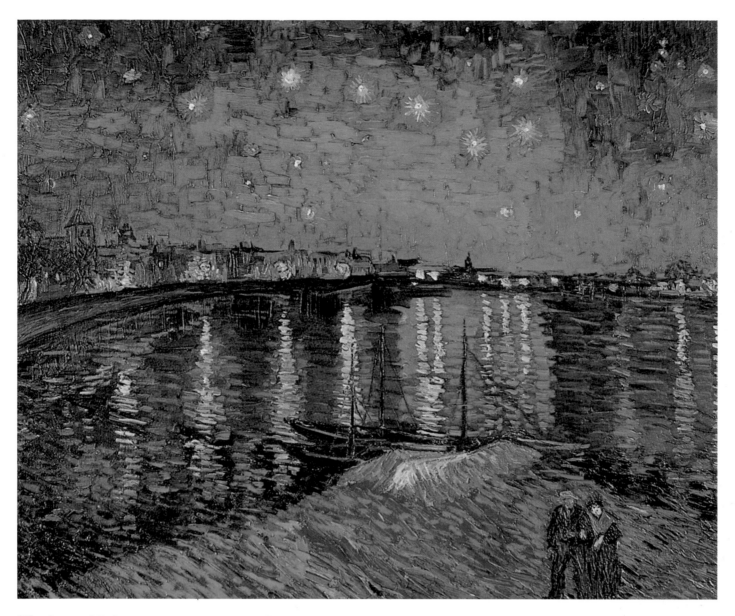

The Starry Night
Arles, September 1888
F474 JH1592
Canvas, 72.5 x 92 cm
Private collection

The Zouave

In June 1888 Van Gogh painted two works and drew three sketches featuring Zouaves, the French foot soldiers who served in North Africa - the corps was founded in Algeria in 1831. One portrait, now in Amsterdam, shows half the figure; the other, *Zouave* (JH 1488; see p. 81), privately owned in America, shows the whole figure. He described his model as: 'A young man of small stature, with a bull's neck and the eyes of a tiger.' The uniform is 'of the sort of blue colour of enamel pots with faded, reddish orange decorations.' The man has 'a cat-like, highly tanned face.' Van Gogh wrote about his two paintings of the Zouave: 'I would be happy to always work on such vulgar and even strident portraits such as these two. I learn something from this work, and this is what I want from my work above all.'

As in his self-portraits, Van Gogh again used the striking contrast between the complementary colours of blue for the jacket and orange for the wide trousers, which were so characteristic of the Zouave uniform.

Meanwhile, in August he made a painting of *Coal Barges* (JH 1570; see p. 82). It is a work which bears some similarity to the painting of *Quay with Men Unloading Sand Barges*, which he had painted earlier.

The painting *The Starry Night* (JH 1592; see p. 83) is a fascinating work.

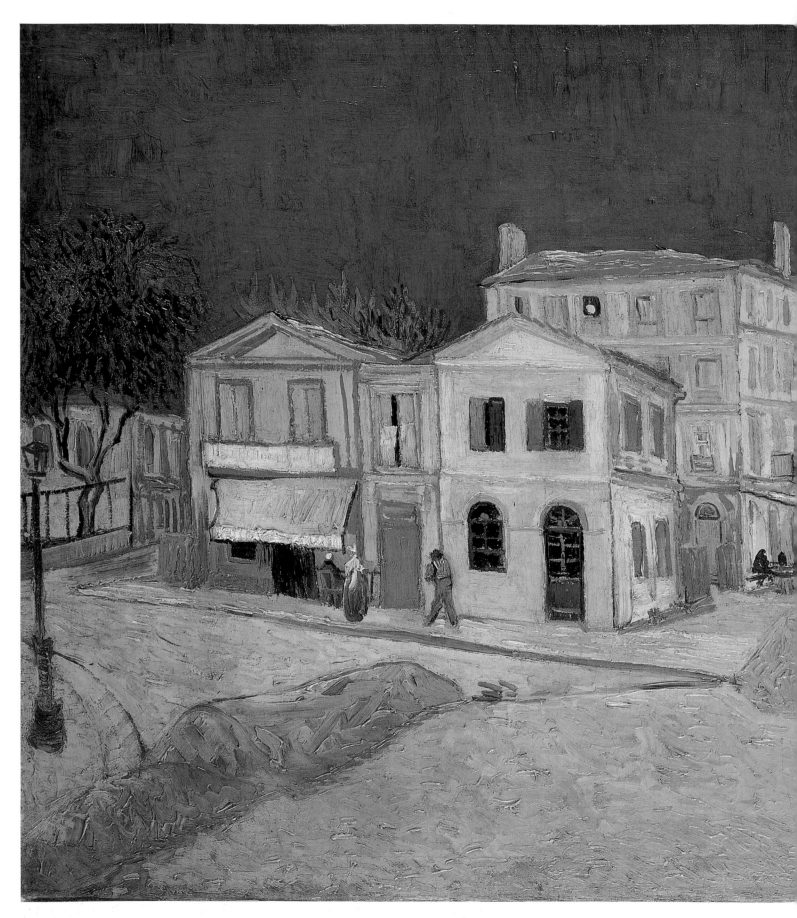

The Yellow House (Vincent's House)
Arles, September 1888
F464 JH1589 Canvas, 76 x 94 cm
Amsterdam, Rijksmuseum
Vincent van Gogh

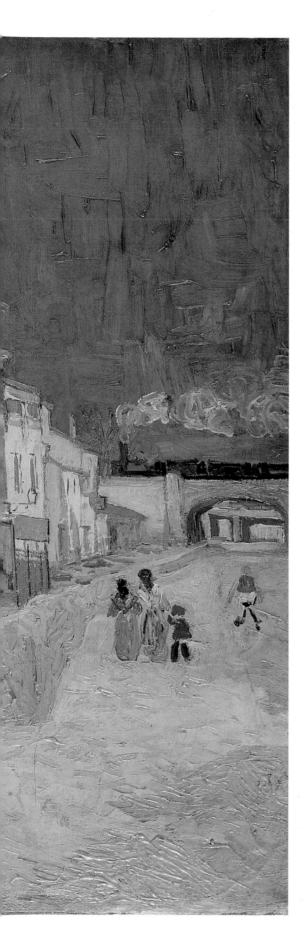

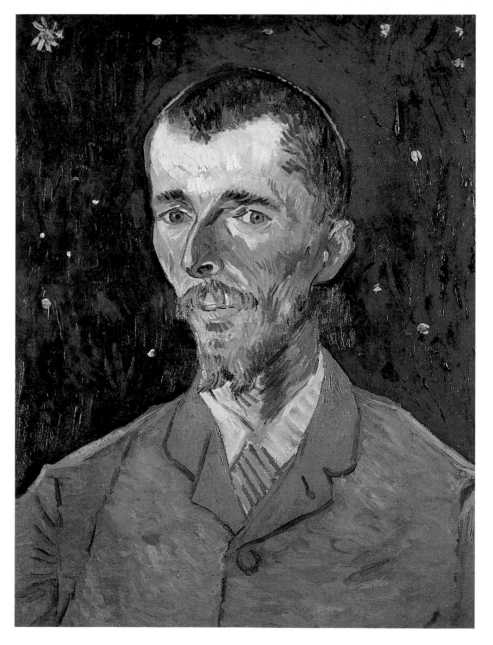

Portrait of Eugène Boch
Arles, September 1888
F462 JH1574
Canvas, 60 x 45 cm
Paris, Musée d'Orsay

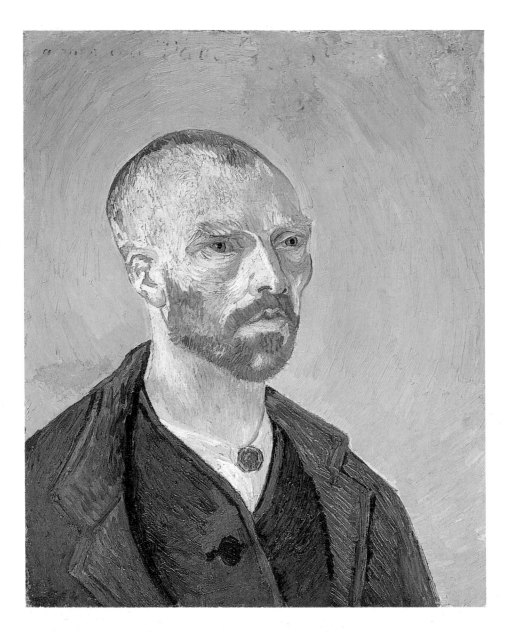

Self-portrait
Arles, September 1888
F476 JH1581
Canvas, 62 x 52 cm
Cambridge, Massachusetts,
Fogg Art Museum, Harvard
University

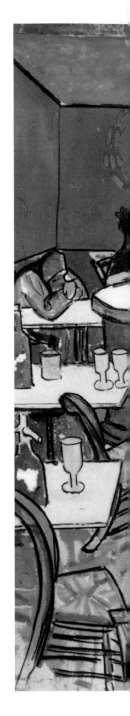

Van Gogh wrote to his brother Theo that it was painted at night by gaslight. (The popular story that he painted it with burning candles on his hat is a fabrication.) On the subject of this work, he wrote (543):

'The sky is bluish green, the water a royal blue, the earth mauve. The city is blue and violet, the gaslight yellow and the reflections are a golden red merging into a bronze green. Against the bluish green heavens the Great Bear blinks with a greenish pink light, and the modest pale glow of the constellation contrasts with the bold gold of the gaslight. In the foreground there are the two colourful figures of a courting couple.'

The Yellow House

At the beginning of May 1888 Van Gogh had rented the Yellow House at 2 place Lamartine, near the station in Arles. This house, with its green shutters and a green door, only exists in his painting of it, entitled *Yellow House* (JH 1589; see p. 84/5), for it was destroyed in June 1944 in the

The Night Café
Arles, August-September 1888
F1463 JH1576
Watercolour, 42 x 61.5 cm
Private collection

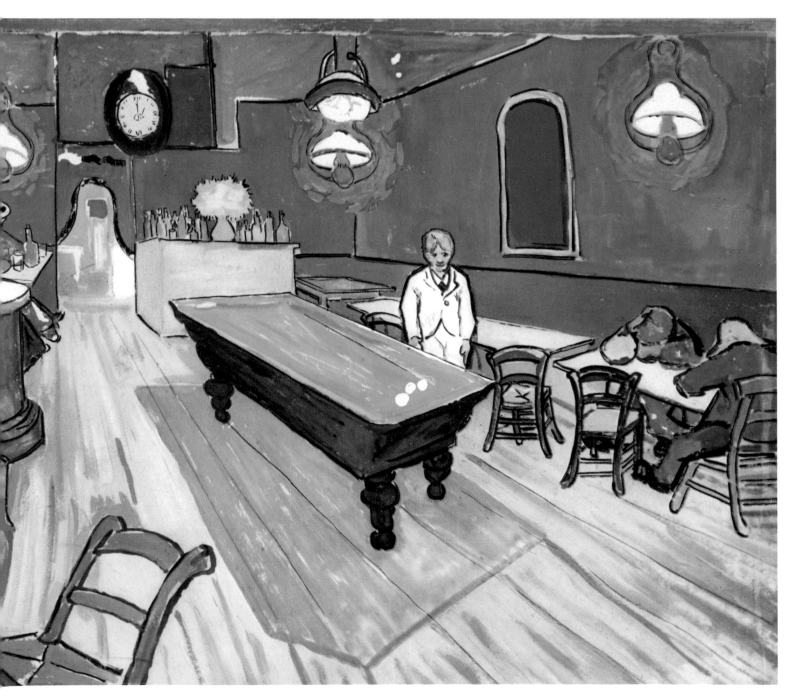

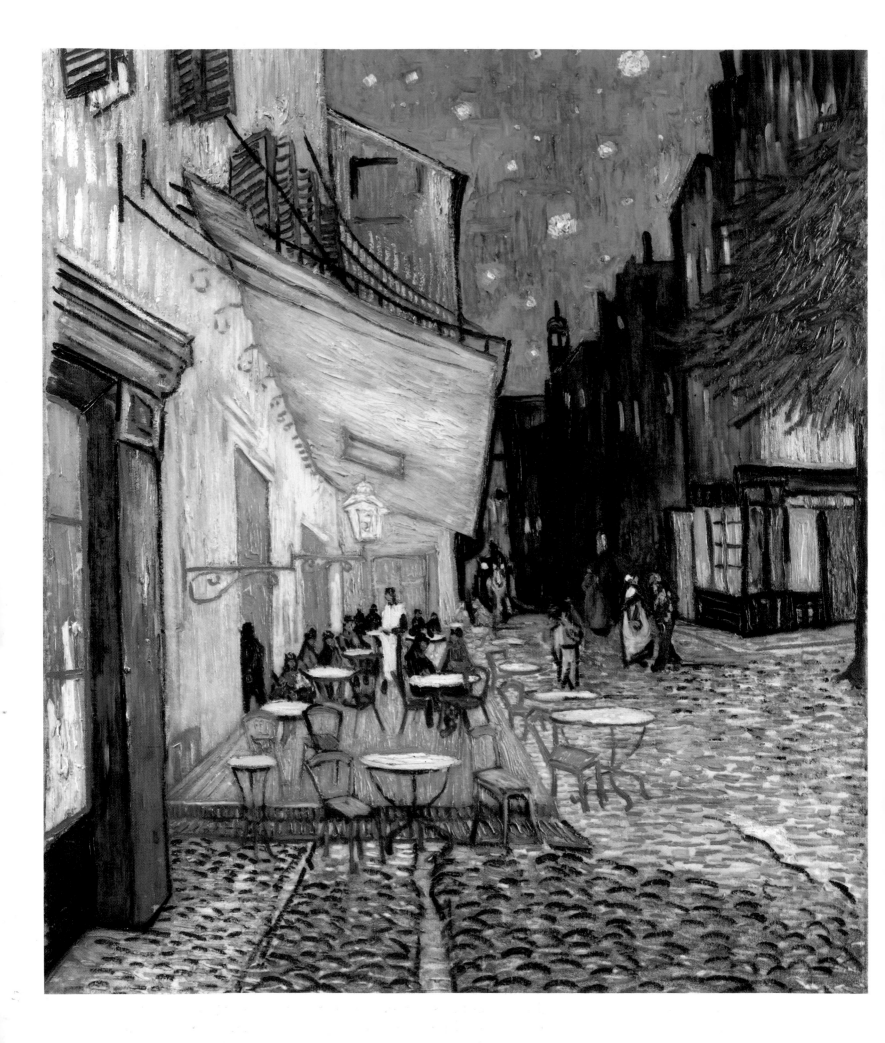

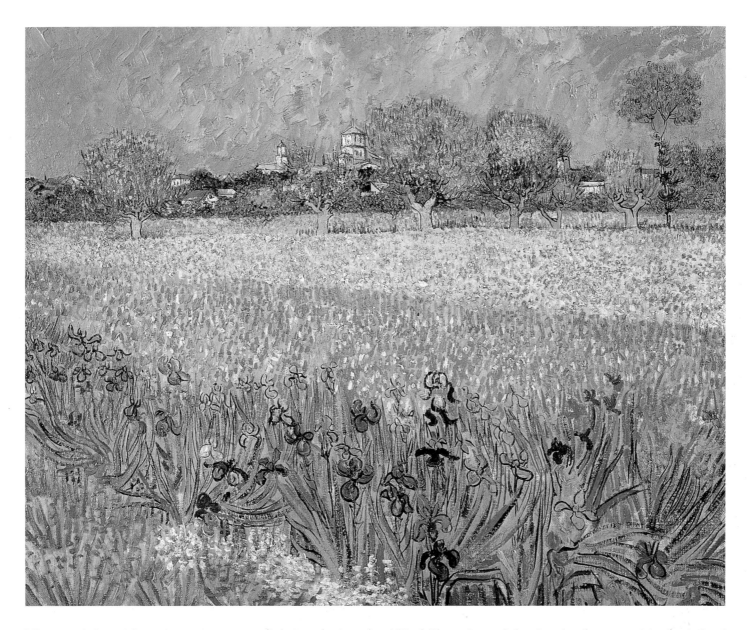

View at Arles with Irises
Arles, May 1888
F409 JH1416
Canvas, 54 x 65 cm
Amsterdam, Rijksmuseum
Vincent van Gogh

Café Terrace at Night
Arles, September 1888
F467 JH1580
Canvas, 81 x 65.6 cm
Otterlo, Rijksmuseum
Kröller-Müller

fighting during the Allied liberation of the South of France. To the left of the Yellow House is a grocer's shop with its awnings down. The word '*Comestibles*' is shown on a watercolour, but not on this painting in oils. To the extreme left, in the shadow of a tree, is the restaurant where Van Gogh ate every day. His friend, the postman Roulin, lived 'at the end of the road, on the left, between the two railway viaducts.' The tall building behind - a restaurant with a red roof - still exists. The railway viaduct in the background is also still recognizable. But while two adults and two children are walking in the middle of the road in the painting, now - over a century later - the traffic is very busy, and the area in the foreground of the painting is a large car park.

In the spring of 1888, Van Gogh described his new house to his sister, Wil (W 4): 'I live in a small yellow house with a green door and shutters, whitewashed inside with very colourful Japanese prints on the white walls and red quarry tiles on the floor - the house catches the sun all day with a strong blue sky above it, and the shadows in the middle of the day are much shorter than they are at home.'

Although Van Gogh had already rented this house unfurnished in May, he did not move in until the middle of September. In the meantime he used the premises as a studio where his models posed for him. He also hung his work there, as well as his Japanese prints. Initially he had no

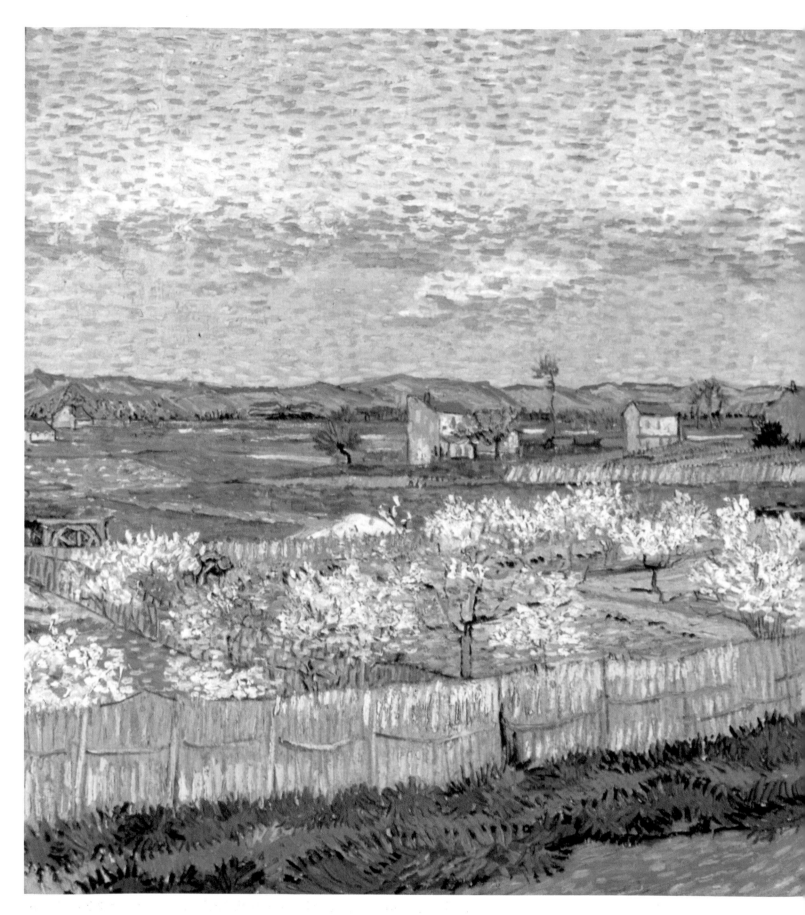

La Crau with Peach Trees in Bloom
Arles, April 1889
F514 JH1681
Canvas, 65.5 x 81.5 cm
London, Courtauld Institute Galleries

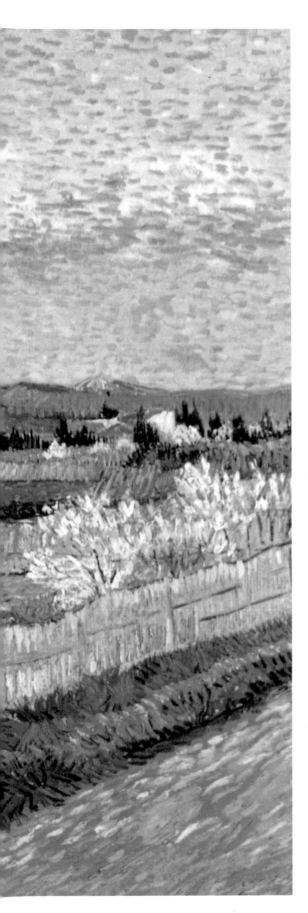

money for furnishing the house, but on 8 September Theo sent him 300 francs. (Theo was able to send him this sum because he had just had an inheritance from his Uncle Vincent.)

On about 8 September he wrote to Wil about the house again, this time not in Dutch, but in French (W 7): 'The house is situated on a square with a green garden of plane trees, pink laurels and acacias. In this house I can live and breathe, think and paint. I think I would rather go further south than go back to the north, for I have a great need of a lot of warmth for my blood to circulate normally. I feel much better here than in Paris.'

Like a nobleman

On Sunday, 2 September 1888 Van Gogh painted *Portrait of Eugène Boch* (JH 1574; see p. 85). The Belgian artist posed for Van Gogh in the Yellow House after they had been to a bullfight, held in the arena in Arles, followed by a long walk. Van Gogh later painted a portrait of his friend in words, saying that he had 'a face like a razor blade, with green eyes and a distinguished appearance. His head looks like that of a nobleman in the days of William the Silent' (505). The man was 'dressed in a short yellow jacket with a collar of unbleached linen and a striped tie' (531). He painted the artist against a background of 'a deep ultramarine starry sky' (531). There is a shrill and challenging contrast between the orange-yellow figure and the blue background. Van Gogh wrote (520): 'Instead of the wall of the miserable dwelling, I am painting a simple background behind the head in the richest and most intense blue I can make, and by means of this simple combination of the illuminated blond head against the deep blue background, I have achieved a mysterious effect like that of a star in the deep azure.'

The portrait of Boch is quite similar to *Self-portrait* (JH 1581; see p. 86), dating from the same period - September 1888. Van Gogh often had no model, so bought a mirror in order to paint self-portraits. He was working very hard at this time, sometimes working without interruption on one painting for twelve hours, and completing three canvasses a week. Once he almost finished two in a day. But during a week of feverish activity he still found time to write letters. In a letter to his friend, the painter Paul Gauguin, he wrote (553a): 'I have done an ash coloured self-portrait. I obtained this ashen colour by mixing Veronese green with orange. The painting has a pale background in Veronese green which is in harmony with the reddish brown clothes. I do not represent myself in an exaggerated way: I wanted my character to be that of a bigshot, a simple worshipper of the eternal Buddha.'

Before moving into the Yellow House in the middle of September 1888, Van Gogh had spent several months in a room in the nearby Café de la Gare, which belonged to Joseph and Marie Ginoux. This café was situated at 30 place Lamartine. It was a *café-de-nuit* - it stayed open all night - and homeless wanderers would often congregate there. Van Gogh captured this scene in *The Night Café* (JH 1576; see p. 86/7). Sometimes drinkers would sleep off their intoxication with their heads on the table. At the beginning of September Van Gogh stayed awake for three nights, sleeping during the daytime, in order to paint the interior of the café at night. He told Theo how he depicted terrible human passions in complementary colours of red and green (533): 'The room is a blood red colour, with dark yellow and a green billiard table in the middle, four lemon yellow lamps

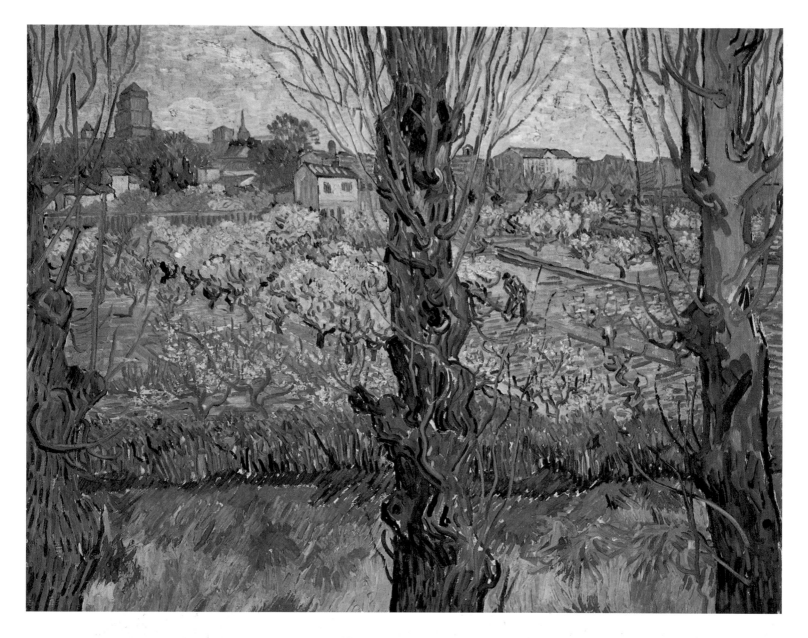

with a glow of orange and green. Everywhere there is a contrast between
the most desperate shades of red and green, in the figures of the sleeping
wanderers, in the empty desolate room, in purple and blue. For example,
the blood red and yellow-green colours of the billiard table contrast with
the soft tender Louis XV green of the bar.'

Following this interior of a café, Van Gogh painted an exterior: *Café
Terrace at Night* (JH 1580; see p. 88). This work, which also dates from
September 1888, hums with activity. He wrote to Wil (W7):

'On the terrace there are the figures of people drinking ... An enormous
yellow lantern illuminates the terrace, the front of the café, the pavement,
and the lantern even casts its light over the cobbles of the street, which is
a pinkish violet colour. The fronts of the houses in a street below a sky-
blue starry sky are dark-blue or violet with a green tree. This is a night
painting without black, with only beautiful blue, violet or green, and in
these surroundings the illuminated square takes on the colour of a pale
sulphur or lemon yellow. I really enjoy painting the square *in situ*. In the
past, you would first do a drawing (*in situ*) and then do the painting in
the daytime, based on the drawing. But it suits me very well to paint this
sort of thing directly.'

For this canvas Van Gogh had been inspired by the novel *Bel Ami*, by
Guy de Maupassant, which contains a description of a starry night with

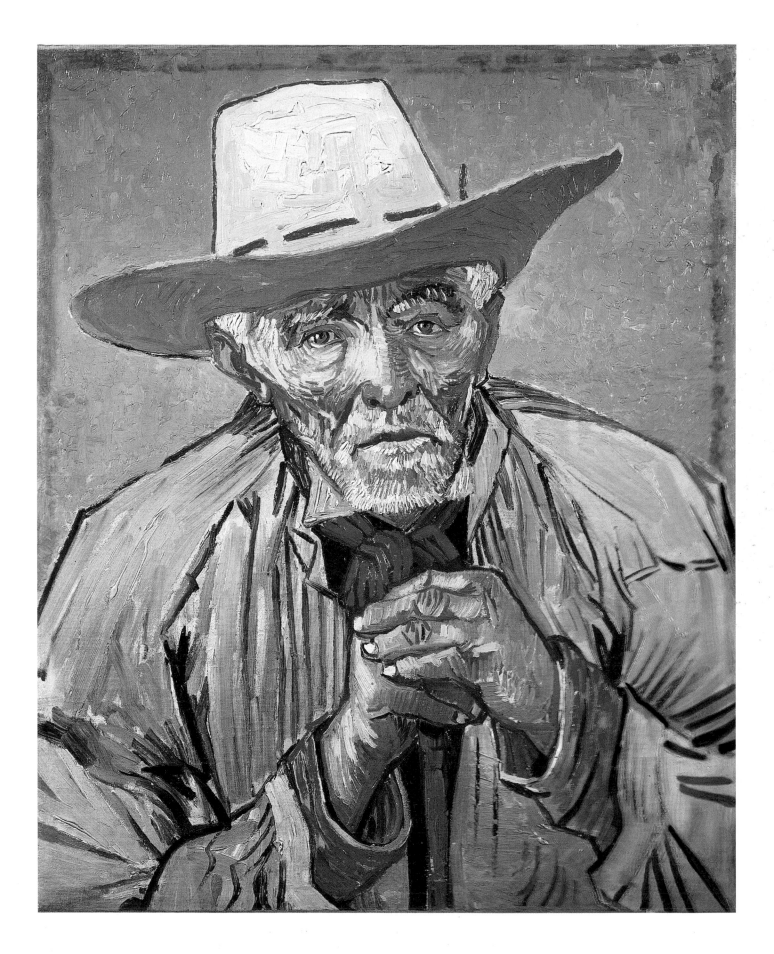

Patience Escalier with Walking Stick
Arles, August 1888
F444 JH1563
Canvas, 69 x 56 cm
Private collection

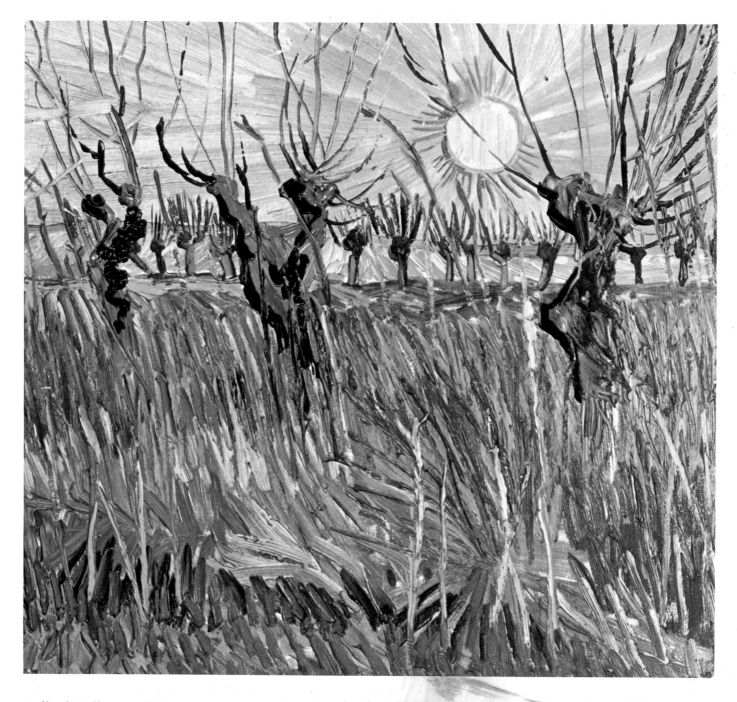

Pollard Willows with Setting Sun
Arles, October 1888
F572 JH1597
Canvas on cardboard,
31.5 x 34.5 cm
Otterlo, Rijksmuseum
Kröller-Müller

an illuminated café. (This book can be seen in one of his still lifes, JH 1349, in the Kröller-Müller Museum, Otterlo.) *Café Terrace at Night* is reminiscent of a similar scene of Paris by his friend, the painter Louis Anquetin.

Pastoral mode

As we have already seen, Van Gogh always alternated his paintings of towns - by night and by day - with paintings of the countryside. In *View at Arles with Irises* (JH 1416; see p. 89) he portrayed meadows full of yellow buttercups with a diagonal row of purple flowers with green leaves in the foreground, and in the background, a horizontal line of red roofs and the spire of the St Trophime, partly concealed behind fig trees. Van Gogh always made a distinction between a study and a painting. For him this was a study (B 5): 'They were cutting the grass while I was painting, and that is why it is only a study and not a completed painting, as I had wished.'

The landscape *La Crau with Peach Trees in Bloom* (JH 1681; see p.

90/91) is another spring scene, dated April 1889, and so painted a year later than the previous view. Van Gogh was still working in Arles and the surrounding countryside. There are some similarities between the composition of the two paintings: in the foreground there is the same diagonal line of flowering trees (this time from left to right), while the houses and their red roofs form a horizontal line in the background. It is a gay and lively painting.

A *View of Arles* (JH 1685; see p. 92), also known as *Orchard in Bloom with Poplars in the Foreground*, was painted in that same month. Once again we see the spire of the church, but in this version the town is much closer. The composition is very strange: the vertical black lines of the trees dominate the canvas, and yet our eyes are drawn to the distant houses and the spire.

The beautiful portrait of *Patience Escalier with Walking Stick* (JH 1563; see p. 93), a former herdsman in the Camargue, is still in the pastoral mode. At the time Van Gogh painted him, he was a gardener for someone living in Crau. He was painted 'in the heat of the harvest as though the whole of the Midi is around him.' Here, Van Gogh's aggressive use of complementary colours is extremely provocative, and marks his rejection of the Impressionist style which he had learned in Paris. The effect of the blue smock against the plain orange background is overpowering. But the eyes of this simple, old peasant form the focal point of the work. His face, in the shadow of a broad-brimmed yellow hat, has a resigned as well as an exhausted expression.

During his years in Brabant, Etten and Nuenen, Van Gogh drew and also painted a number of heads of farmers and peasants using dark colours. But this portrait radiates the light of a hot summer in Provence, whilst revealing the same empathy with those who earn their bread by physical labour, and whose faces show the effects of diligent work.

Source of light and life

On 7 October 1888, Van Gogh wrote that he had painted a sunset the previous day. *Pollard Willows with Setting Sun* (JH 1597; see p. 94) might easily have been a Dutch landscape. As in the *View of Arles* (see p. 92), the trees dominate with their broad, dark vertical lines perpendicular to the horizontal blue line just above the centre. Yet our eyes are drawn to the background - in this case, to the sun - which is depicted in an almost primitive way as a yellow disc surrounded by orange lines radiating in every direction. The painting is obviously about the sun as a symbol of the source of light and life. During this stage of his artistic development - the periods in Arles and Saint-Rémy - Van Gogh often painted the sun as a yellow disc in the sky and used this image in his paintings of sowers, including *Sower with Setting Sun* (JH 1627; see p. 96), now in Zurich. This image was a highly personal one: an object which fascinated and obsessed him, and which had a religious significance.

In a letter with a drawing which he sent to Theo, dated 25 November 1888 (558a), he described the sun in this last work as: 'an enormous lemon yellow disc' against 'a greenish yellow sky with pink clouds. The field is violet, the sower and the tree are Prussian blue.' He thought this sower was much better than the one he had painted in June with an orange-blue field in the foreground, a painting which he himself considered 'a failure' at the time. However, he was satisfied with the later version. It is signed

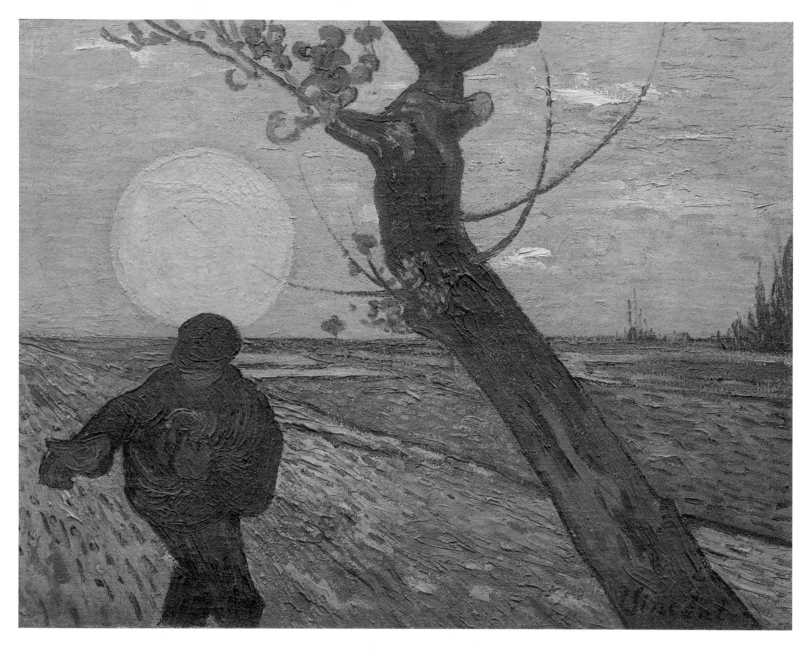

Sower with Setting Sun
Arles, November 1888
F450 JH1627
Burlap on canvas, 73.5 x 93 cm
Zurich, Foundation E.G. Bührle
Collection

'Vincent' at the bottom of the tree. For this painting he first made a *pochade*, or preliminary study in oils, which is half the size of the painting now in the Van Gogh Museum in Amsterdam. The differences between the works can only be discerned on careful examination, which reveals the work from Zurich to be superior.

The composition is that of a Japanese woodcut by Hiroshige or Hokusai. The picture is perfectly divided by the diagonal tree next to the sower, whose stretched out right arm forms an opposing diagonal which is continued in a branch of the tree. The symbolic images of sower and sun are closely related: the seed that is sown must germinate and grow in the heat of the sun. What is sown by man can only grow in the warmth and light of love, God's love, and mercy.

Vineyards

In the autumn of 1888 Van Gogh painted several vineyards, one of which was *The Green Vineyard* (JH 1595; see p. 98). At the beginning of October he wrote (544): 'The vineyard I have just painted is green, dark purple and yellow with purple bunches of grapes hanging on black and orange vines.

On the horizon there are several greyish blue willows, and in the far distance the wine press with its red roof, and far away, the lilac silhouette of the town. In the vineyard there are figures of ladies with red parasols, and other figures of grape pickers with their cart.'

The second painting is entitled *The Red Vineyard* (JH 1626; see p. 99). At the beginning of November 1888, he wrote (561): 'I have completed a canvas of a vineyard which is completely purple and yellow, with figures in blue and violet and a yellow sun.' In *The Green Vineyard* the two main figures, the women with the red parasols, are not working but are taking a relaxed stroll, while here there is a hive of activity with women picking grapes, and in the background a man ready with his horse and cart.

Two sales

For a long time it was said that *The Red Vineyard* was the only painting which was sold during Van Gogh's lifetime. In February 1890 there was an exhibition in Brussels by a group of artists who called themselves Les Vingt. Van Gogh contributed six paintings, one of which was sold for 400 Belgian francs, as Theo noted in a letter to his brother of 14 February. One of the contributors to the exhibition, the artist Anna Boch, a sister of Eugène Boch, bought a painting. However, it is not certain whether or not this was *The Red Vineyard*. The Van Gogh expert, Ronald Pickvance, believes that Anna Boch bought this work after Van Gogh's death, but that one of his paintings was certainly sold in Brussels. Another Van Gogh authority, Marc Edo Tralbaut, recounts that at least one other Van Gogh painting was sold during his lifetime. On 3 October 1888, Theo wrote to the London art dealers, Sulley & Lori: 'We are pleased to inform you that we have sent you the two paintings which you bought and which you paid for promptly: a landscape by Camille Corot, and a self-portrait by V. van Gogh.' This shows that fifteen months before the sale of a Van Gogh painting in Brussels, another work had been sold in London. Thus the artist must have known that two of his paintings had been sold, although this is an extremely small proportion of his production of approximately 825 paintings.

A rest cure is recommended

Meanwhile Van Gogh had furnished his Yellow House. The gas had been connected in the studio for 25 francs, and he had employed a housekeeper. He painted his bedroom several times whilst in Saint-Rémy in October 1888, and in the summer of 1889 he completed *Vincent's Bedroom in Arles* (JH 1771; see p. 100), a work he copied twice.

On 16 October 1888 Van Gogh wrote to his brother Theo (554):

'Today I am fine again. My eyes are still tired, but I've had a new idea ... I have painted my bedroom; it all depends on the colours, and by simplifying things I am giving them more style. I want to create an impression of rest, or sleep in general. When you look at the painting, your brain or your imagination should feel rested. The walls are a pale violet colour, the floor is made of red tiles, the wood of the bed and the chairs is the colour of fresh butter, the sheets and pillows are a very pale lemon yellow. The blankets are scarlet, the window green; the dressing table is orange, the washbasin blue, the doors lilac. That is all. There is nothing special in this room with its closed shutters. The thick lines of the furni-

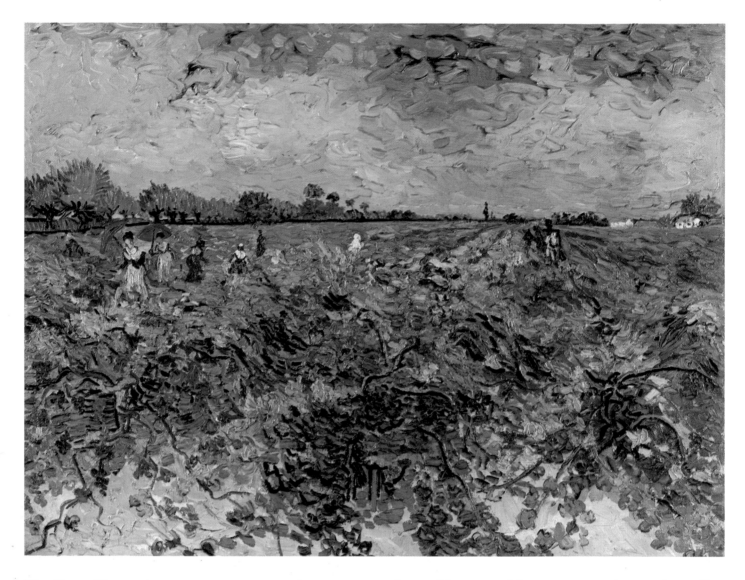

The Green Vineyard
Arles, September 1888
F475 JH1595
Canvas, 72 x 92 cm
Otterlo, Rijksmuseum
Kröller-Müller

ture also express an intangible peace. There are portraits on the wall, a mirror, a towel and some clothes. The frame should be white because there is no white in the painting.'

Finally Van Gogh noted the contrast between this painting and that of the *Night Café* (see p. 86/7). In October he also wrote to his friend Paul Gauguin about this painting of his bedroom, describing how he wished to express 'complete rest' through his use of colour.

With Gauguin

On 23 October 1888 Paul Gauguin (1848-1903) arrived at the Yellow House, where he stayed for nine weeks. He left his temperamental friend on 26 December after several serious disagreements and incidents. Van Gogh had wanted Gauguin, whom he had met in Paris in November 1887, to come to Arles ever since May 1888, so that they could work together. It was finally possible when Theo sold some of Gauguin's work for 300 francs, which helped to pay the train fare from Pont-Aven in Brittany and other expenses. Van Gogh painted six views of sunflowers to brighten up his guest's bedroom.

For more than a month the two friends got on fairly well. Van Gogh did the shopping and Gauguin the cooking. They often painted the same subject. But then tension started to build up. Van Gogh's dream of an artists' colony in Arles, which was to include the artists Laval and Ber-

for many years.) The seventeen-year-old Armand looks at the world candidly. The blue hat and greenish yellow jacket against the green background are wonderfully effective. The boy's face stands out strongly in the midst of all these bright colours. This painting has sometimes been compared with the portraits by Edouard Manet.

At that time Armand was a blacksmith's apprentice, but later he became an officer in Tunisia. While he is shown in this portrait - now in Essen - as a strong boy who will carve out a place for himself in society, another portrait of Armand in the Boymans-Van Beuningen Museum in Rotterdam, this time in profile, shows him as a thoughtful dreamy figure, no doubt another aspect of his character. This is a work with a simple contrast of blue and green, in which the red and brown face with blue eyes stands out clearly.

La Berceuse

Van Gogh called his third family portrait, that of Madame Roulin, *La Berceuse* (JH 1669; see p. 106) - the lullaby. The woman is holding a rope between her hands to rock the cradle for the newly-born Marcelle. In a letter of around 29 January 1889 to his friend A.H. Koning, the Dutch artist (571a), Van Gogh mentioned that he had 'a portrait of a woman on the easel'. He described this work as follows:

'She is a woman dressed in green, with an olive green top and a Veronese green skirt. Her hair is a bright orange colour and plaited. Her complexion is done in chromium yellow, though obviously with some shading to model the features. The hands holding the rope for the cradle are the same. The background is vermilion at the bottom, representing a simple flagged or stone floor. The wall is papered, which I have of course worked out to be in harmony with the rest of the colours. This wallpaper is bluish green with pink dahlias, dotted with orange and ultramarine.'

In this painting, Van Gogh 'sang a lullaby in colours'. He was inspired by the music of Richard Wagner and Hector Berlioz, a novel by Pierre Loti entitled *Pêcheur d'Islande* (1886), and the work of the Dutch writer, Frederik van Eeden. He saw this painting as the centrepiece of a triptych; *La Berceuse* was to have had a painting of sunflowers on either side. He even made a sketch of this arrangement in a letter to Theo (592). For him, this was like a painting of the Virgin Mary between two candles.

Van Gogh copied this painting no fewer than five times with small variations. It is only in this portrait shown here that the right hand rests on the left hand; in the other four it is the other way round. Of the five Berceuses, two are in the Netherlands: one in the Kröller-Müller Museum in Otterlo, and one in the Stedelijk Museum in Amsterdam. The other three are in America: in the Museum of Fine Arts in Boston, the Art Institute in Chicago, and a private collection. The portrait illustrated here was probably painted first. This would also have been the work that he gave Madame Roulin as a present, while he sent the other four to Theo in Paris for sale.

In all the versions of this painting the complementary colours red and green are predominant. The figures have been clearly outlined, a characteristic of *cloisonné* style, which takes its name from '*email cloisonné*' or cloisonné enamel, a technique in which the blocks of colour are divided by lines of copper. Thus the style in which this painting was executed is far removed from the Impressionist style of Van Gogh's Parisian period.

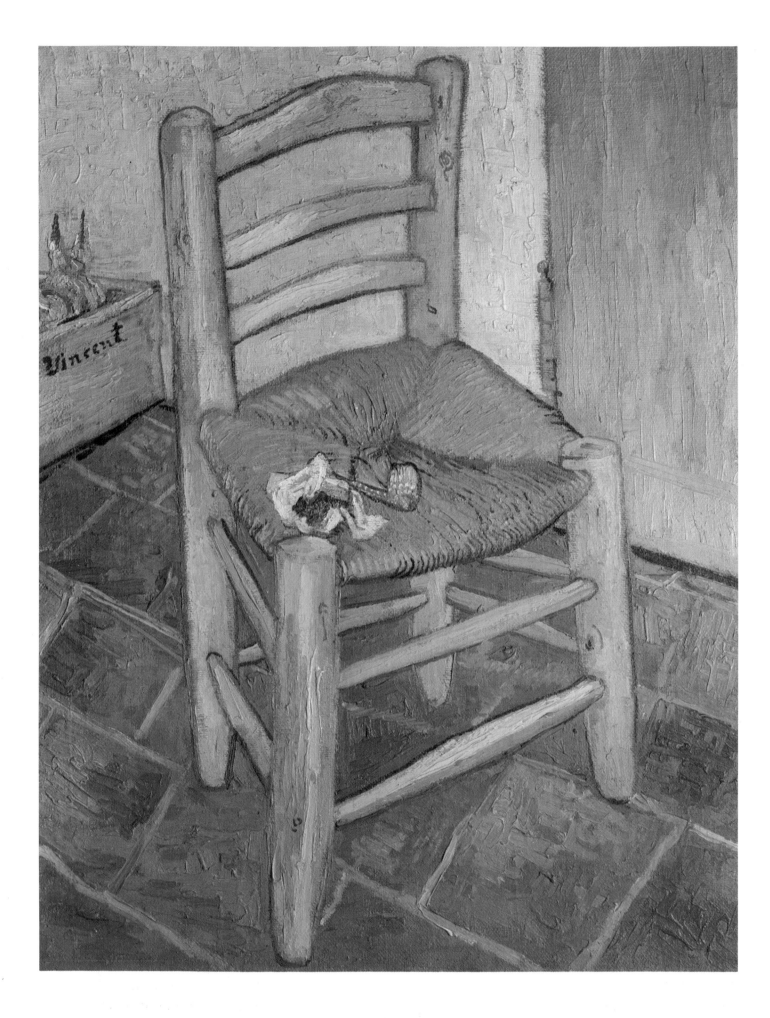

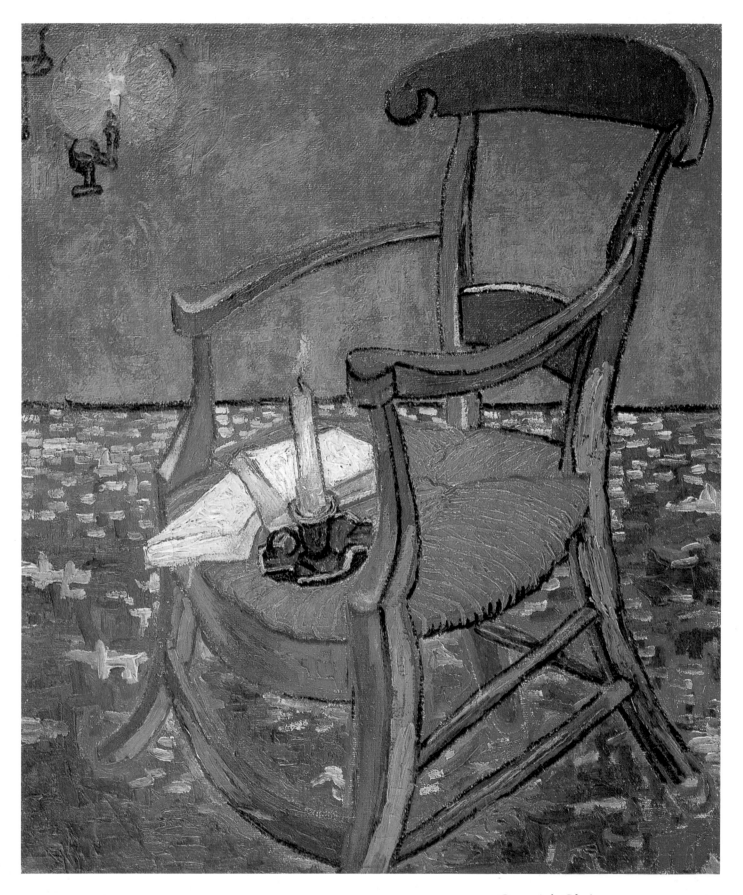

Vincent's Chair
Arles, December 1888
F498 JH1635
Canvas, 93 x 73.5 cm
London, The Tate Gallery

Gauguin's Chair
November-December 1888
F499 JH1636
Canvas, 90.5 x 72 cm
Amsterdam, Rijksmuseum
Vincent van Gogh

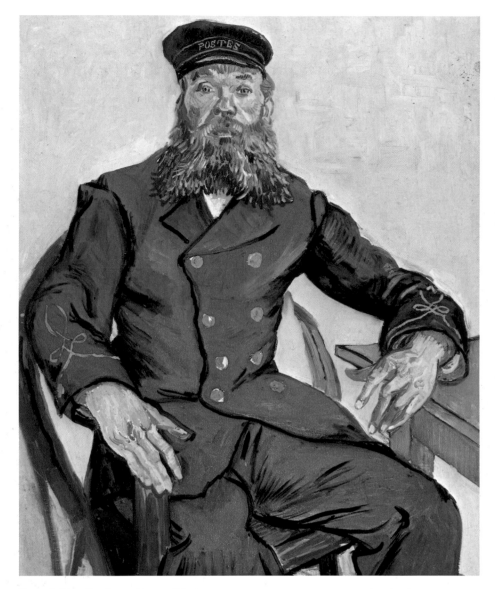

Joseph Roulin in a Cane Chair
Arles, July 1888
F432 JH1522
Canvas, 81 x 65 cm
Boston, Museum of Fine Arts,
Gift of Robert Treat Paine

Armand Roulin
Arles, December 1888
F492 JH1642
Canvas, 66 x 55 cm
Essen, Folkwang Museum

For some time he had planned to do a coloured print of this work, a 'chromolitographie de bazar', which could then be sold to fishermen to hang up in their cabins. It was to be a print which would console them in their loneliness and their fear of the dangers at sea. For Van Gogh, this painting had a religious dimension. He thought the mother figure could be seen as a Blessed Virgin, a Stella Maris, by these fishermen.

Madame Roulin was also painted on various occasions holding her baby, while the portrait of the baby on its own, *Marcelle Roulin* (JH 1641; see p. 107), has two variations.

Finally, Van Gogh painted the eleven-year-old Camille. There are at least three portraits of him. The one shown here, *Camille Roulin* (JH 1645; see p. 108), now in the Van Gogh Museum in Amsterdam, is a portrait of Camille wearing a cap: a pleasant, lively lad, whose expression is similar to that of his mother's. There is a comparable portrait of Camille in the Philadelphia Museum, and a completely different portrait in the Museum of Sao Paulo in Brazil, painted in complementary colours of blue and orange, in which the boy is painted in profile, wearing a cap. (This painting is not recognized as a portrait of Camille Roulin by Jan Hulsker, though Ronald Pickvance attributes it as such.) In these works Van Gogh shows that he was an Expressionist before his time, anticipating twentieth-century painting - not only Expressionism, but also the Fauvism of artists such as Henri Matisse.

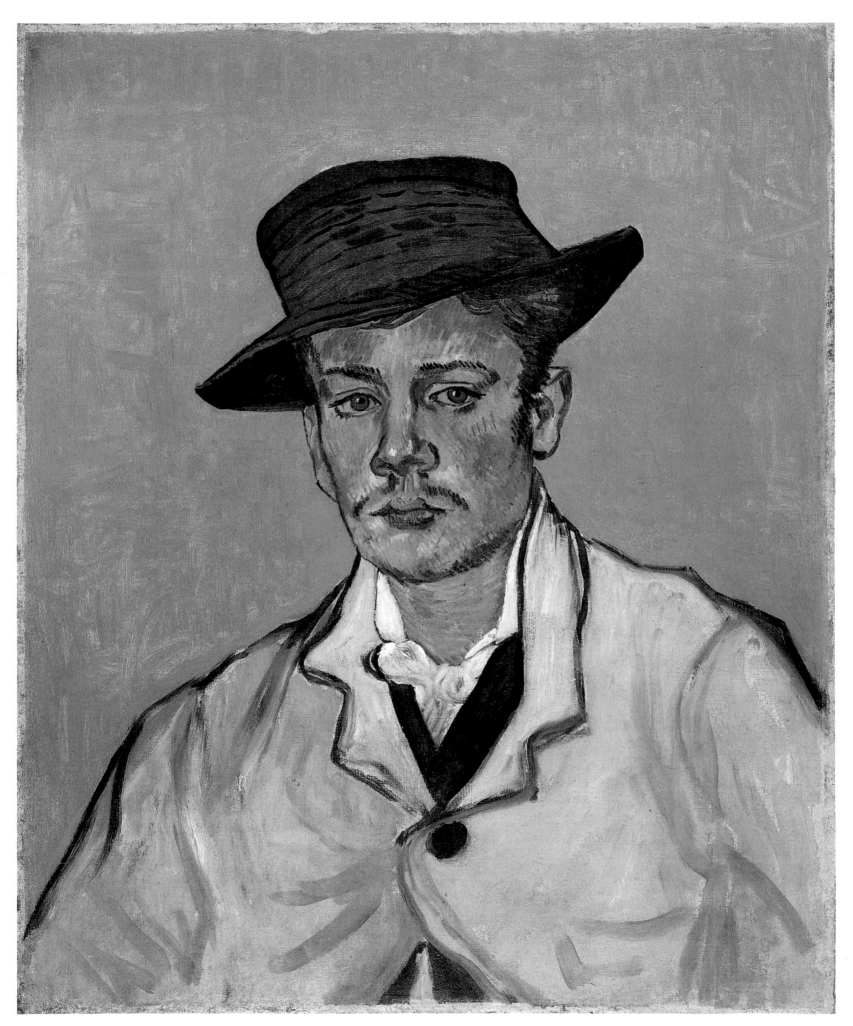

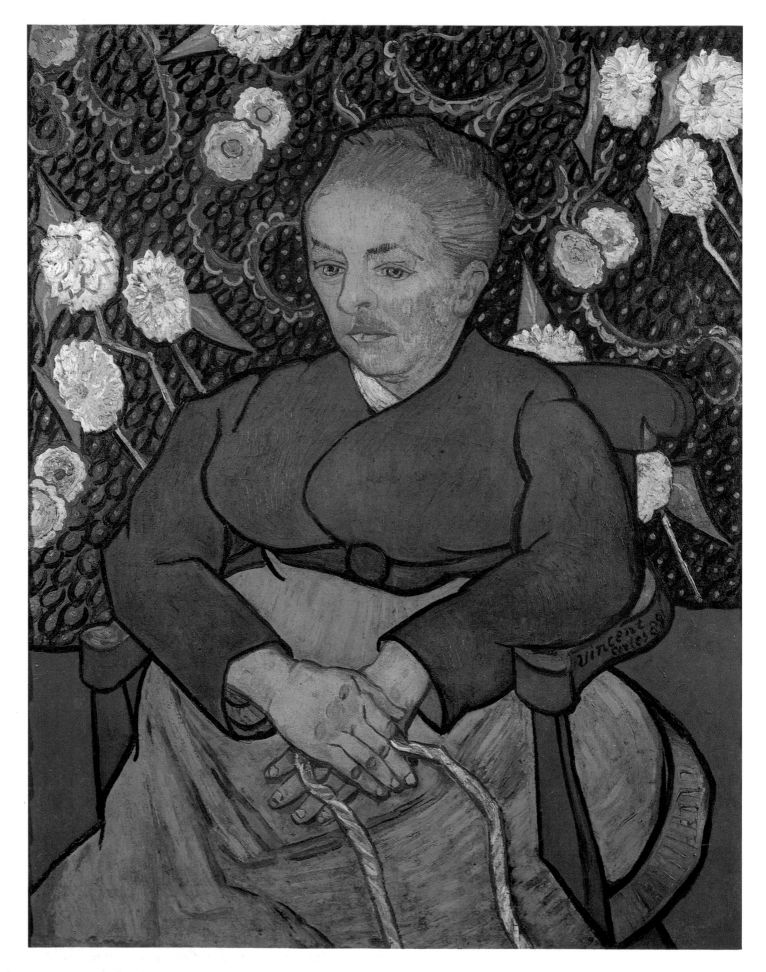

Augustine Roulin, 'La Berceuse', Arles, January 1889
F505 JH1669 - Canvas, 93 x 74 cm. Private collection

Marcelle Roulin
Arles, December 1888
F441 JH1641
Canvas, 35.5 x 24.5 cm
Amsterdam, Rijksmuseum
Vincent van Gogh

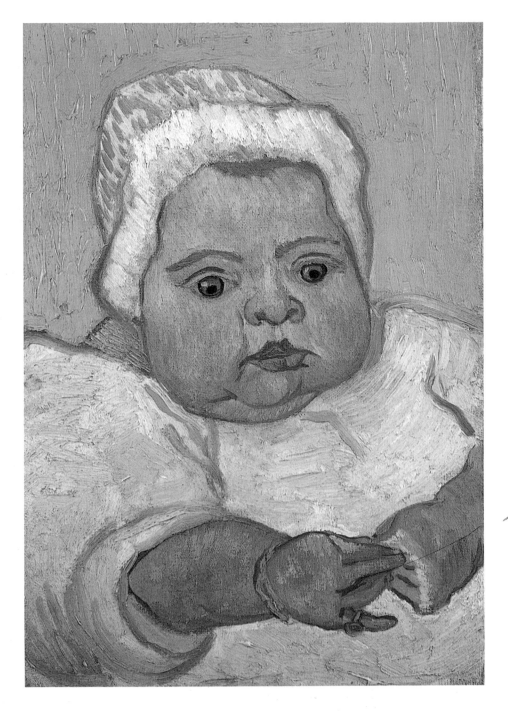

True friends

Joseph Roulin and his wife Augustine, who was ten years younger, meant a great deal to Van Gogh. Even when he was admitted to hospital in Arles, they proved to be true friends with a great deal of patience and understanding for his highly unsociable behaviour, and even showed appreciation for his work, though it was only understood by very few at that time. These so-called simple people had more insight into the qualities of Van Gogh than many intellectuals, art dealers and collectors.

Apart from Joseph Roulin, Paul-Eugène Milliet, second lieutenant in the 3rd Zouave Regiment, was another faithful friend of Van Gogh's, who gave him lessons in drawing. (This is not the Zouave described previously.) Early in July 1888, Van Gogh had gone out for the day with Milliet, visiting the ruins of the ancient abbey of Montmajour. Halfway through August, Milliet was on leave and went to the north of France. He took a package of thirty-six rolled up paintings with him for Theo in

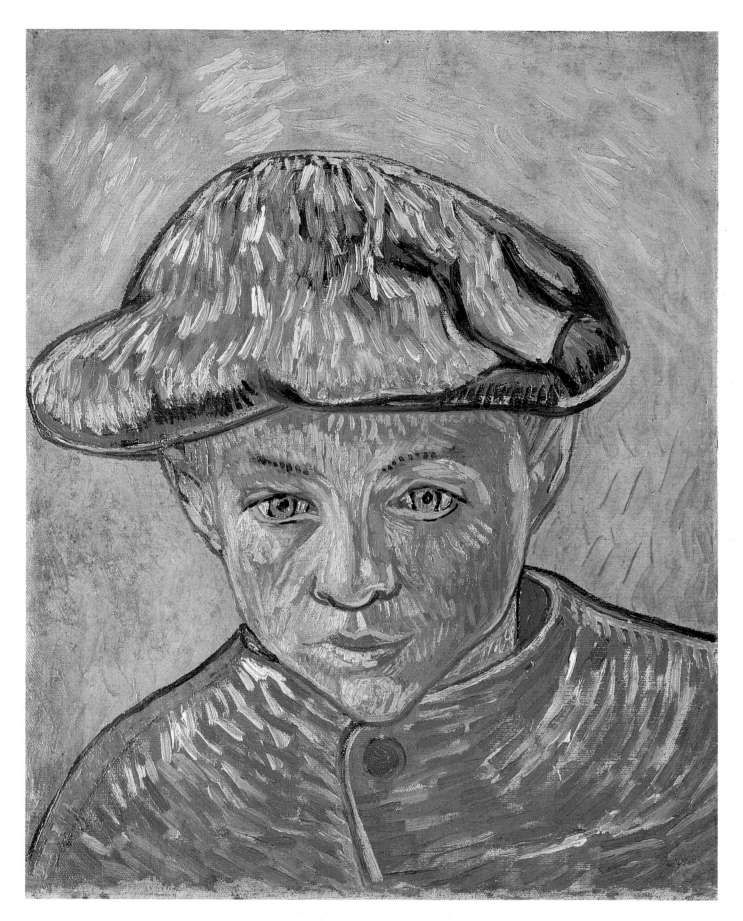

Camille Roulin
Arles, December 1888
F538 JH1645 Canvas, 37.5 x 32.5 cm
Amsterdam, Rijksmuseum Vincent van Gogh

Lieutenant Milliet
Arles, September 1888
F473 JH1588
Canvas, 60 x 49 cm
Otterlo, Rijksmuseum
Kröller-Müller

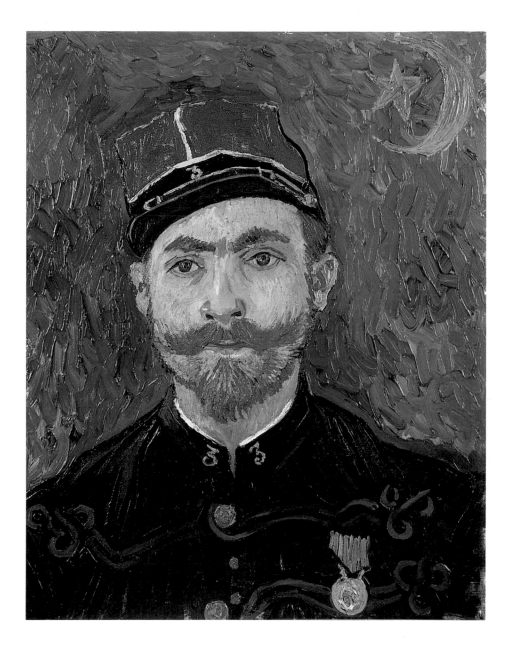

Paris. On the journey back to Arles, he called in on Theo again, and was given a package of Japanese prints, lithographs and illustrated magazines for Van Gogh, which he gave to him on about 20 September.

The portrait of *Lieutenant Milliet* (JH 1588; see p. 109) was painted shortly afterwards. The complementary colours, red for the cap, and green for the background, are predominant. The medal on the uniform was a decoration for an expedition to Tonkin in French Indo-China, the place from which Milliet had returned in February 1888 to be quartered in the Zouave barracks in Arles. The yellow half moon and the five-pointed star formed the insignia of Milliet's regiment. Van Gogh described him as a 'young, good-looking man with an easy carefree manner. He would be a good model for a painting of a lover. I have promised him a work for his trouble, but he can't sit still.' Finally, however, Milliet did pose for him. Like the portrait of Eugène Boch, the portrait of Milliet was framed and hung on the wall of Van Gogh's bedroom.

Madame Ginoux was also a dear friend of Van Gogh's and he painted her twice as *The Arlésienne* (JH 1624 and JH 1625; see p. 110, p. 111), once with books and once wearing gloves with a parasol. The second work was probably the one which Van Gogh wrote about in his letter to Theo of 6 November 1888: 'I have finally found an Arlésienne, a figure I got down

109

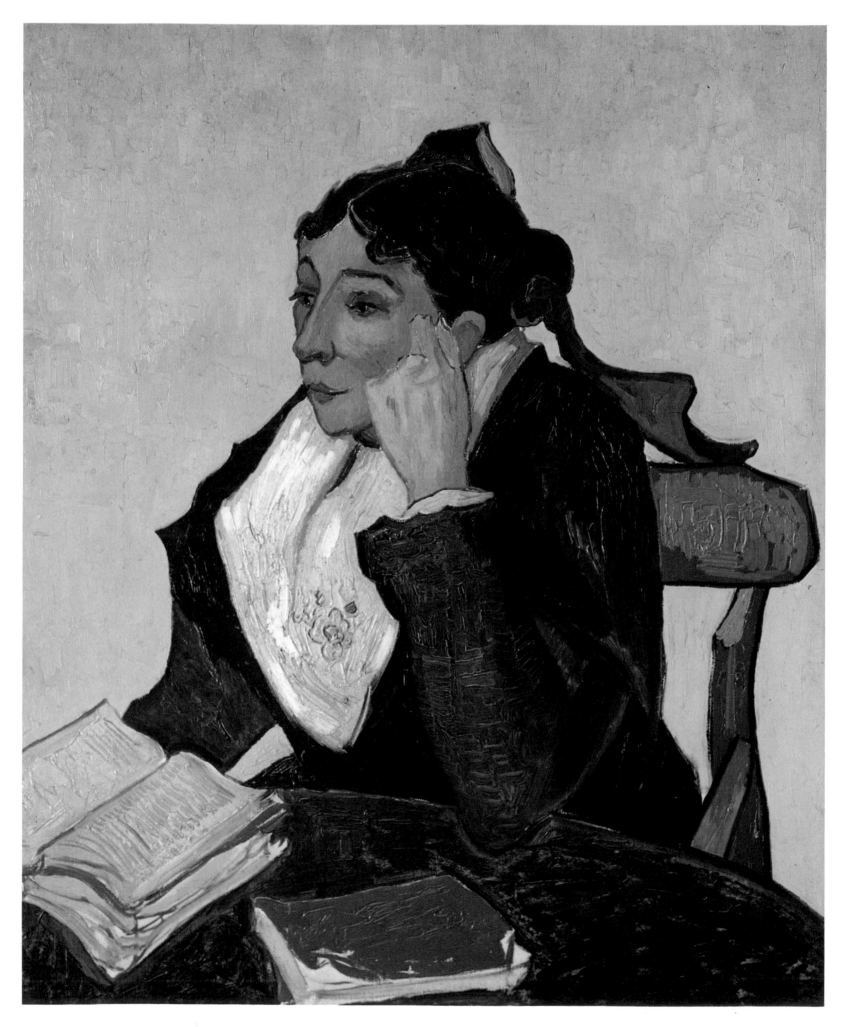

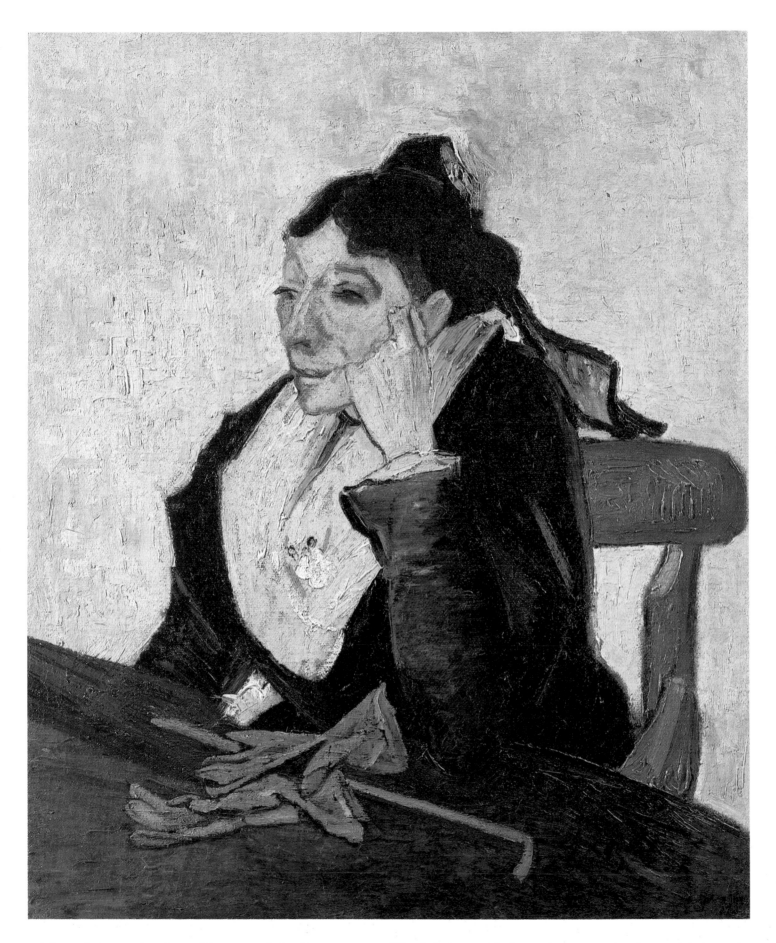

The Arlésienne, Madame Ginoux with Books
Arles, November 1888
F488 JH1624 - Canvas, 90 x 72 cm
New York, Metropolitan Museum of Art

The Arlésienne, Madame Ginoux with Gloves and Parasol
Arles, November 1888
F489 JH1625 - Canvas, 93 x 74 cm
Paris, Musée d'Orsay

111

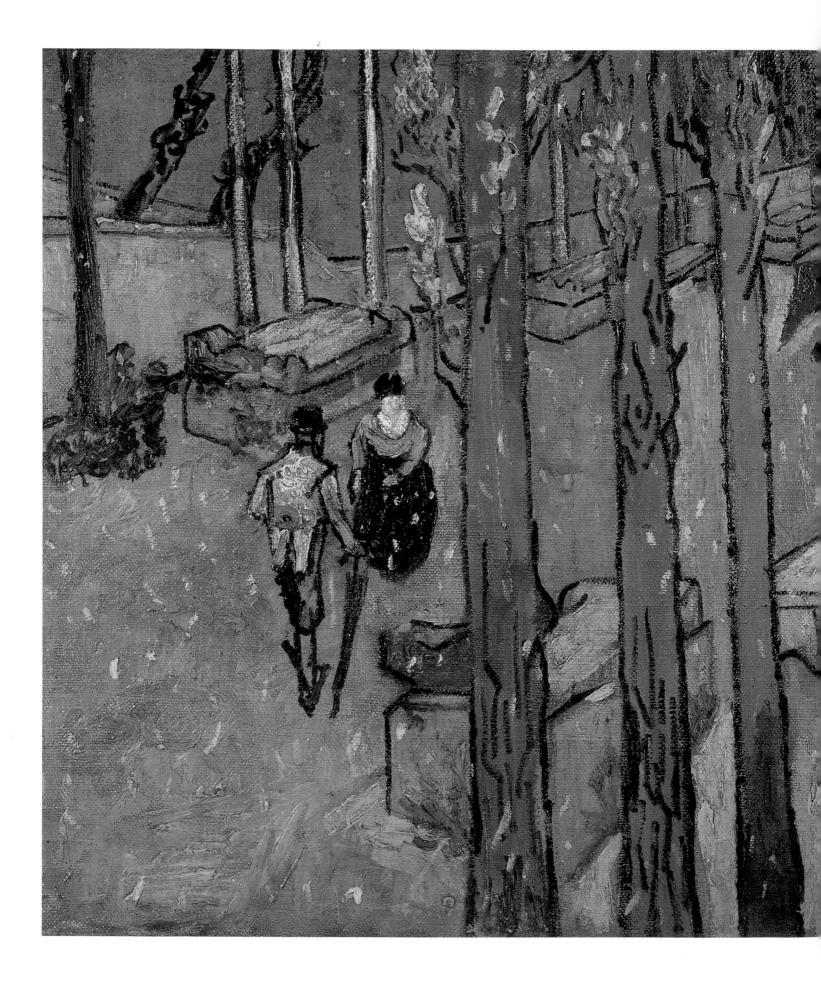

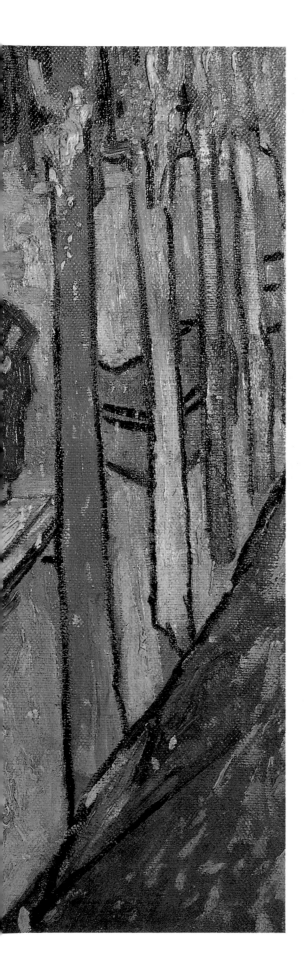

The Alyscamps, Avenue at Arles
Arles, November 1888
F486 JH1620
Canvas, 73 x 92 cm
Otterlo, Rijksmuseum
Kröller-Müller

113

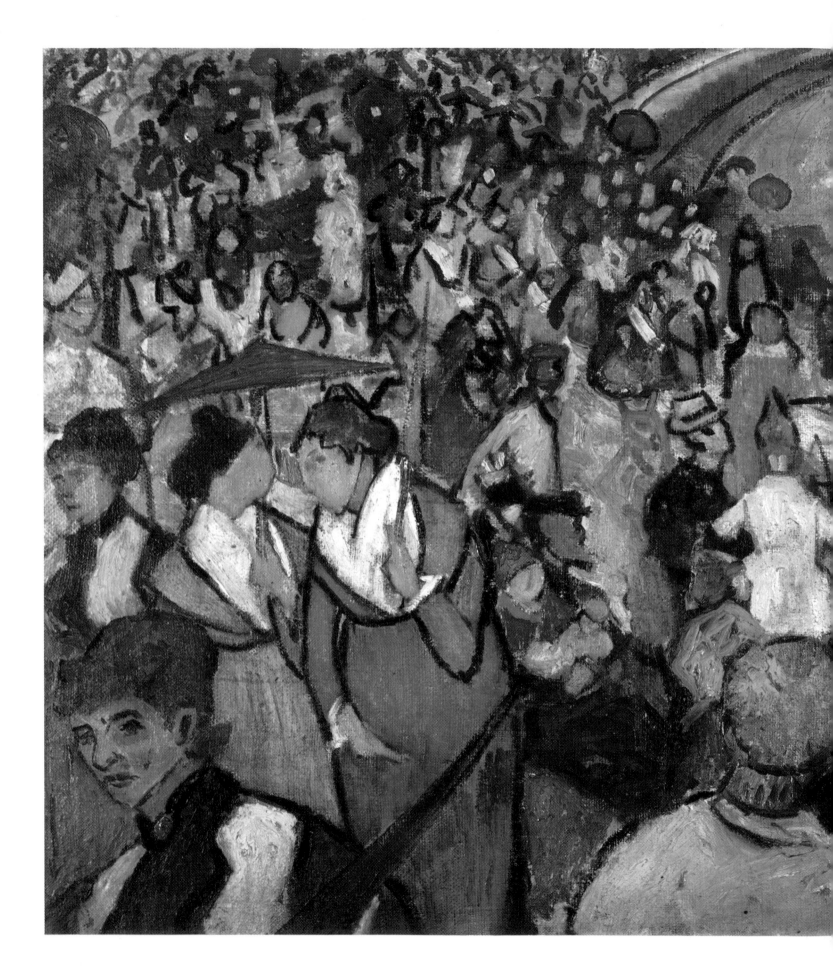

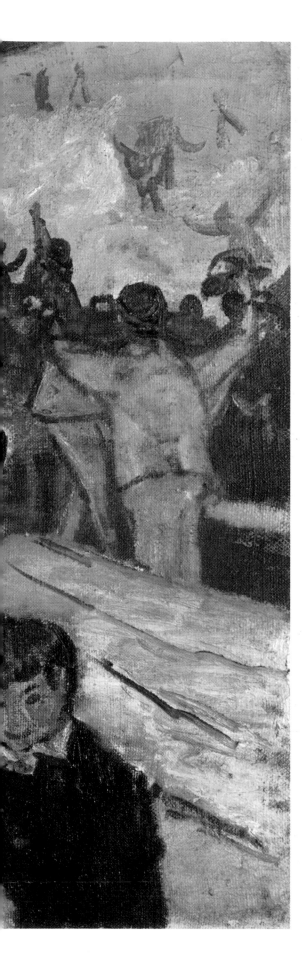

Spectators in the Arena
Arles, December 1888
F548 JH1653
Canvas, 73 x 92 cm
Leningrad, The Hermitage

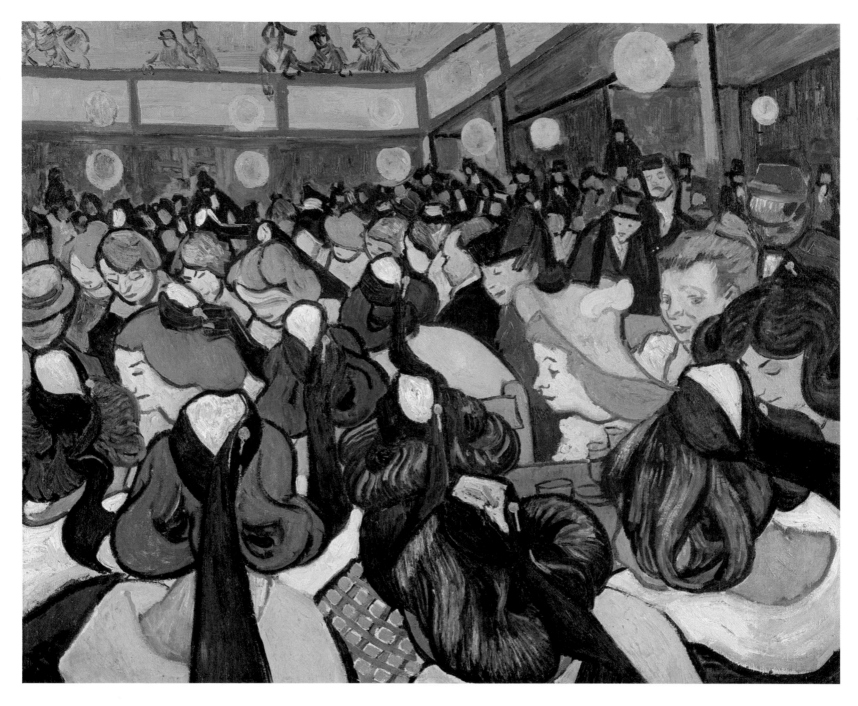

The Dance Hall
Arles, December 1888
F547 JH1652
Canvas, 65 x 81 cm
Paris, Musée d'Orsay

in paint in one hour, against a lemon yellow background, with a grey face, and her clothes are black, black, black, with Prussian blue, very rough. She is leaning on a green table and sitting on an orange wooden stool.' In a later letter he asked Theo: 'In your hurried visit to Arles, did you see the portrait of Madame Ginoux in black and yellow? That portrait was painted in three quarters of an hour.'

Whether it was done in an hour or in three-quarters of an hour, it was certainly painted very quickly. Van Gogh knew that some art dealers criticized him for working too fast, but he was unconcerned. It was his preferred way of working.

For Van Gogh, Madame Ginoux was just as fascinating a subject as Madame Roulin, and he did a series of paintings of this Arlésienne. Apart from these two works from Arles, another five were painted in Saint-Rémy in February 1890, after a drawing by Gauguin done in Arles the previous November - the same time that Van Gogh was painting his rapidly executed portraits. For Gauguin, this drawing was a preliminary study for a painting of Madame Ginoux in her night café, which was also immortalized by Van Gogh. This was the Café de la Gare at 30 place Lamartine in Arles. Van Gogh had rooms there from May to mid-September 1888. Then he moved to the Yellow House at 2 place Lamartine, but he was still living in the same square so Van Gogh, the Roulins and the Ginoux were all close neighbours.

The Alyscamps

During his stay in Arles, Van Gogh was inspired to make three paintings at The Alyscamps, a 2,000-year-old cemetery with gravestones dating from classical antiquity and the early Christian era. Dante and Ariosto referred to it. The word 'Alyscamps' has the same meaning as Champs Elysées, or Elysian Fields. Unfortunately, a great deal of its beauty was lost over the years, particularly when a railway line was constructed through it in the nineteenth century. Some of the most beautiful tombs were simply given away by the dignitaries of Arles at various times. But Van Gogh, who did not have much feeling for historical monuments, simply saw the cemetery as a picturesque subject to be painted. For him, *The Alyscamps* (JH 1620; see p. 112) was 'a study in falling leaves in a lane of poplars.' An evocation of autumn, executed in the complementary colours of bluish lilac and orange, red and green.

On about 6 November 1888, he wrote to Theo (559): 'I think you will enjoy the way I have painted the falling leaves. The lilac trunks are of poplars which have been cut off where the leaves start by the frame of the painting. These trunks border a lane with rows of ancient Roman tombs in lilac blue on the left and right, rather like pillars. The earth is covered with a thick layer of orange and yellow leaves like a carpet. They just go on falling like snowflakes.'

This work was painted from a high vantage point. Van Gogh's easel was placed on the two-metre-high dyke between the canal of Craponne and The Alyscamps. He did another version of this horizontal painting, which is now in the Niarchos collection in Athens. A third study of this subject is a vertical work in orange and blue, and red and green. In the background we see the Church of Saint-Honorat and the tall, smoking factory chimneys of the railway yard. Paul Gauguin also made a painting of The Alyscamps, which is now in the Musée d'Orsay in Paris. When you walk round Arles nowadays, you can still see The Alyscamps more or less as it was in Van Gogh's time.

You can also visit another ancient monument in Arles, the arena, which Van Gogh painted in the autumn of 1888: *Spectators in the Arena* (JH 1653; see pp. 114/115). The restoration of this monument, which dates from approximately 50 BC, had started over sixty years earlier. This canvas did not receive much mention in Van Gogh's letters, so there is little information available about it. One would suspect that the figure on the right under the red parasol is Madame Ginoux, and others have identified the Roulin couple with little Marcelle in the middle of the painting. This work is a scene of a large crowd of people, again viewed from a high vantage point. As regards its subject and the style of painting, it bears a close resemblance to *The Dance Hall* (JH 1652; see p. 116). The *cloisonné* style was adopted in both works, that is, the figures and blocks of colour are sharply outlined, almost like stained glass windows. This style was developed by Gauguin and Bernard in Pont-Aven.

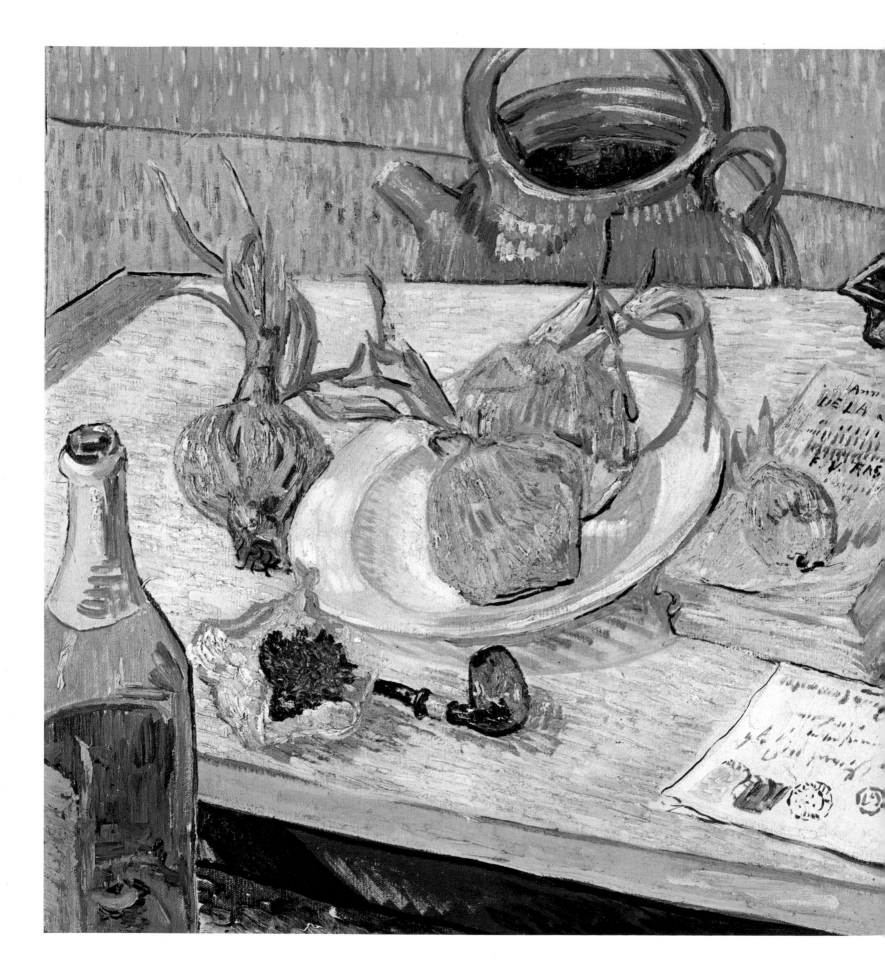

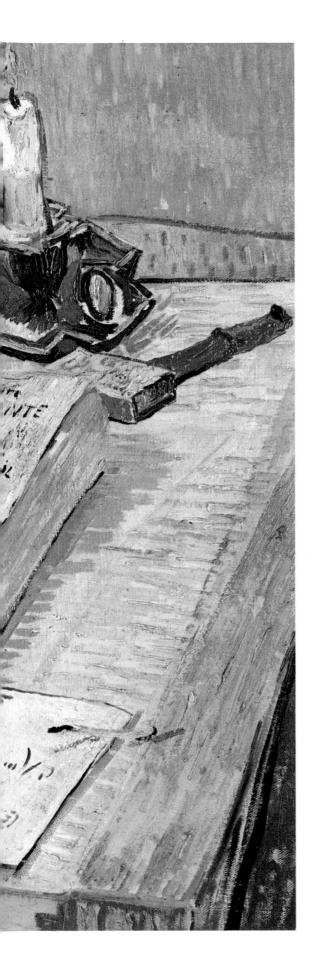

Plate with Onions, 'Annuaire de la Santé' and Other Objects
Arles, January 1889
F604 JH1656
Canvas, 50 x 64 cm
Otterlo, Rijksmuseum
Kröller-Müller

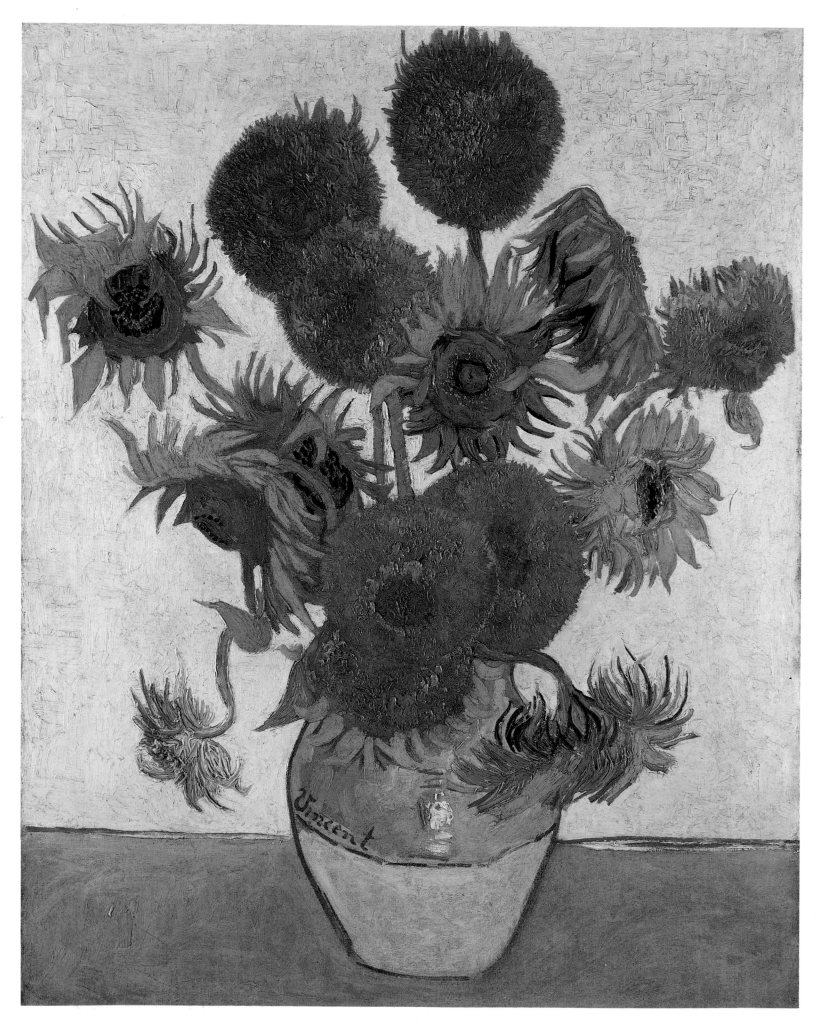

Influence of Bernard

Van Gogh was extremely impressed by a painting by Emile Bernard of Breton women and children. Gauguin took it with him to Arles, having exchanged it with Bernard for one of his own. Enthusiastically Van Gogh made a copy of this painting in watercolours - not a faithful replica, but rather a free interpretation. The colours have been changed and the figures in the foreground enlarged.

Bernard's distinct *cloisonné* style clearly influenced Van Gogh's paintings of the arena and the dance hall with their multicoloured flurries of colourful figures. In *Spectators in the Arena* the complementary colours used are orange and blue, and in *The Dance Hall* red and green for the balcony, and purple and yellow for the women in the foreground.

In these two works Van Gogh painted a crowd of people, which was unusual for him. In this sense these works look like some of the Parisian paintings of Impressionists such as Renoir and Toulouse-Lautrec. However, this only applies to the subject matter and certainly not to the style in which the subject matter has been painted, which - particularly in *The Dance Hall* - looks forward to Fauvism and Expressionism.

A few weeks later, Van Gogh painted a still life: *Plate with Onions, 'Annuaire de la Santé', and Other Objects* (JH 1656; see p. 118/9). It is another *nature morte*, full of symbolism like a modern version of a sixteenth or seventeenth-century *vanitas* painting in which the viewer is made aware of the transience and impermanence of life. It can also be read as a sort of self-portrait. Van Gogh was drinking and smoking too much (symbolized by the half-empty wine bottle and the pipe and tobacco), so he had to watch his already weakened health to an even greater extent. This is why he consulted the book *Manuel annuaire de Santé ou Médicine et pharmacie domestique*, of which there had been a new edition every year since 1847. The author was the homeopathic doctor, F.V. Raspail. A red bar of sealing wax alongside the candle and matches represents the many letters which he wrote to Theo.

It could also be argued that this painting shows Van Gogh and Gauguin, who had by now left Arles and the Yellow House. In this case, the burning candle in the candle holder refers to the same object on *Gauguin's Chair* (see p. 103), while the pipe and tobacco echo the objects on *Van Gogh's Chair* (see p. 102) - the two paintings which had been painted a few weeks earlier. This work is interesting from the artistic point of view because it was executed in a different style from the *cloisonné* paintings discussed earlier, such as *The Dance Hall* and *Madame Ginoux*. This still life is in the Pointillist style: horizontal yellow dashes for the table with blue lines for the shadows. The background is blue with short vertical yellow and red dashes.

The sunflowers

Of all Van Gogh's paintings of flowers, those with sunflowers are the most famous. *Vase with Fourteen Sunflowers* (JH 1666) was sold by Christie's in 1987 for £22 million to a Japanese buyer. It is no coincidence that there is so much interest in Van Gogh's work in Japan, for he had a boundless admiration for the Japanese woodcuts of Hiroshige and others.

Van Gogh painted his finest picture of sunflowers in the summer of 1888. On 18 August he wrote to Emile Bernard (B 15): 'I am thinking of

Fourteen Sunflowers in a Vase
Arles, August 1888
F454 JH1562
Canvas, 93 x 73 cm
London, National Gallery

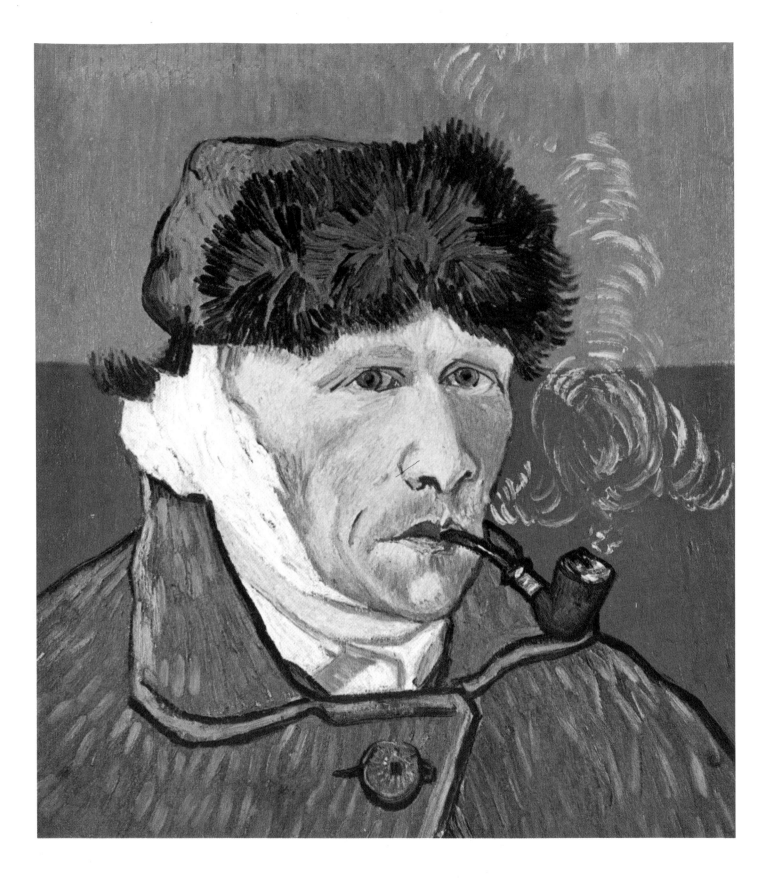

Self-portrait with
Bandaged Ear and Pipe
Arles, January 1889
F529 JH1658
Canvas, 51 x 45 cm
Private collection

decorating my studio with half a dozen paintings of sunflowers, a decoration in which the unmixed or broken chromium yellow will show up exuberantly against various different backgrounds: blue, the palest Veronese green, to royal blue, with the whole thing framed in an orange painted frame. This should produce the effect of stained glass windows in a Gothic church.'

Van Gogh later wrote to Theo (526): 'I am painting with the passion of someone from Marseilles eating bouillabaisse, which won't surprise you because I am painting large sunflowers.' He went on to say that he was working on three different paintings. He was hoping to live and work with Paul Gauguin, together in one studio, and he wanted to decorate the wall of the studio with 'nothing but sunflowers'.

'When I have carried out my plan, I will have a dozen of these paintings. The whole thing will be a symphony of blue and yellow. I am working on them every morning from sunrise, because the flowers wilt quickly, and I must finish the whole thing in one stretch.'

We know that of four paintings completed during August, *Five Sunflowers in a Vase* (JH 1560) was destroyed in Japan and no longer exists. *Three Sunflowers in a Vase* (JH 1559) is in a private collection in the United States, *Twelve Sunflowers in a Vase* (JH 1561) is in the Neue Pinakothek in Munich, and *Fourteen Sunflowers in a Vase* (JH 1562; see p. 121) is in the National Gallery in London. These works were quickly painted from nature. Using them as studies, he painted another three works of sunflowers in January 1889. First, the *Vase with Fourteen Sunflowers*, which was auctioned in 1987 and went to Japan; then *Vase with Fourteen Sunflowers* (JH 1667), which is in the Van Gogh Museum in Amsterdam, and finally *Vase with Twelve Sunflowers*, which is in the Philadelphia Museum (JH 1668). Two of these sunflower paintings were intended to hang on either side of the *Berceuse*.

It is interesting to note that in December 1888, Gauguin did a painting of Van Gogh painting sunflowers (this work is in the Van Gogh Museum in Amsterdam). Regarding it, he told Gauguin: 'It's definitely me, but you've painted me as a madman.'

Van Gogh loved sunflowers even more than irises. When his body was laid out in the bar room of Ravoux's inn at the end of July 1890, sunflowers filled the room.

Bandaged ear

Van Gogh painted himself twice with a bandaged right ear. One of the paintings, in which he holds a pipe, is in Chicago, privately owned; the other, without a pipe, is in the Courtauld Institute Gallery in London.

The Self-portrait with Bandaged Ear and Pipe (JH 1658; see p. 122) is a striking example of the use of complementary colours: in the bottom half of the canvas there is a green jacket against a red background, and above this a blue hat against an orange background. Both canvasses were painted in the middle of January 1889.

This is the story behind the creation of these strange and provocative portraits. During the second half of December 1888, Van Gogh visited the Musée Fabre in Montpellier with Gauguin. Amongst other works, they admired paintings by Eugène Delacroix and Gustave Courbet. If you visit the museum today, these paintings can still be seen. One work by Courbet, entitled '*Bonjour, Monsieur Courbet*', shows the artist talking to a peasant. Gauguin used this theme for his own version, which he called '*Bonjour, Monsieur Gauguin*'.

Van Gogh wrote about this visit to Montpellier in a letter to Theo (564). The two of them, Van Gogh and Gauguin, discussed Delacroix and Rembrandt. 'The discussion was charged with enormous electric tension, and when we finally stopped, our heads were as tired as an electric battery after it's been drained.' On the evening of Sunday 23 December, Van Gogh and Gauguin quarrelled. Gauguin had already threatened to leave

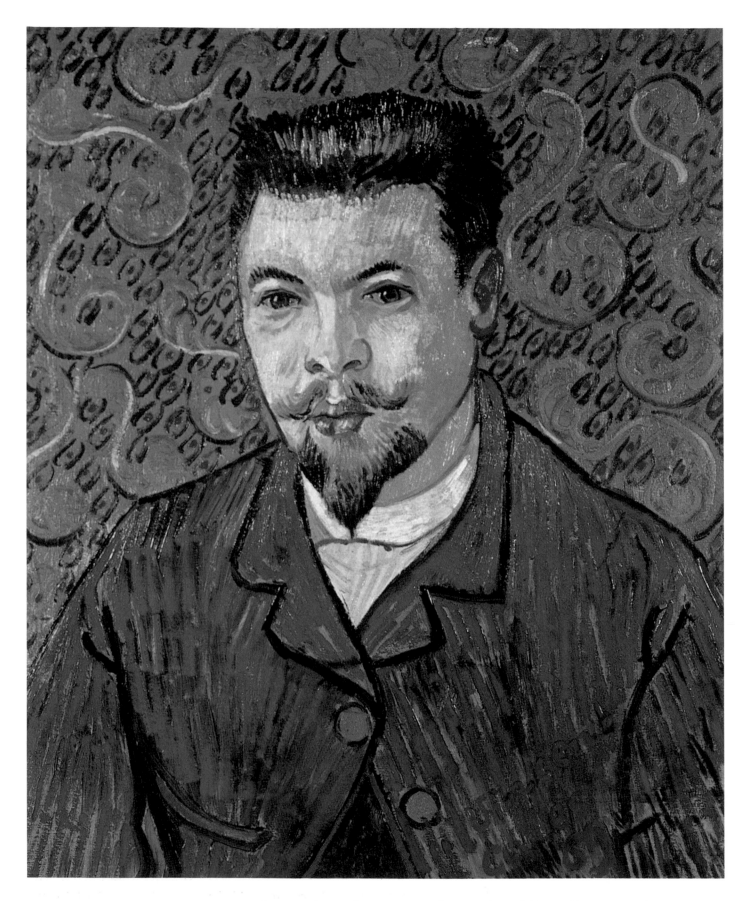

Doctor Félix Rey
Arles, January 1889
F500 JH1659
Canvas, 64 x 53 cm
Moscow, Pushkin Museum

because he no longer wanted to work and live with Van Gogh. The dramatic events of that day were briefly described a week later in the Arles Sunday newspaper, *Le Forum Républicain*, in the column *Chronique Locale*:

'Last Sunday at half past eleven in the evening, a certain Vincent Vangogh, an artist from Holland, appeared at the brothel at no. 1, where he asked for a certain Rachel, to whom he then gave his ear with the words:

124

"Keep this object carefully." Then he disappeared. When the police had been informed - it could only have been the deed of an unfortunate madman - they went to see this individual the following morning. He was found in bed and barely showed any sign of life. The poor man was admitted to hospital as an emergency case.'

In fact, Van Gogh only cut off the bottom half of his ear, but that was enough. Before this serious incident, he had been to the café with Gauguin. In anger at Gauguin's threatened departure, he threw a glass of absinthe at his head, but Gauguin managed to avoid it. The next evening, when Gauguin went for a walk, Van Gogh followed him, which Gauguin found threatening. Van Gogh was finally admitted to hospital, the Hôtel Dieu on the place du Marché-Neuf in Arles. But while Van Gogh was obviously seriously distressed, and perhaps drunk, when he cut off part of his ear, he was not insane. Theo, informed of this event by Gauguin by telegraph, immediately came to Arles to visit his brother. On Christmas Day Van Gogh's condition seemed critical, and when Theo returned, he feared that his brother would not recover from the crisis. But by New Year's Eve the patient was getting better.

The concern of the postmaster Roulin and his wife for their friend was very moving. They visited Van Gogh many times, and Joseph Roulin wrote to Theo to keep him up to date with what was happening. Meanwhile, Gauguin had left for Paris with Theo on Wednesday 26 December. He did not return to Arles, and never saw Van Gogh again, although they continued to correspond.

Dr Félix Rey

In the hospital in Arles Van Gogh was treated with a great deal of devotion by a young doctor, Félix Rey. Rey even showed an interest in and appreciation for Van Gogh's work. The artist did a portrait of him, *Doctor Félix Rey* (JH 1659; see p. 124) which has a similarly restless background to the portraits of the Roulin couple. However, it does not have a floral background. The motif is more like that of a treble clef in musical notation. It is significant that this portrait is dominated by the colours green and bluish purple, not complementary colours as in the self-portrait with the bandaged ear. The painting is signed in large red letters on the bluish purple background of the jacket: 'Vincent, Arles 89'.

Van Gogh gave the portrait to Dr Rey as a memento, but the young doctor's mother thought it was so hideous that she used the painting to close a hole in the chicken house. It was discovered there by an art dealer in 1901. That year Dr Rey sold the canvas, as well as five others by Van Gogh, to an art dealer in Marseilles, after which they became the property of the artist, Ambroise Vollard. The portrait of Rey is now in the Pushkin Museum in Moscow.

On Monday, 7 January 1889, Van Gogh was permitted to leave the hospital and return to the Yellow House. He resumed his hard work. The fact that he was not insane is clear from the work he did and from his letters. But then he suffered another crisis and was admitted to hospital again on 7 February. On 17 February he was provisionally released.

A very tragic development followed. Van Gogh's behaviour had upset his neighbours and other people in Arles. Thirty people sent a petition to the mayor declaring that Van Gogh was insane, that he drank too much and that he was a danger to women and children. He should therefore

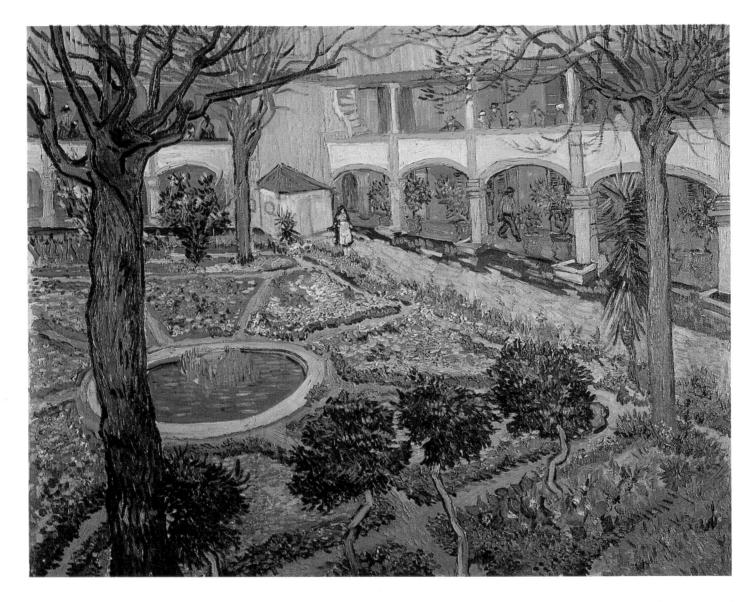

The Courtyard of the Hospital
Arles, April 1889
F519 JH1687
Canvas, 73 x 92 cm
Winterthur, Oskar Reinhart
Collection

return to his family or be committed to a lunatic asylum. The result of this was that Van Gogh was apprehended by the police, and his house was locked up. In the hospital he was put in an isolation cell. Theo was told about this by the pastor of the Église Réformée, Frédéric Salles, who had concerned himself with the artist's fate.

Van Gogh did a drawing and also two paintings of the Hôtel Dieu, the hospital in Arles: *The Courtyard of the Hospital* (JH 1687; see p. 126), which was viewed from a great height, and *Dormitory in the Hospital* (JH 1686; see p. 127). In the middle of the courtyard there is a pond with goldfish, and in the background walks a Reverend Sister. The dormitory reveals a long room with beds behind curtains. Two nuns, who are clearly nurses, as was customary in the last century and long after, are walking through the dormitory. Some of the patients who are not bedridden are sitting round a stove. One of them is reading a newspaper. These are the last but two paintings from the Arles period. Van Gogh was still to paint a *Lane with Chestnut Trees* and a *Road with Pollarded Willows* (both paintings are in private collections).

In his solitary cell in the hospital in Arles, Van Gogh had no books. He was not allowed to smoke a pipe, and had nothing to paint with. He did not write to Theo for almost a month, but on Tuesday 19 March (579) he wrote to his brother: 'I am in a cell under lock and key and guarded all day long, though my guilt has not been proved.' A few days later on

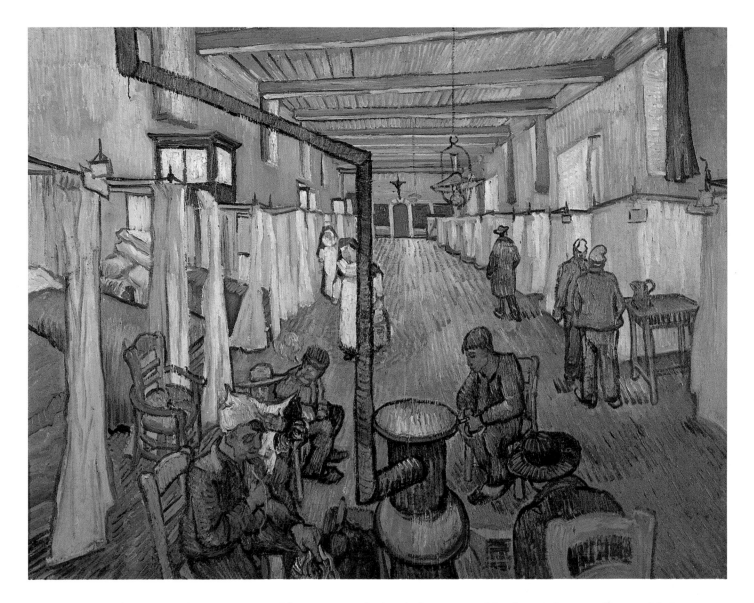

Dormitory in the Hospital
Arles, April 1889
F646 JH1686
Canvas, 74 x 92 cm
Winterthur, Oskar Reinhart
Collection

Friday 22 March (580), he wrote: 'As far as I can tell myself, I am not really insane. You will see that the canvasses which I have done in the meantime are calm and in no way inferior to the others.' He was then visited by his friend Paul Signac, which raised his spirits. When he was permitted books again, he read *Uncle Tom's Cabin*, Harriet Beecher Stowe's book on the slave trade, Charles Dickens's *Christmas Stories*, and *Germinie Lacerteux* by the Goncourt brothers. In April Van Gogh became convinced that it would be better for him to go to an asylum in Saint-Rémy for several months. Accompanied by Pastor Salles, he finally left Arles on Wednesday 8 May to go to the Saint-Paul-de-Mausole asylum in Saint-Rémy-de-Provence.

Most productive period

Van Gogh had lived in Arles for almost fifteen months. This was the greatest period of productivity during his ten years as a painter. On average he did more than three paintings each week, amounting to a total of some 200 paintings, over 200 drawings and watercolours, as well as about 200 letters. These paintings include such masterpieces as *The Drawbridge*, *Harvest Landscape*, *Fishing Boats on the Beach*, *Vincent's Bedroom*, *Night Café*, the Sunflower series, and the *Berceuse*.

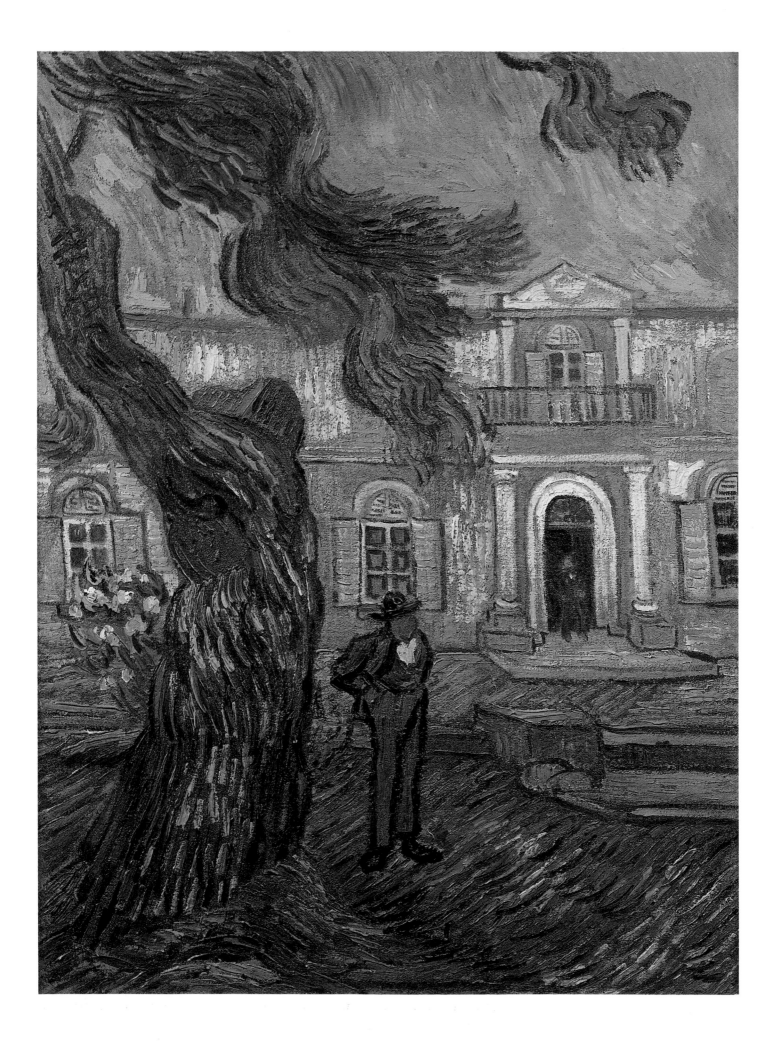

Chapter V

Translations into colour
Saint-Rémy-de-Provence

On their arrival at the asylum of Saint-Paul-de-Mausole, Pastor Salles bade Van Gogh farewell and returned to Arles. The asylum, which was founded at the beginning of the century by Dr Mercurin, was still a private institution in 1889. It was a converted monastery dating from the twelfth century, with later additions. In Van Gogh's time, and to this day, there was a Romanesque church of which the tower is sometimes shown in his work. In a prospectus the institution was officially entitled '*Maison de Santé au traitement des aliénés de deux sexes*' (Sanatorium for the Treatment of the Insane, both Men and Women). But Van Gogh was not insane. He wrote to Theo that the doctor who was treating him told him that he was 'not really mad'. He was probably suffering from a type of epilepsy; now and again he would suffer a crisis, but during the periods in between these crises he was perfectly lucid. The doctor who treated him was the 62-year-old Dr Théophile Peyron, who wrote in a medical report on his patient: 'He suffers acute manias with hallucinations of images and sounds, which led him to inflict an injury on himself by cutting off a piece of his right ear. At the moment he seems to be in his right mind, but he does not think he has enough strength and courage to live on his own. He asked to be admitted to this institution of his own free will. As he suffers from epileptic fits at extremely irregular intervals, I think it is advisable to keep him under observation for a long time.' Patients were treated with hydrotherapy, amongst other things. Van Gogh wrote: 'I now take a bath twice a week and stay in the water for two hours. My stomach is feeling infinitely better.' *Pine Tree in Front of the Entrance to the Asylum* (JH 1840; see p. 128) shows Dr Peyron in the foreground wearing a hat, with his right hand in his trouser pocket, while Van Gogh himself is standing in the doorway. This painting is now in the Musée d'Orsay in Paris, and there is a very similar painting in the Folkwang Museum in Essen: *Garden of the Asylum with a Sawn-off Pine Tree* (JH 1849; see p. 130). Van Gogh was fascinated by these pine trees with the stone bench underneath, and he did a series of paintings on this subject.

But on 22 May 1889, two weeks after his arrival, Van Gogh wrote a letter to Theo from Saint-Rémy (592): 'Since I've been here I've had enough to do with the cheerless garden with its tall pine trees and its high, badly maintained lawn and all sorts of weeds, and I have not even been outside the garden. Meanwhile, the landscape of Saint-Rémy is very beautiful and gradually I will make some trips I think.'

A beautiful bust of Van Gogh by the sculptor Zadkine now stands on the drive of Saint-Paul-de-Mausole. It shows Van Gogh receiving a letter from Theo. (Zadkine also made statues of Van Gogh in Zundert, the Borinage and Auvers.)

Pine Tree in Front of the Entrance to the Asylum
Saint-Rémy November 1889
F653 JH1840
Canvas, 58 x 45 cm
Paris, Musée d'Orsay

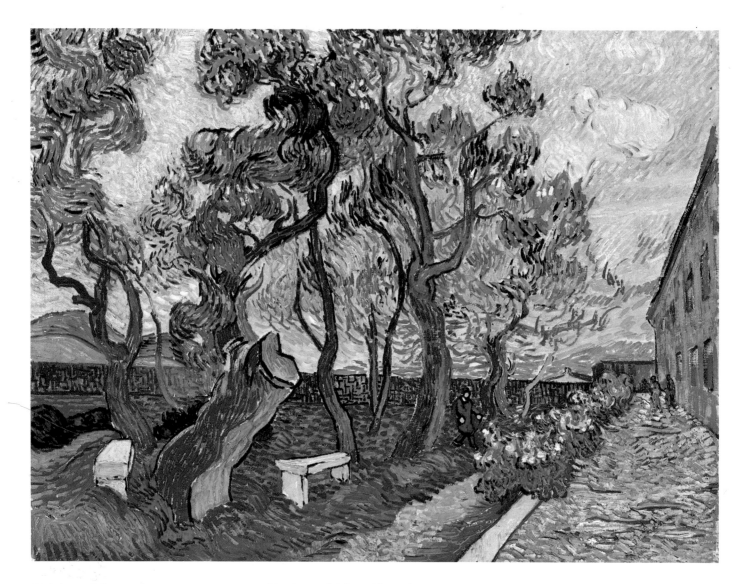

*Garden of the Asylum with a
Sawn-Off Pine Tree*
Saint-Rémy, November 1889
F660 JH1849
Canvas, 73.5 x 92 cm
Essen, Folkwang Museum

'As it could have been'

Van Gogh wrote about his room in the asylum (592):
'I have a small room with greyish green wallpaper and two sea-green curtains with very pale roses, brightened up by blood-red lines. These curtains, which were probably left by a rich ruined man who died, have a very nice pattern. The highly worn chair, which is covered with a dotted material in the style of Diaz or Monticelli, brown, red, pink, white, cream, black, forget-me-not blue and bottle green, probably belonged to the same former inmate. Through the window with its iron railings, I can see a fenced wheat field: a view like that in a Van Goyen. Every morning I see the sun rise above this in all its glory. I also have a room to work in here, for there are more than thirty rooms empty.'

This letter is quoted here at length because it gives a good idea of what he felt about the asylum. Clearly he was quite happy at first. The institution, which had been set up for wealthy people, was beginning to run down, but it was still a reasonably pleasant place to live. In fact, in his paintings Van Gogh allows himself some artistic licence for he shows the area to be rather more agreeable than it was in reality. He did paintings of the garden and the asylum in which 'the place looks very attractive. I am trying to reconstruct everything as it could have been.' In one or two paintings the asylum actually looks like a country estate with a splendid park, where the guests of the lord of the manor are taking a relaxed stroll.

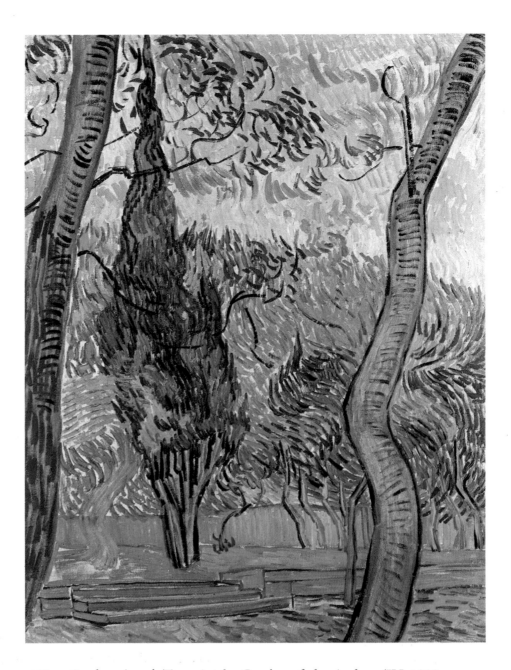

Van Gogh painted *Trees in the Garden of the Asylum* (JH 1800; see p. 131) in the style of earlier works in which he had placed sawn-off tree trunks in the foreground to give added depth. This work, which shows a cypress between two pine trees, also appears in a gouache with black chalk representing Van Gogh's studio in the asylum, with bottles and glasses on the window-sill (JH 1807; now in Amsterdam). Another gouache of *The Vestibule of the Asylum* (JH 1806; see p. 132) shows in the background another picture, *Fountain in the Garden of the Asylum* (JH 1705; see p. 133). So these two works follow on from each other, though they were painted with a six-month interval. In the earlier work, the gouache of the vestibule, the perspective is heightened by the use of warm, advancing colours, such as violet and yellow, for the hall of the building in the foreground; cold colours, green and yellowish-green, are used for the garden behind the doorway, so the background seems further away.

'No reason to complain'

At the beginning of September 1889, Van Gogh wrote a belated letter to his mother to congratulate her on her seventieth birthday (606):

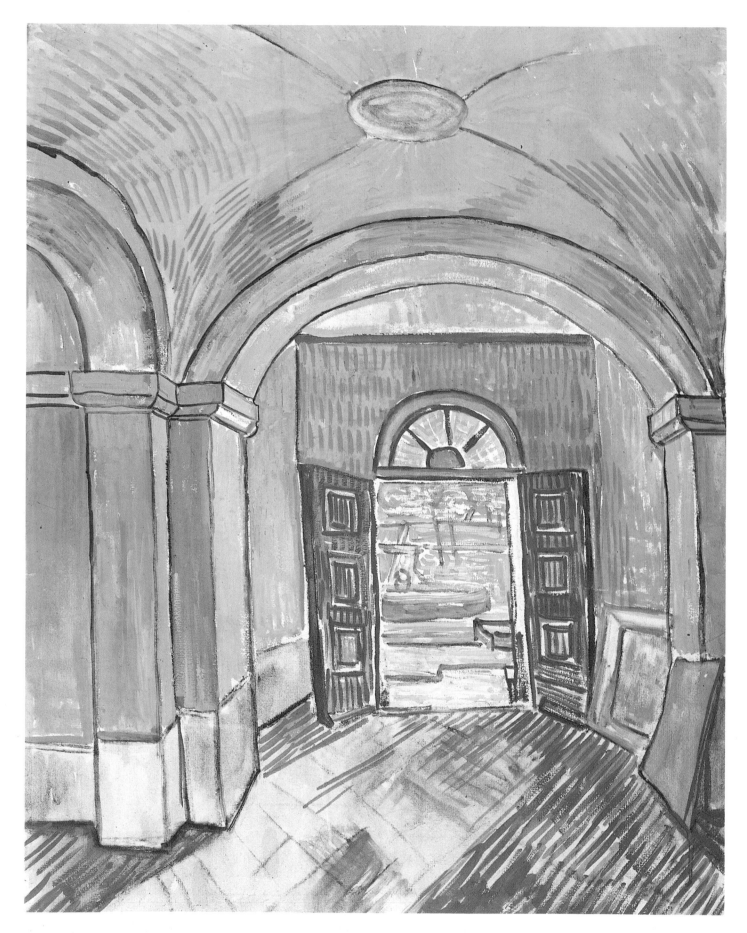

The Vestibule of the Asylum
Saint-Rémy, October 1889 F1530 JH1806
Black chalk, gouache, 61.5 x 47 cm
Amsterdam, Rijksmuseum Vincent van Gogh

132

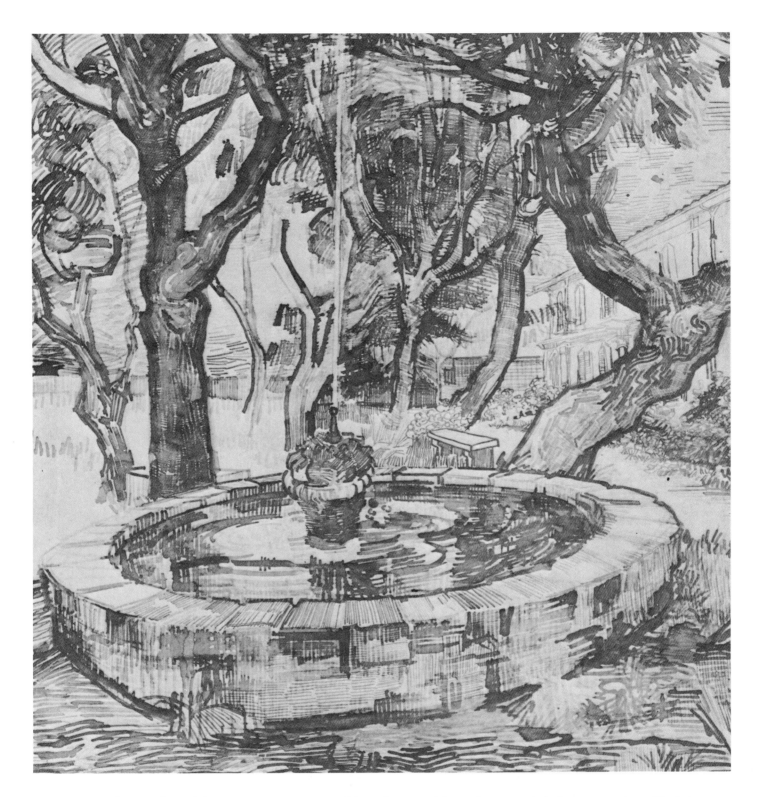

*Fountain in the Garden of the
Asylum*
Saint-Rémy, May 1889
F1531 JH1705
Black chalk, pen, reed pen and
brown ink, 49.5 x 46 cm
Amsterdam, Rijksmuseum
Vincent van Gogh

'I am working almost without interruption from morning till night, one day after another, and I shut myself up in the studio so that I am not distracted. Thus I am greatly consoled that my work is progressing rather than falling behind, and I can do it completely calmly; my thoughts are quite clear and conscious in that respect. Thus, compared to others here who have nothing to do, I certainly have no reason to complain.'

To Theo, he wrote at that time (604):

'I'm working on a painting in my room, which is doing me good. I'm struggling with all my energy to gain control over my work, and I feel sure that if I succeed in this it will be the best lightning conductor for my illness. I look after myself well by carefully shutting myself away. You could say that it is selfish of me not to be more friendly with my fellow

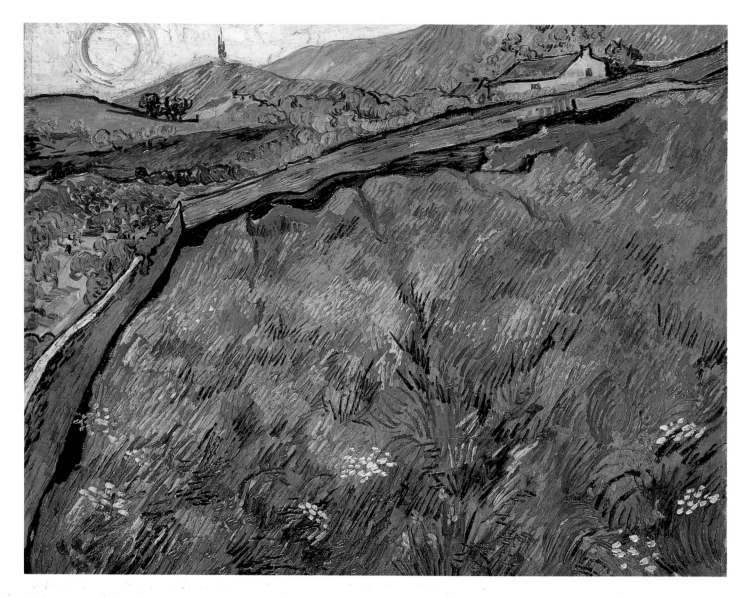

Mountain Landscape
seen across the Walls with
Rising Sun and Green Field
Saint-Rémy, June 1889
F720 JH1728
Canvas, 72 x 92 cm
Otterlo, Rijksmuseum
Kröller-Müller

sufferers here, and to visit them, but in the end I don't feel bad, because my work is progressing, and that is what we need, for it's more important than ever that I do better work than before, as it wasn't adequate then.'

Self-criticism

There is a lot of self-criticism in that last sentence, although we know that even in Nuenen - and especially in Paris and Arles -Van Gogh had already produced magnificent masterpieces like *The Potato Eaters*, *Père Tanguy*, and the *Berceuse*, to mention just three paintings. It is astonishing that despite his illness, and with little recognition, he continued to draw and paint indefatigably, although absolutely nothing was sold. Van Gogh felt for his fellow patients, for he was, after all, a very sensitive and sociable person, but he did not want to be dragged down in their misery. In the asylum of Saint-Paul-de-Mausole he clearly got on well with the chief attendant, the 59-year-old Charles Elzéard Trabu, and his wife, Jeanne. Trabu lived in a small house near the asylum. Van Gogh wrote about him (605): 'He is a man who has seen an enormous amount of suffering and death, and his expression is one of calm observation ... There is something of a military feeling in his small, quick black eyes.' In early September 1889 Van Gogh painted two portraits of Trabu within five days; one for the man himself, and one to send to Theo. He probably painted the first portrait at one sitting without stopping, as was his usual practice. It is as penetrating a portrait as those of Joseph Roulin, Madame Roulin, Madame Ginoux and Patience Escalier from the Arles period. He had an eye for so-called ordinary people whose personalities he expressed powerfully in his portraits.

Van Gogh also painted two portraits of Madame Trabu: one for Madame, and one for Theo (W 14): 'The faded face is tired and marked with smallpox. Her complexion is an olive colour, burnt by the sun, and she has black hair. She is wearing a faded black dress decorated with a soft pink geranium. The background is in a neutral shade between pink and green.'

The original portraits given to the couple were lost. Perhaps they, or their family, did not think much of them, just as Dr Rey's mother thought that her son's portrait was worthless. Fortunately the two copies sent to Theo have survived.

Beautiful view

Van Gogh had a beautiful view of the garden and the mountains beyond, the Alpilles, from the window of his studio on the first floor of the asylum. He saw this landscape through iron bars, but he left these out of his paintings and drawings. *Mountain Landscape seen across the Walls with Rising Sun and Green field* (JH 1728; see p. 134-5), a scene he painted several times, is a very striking, almost Expressionist work. The dominant colours are yellow, green and blue. The painting has depth because of the use of the warm yellow in the foreground and the cool blue in the background. The most striking feature is the long blue wall, which forms a diagonal line across the work. Thus although Van Gogh did not paint the bars, he did emphasize the wall which imprisoned him, and yet like a bird he flew over it towards the mountains in the distance.

He did six pencil drawings of this subject in June 1889, which are all in Amsterdam, as well as two drawings in black chalk, a pen and ink drawing, and four paintings. He was certainly inspired by this subject. In that same month of June 1889, he painted *Fields with Poppies* (JH 1751; see p. 136/7, evidently from a high vantage point. This work, reminiscent of *Garden with Flowers* which he had painted in Arles a year earlier, and *House in Auvers* painted a year later, stands out among the works of the Saint-Rémy period.

The main line of the composition is formed by the row of red poppies in the middle which contrasts with the complementary green tones next to it. From left to right there are a number of lines which converge at a single point, and which run from the foreground to the background, creating a powerful perspective. This canvas of a field of poppies, which was exhibited in the Gallery Bernheim Jeune at a large one-man exhibition of Van Gogh's work in 1901, eleven years after Van Gogh's death, indicates his admiration for Claude Monet, who was already a celebrated Impressionist painter, and who had painted so many landscapes and gardens.

The reaper

The *Enclosed Wheat Field with Reaper* (JH 1753; see p. 138), now in Otterlo, also dates from June 1889, and is a much more emotionally charged landscape than the serene and peaceful field of poppies. This was probably the field behind the asylum. Van Gogh wrote of it (596): 'I have painted

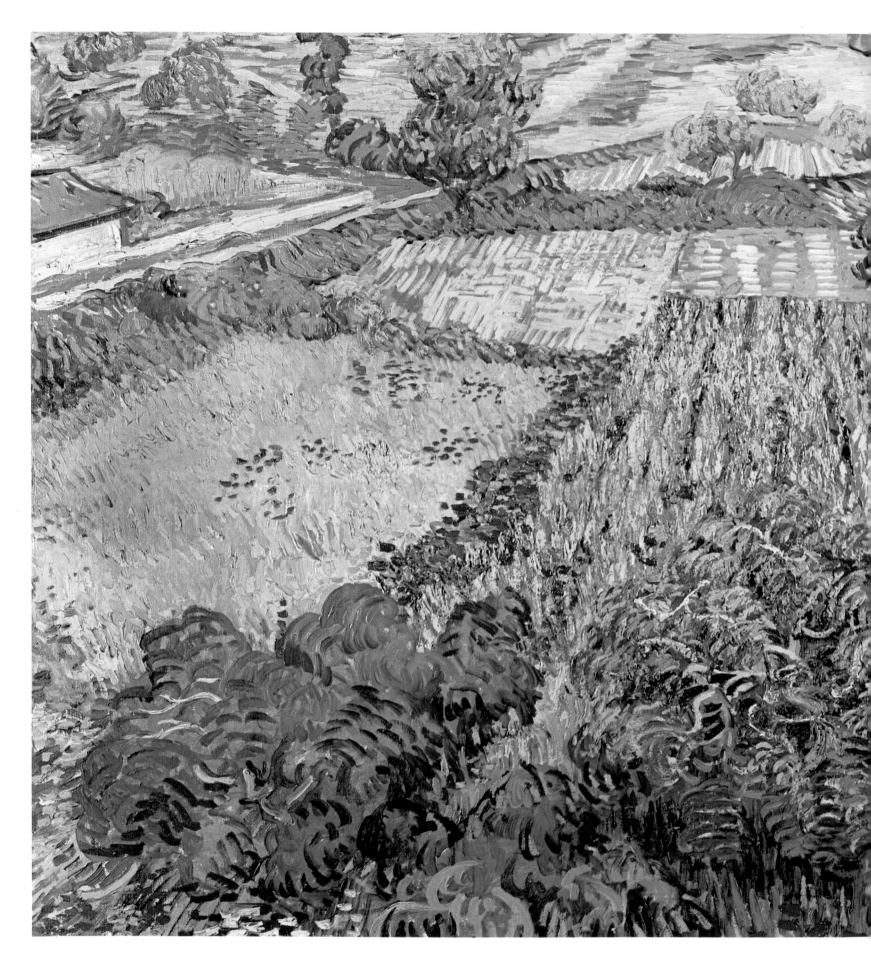

Fields with Poppies, Saint-Rémy, June 1889
F581 JH1751 - Canvas, 71 x 91 cm
Bremen, Kunsthalle

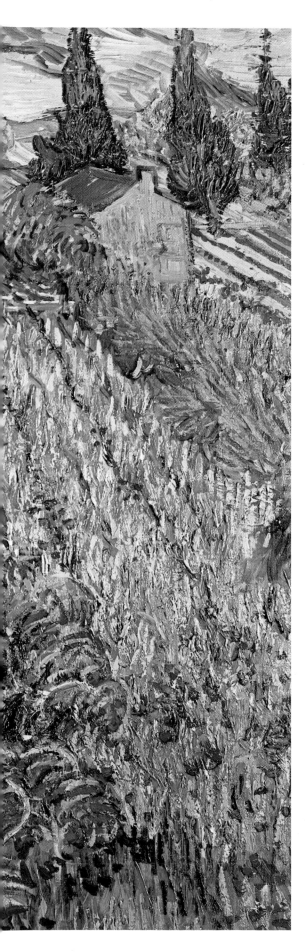

a wheat field, very yellow and very bright, possibly the brightest work I have ever done.' In his next letter to Theo he wrote (597): 'The last painting I have started is the wheat field, which shows a small reaper and a large sun. The canvas is completely yellow with the exception of the wall and the background of purplish hills.'

He did various versions of this painting, which also has a deeper significance. Just like the *Mountain Landscape seen across the Walls with Rising Sun and Green Field*, and the paintings of reapers from Arles, the sun is again seen as an outlined round yellow disc. The reaper is almost entirely lost in the field in which he is working.

Van Gogh took up this theme again several months later, having just recovered from a lengthy and severe crisis. On 6 September 1889 he wrote to Theo (604):

'The work's going fairly well - I am struggling with a canvas [JH 1773], which I started several days before my illness, a reaper. The study is all yellow, terribly thickly painted, but the design was good and simple. At the time I saw in this reaper a vague figure like that of a devil, fighting in great heat to finish his job. I saw in him the image of death, in the sense that humanity was the wheat that he was reaping ... However, there is no sadness in this death, it takes place in full sunlight, with a sun which floods everything with a light of fine gold.'

Van Gogh added to this explanation that he only wrote in the intervals between his work: 'I am working like someone who's really possessed, more than ever I am filled with a dull mania for work, and I believe that this will contribute to my recovery.'

Van Gogh interrupted the letter to continue work on the painting. Then he took up his pen again and wrote: 'At last. The mower is done. I think it is a painting that you will want at home. It is an image of death, like that referred to in the great book of Nature. But I was looking for an almost smiling image. It is completely yellow. This is funny because I saw it through the iron bars of my cell.' He is referring here to the painting *Enclosed Field with Reaper at Sunrise* (JH 1773; see p. 140/141), which is now in the Van Gogh Museum in Amsterdam, and careful examination reveals that it is different from the painting in Otterlo. In the later painting the reaper is more clearly delineated in greyish-green clothes against the yellow background of the wheat field, and the sun is higher in the sky.

He also made a smaller copy of this painting with some minor changes (JH 1792; see p. 139). At the same time he made copies of three other paintings: *Vincent's Bedroom*, *Wheat Field and Cypress* and *Olive Trees*. He sent these to his mother and to his sister Wil, though they did not much care for them. When Van Gogh died less than a year later, his mother and sister were saddened by his tragic fate, but were completely disinterested in his paintings, as they never considered him to be a true artist.

Van Gogh took up the theme of the *Enclosed Field with Young Wheat and Rising Sun* (JH 1862; see p. 142) at the end of the year. This time it is a field of young wheat, and the predominant colour is not yellow, but green. The purple and the yellow sun, again seen as a sharply outlined, perfectly round circle, is surrounded by a series of concentric yellow circles, which represent its rays.

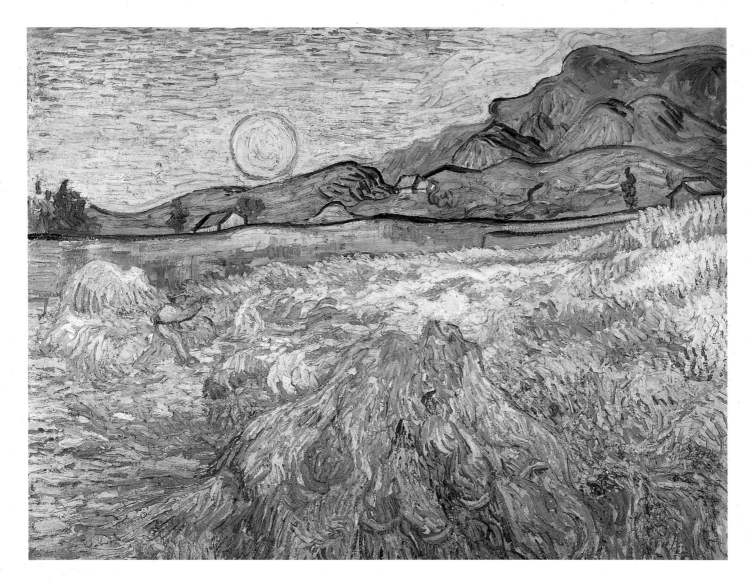

Enclosed Wheat Field with Reaper
Saint-Rémy, June 1889
F617 JH1753
Canvas, 72 x 92 cm
Otterlo, Rijksmuseum
Kröller-Müller

The sun

The sun plays an important role in the Provence paintings. In 1988 Tsukasa Kodera, the Japanese critic, stated in his thesis on the themes in Van Gogh's work, *Christianity versus Nature,* that Van Gogh wished to replace the Christianity of pastors with nature. Where his early landscapes had a church spire, his later work contains a radiant sun as a religious symbol, a symbol of Light shining in the darkness. Perhaps he was thinking about the Light referred to by the apostle John.

In the autumn of 1889, Van Gogh did a painting of a landscape which is quite different from his views of wheat fields, olive groves and cypresses. This was *Two Poplars* (JH 1797; see p. 143) in blue, green, yellow and brown. It is a wild and capricious work, and the details of the representation are not immediately clear. It is an evocation of autumn in Provence. The work does bear some similarity as regards its subject and style to *Trees in the Garden of the Asylum,* which dates from the same period, October 1889.

Irises

In the middle of May 1889, during the very first week of his stay in the asylum at Saint-Paul-de-Mausole, Van Gogh completed his painting of *The Irises* (JH 1691, F 608; see p. 144/145). He painted this work in the

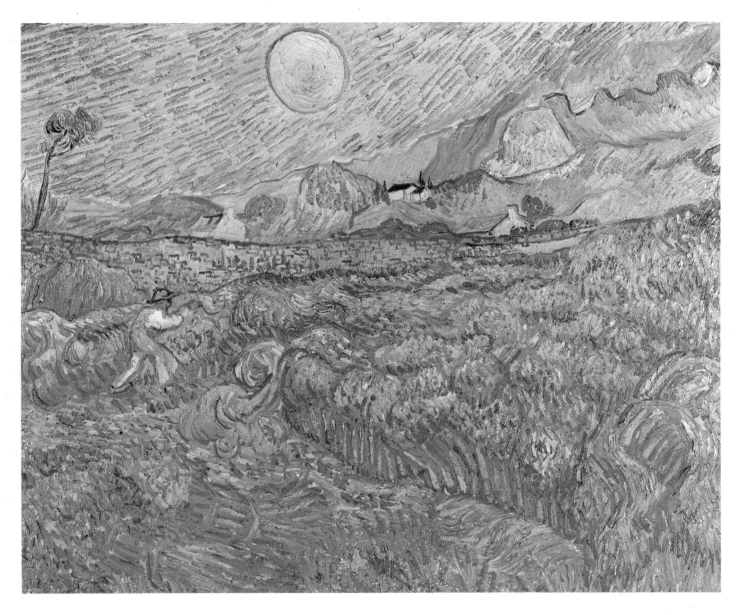

Enclosed Field with Reaper at Sunrise
Saint-Rémy, September 1889
F619 JH1792
Canvas, 59.5 x 73 cm
Essen, Folkwang Museum

large garden to the south of the men's ward (591): 'When I'm working in the garden they all come and look', he wrote to Theo about his fellow patients, 'and I assure you that they are modest and well-mannered and leave me alone - they disturb me less than the good people in the town of Arles did, for example.'

During that spring he completed general views of the garden of the asylum, but he also painted close-ups, such as *Death's Head Butterfly on an Arum Lily,* now in the Van Gogh Museum in Amsterdam. This painting of irises is also a close-up; the flowers are life-size. It is a composition in blue and green, with contrasting elements such as the reddish green in the foreground and the orange flowers in the background.

Van Gogh liked to paint flowers in nature in addition to flowers in vases. This painting was executed particularly well. When Claude Monet saw it at an exhibition, he said: 'How can someone who loves flowers and light so much, and is able to depict them so well, be so unhappy?'

About two months later, Van Gogh sent this canvas to Theo with ten other paintings. In September, Theo arranged for the work to be shown at the Salon des Indépendants in Paris. The work then came into the possession of Van Gogh's Parisian friend, Julien Tanguy, who sold it in 1892 to the Symbolist author Octave Mirbeau, one of the earliest admirers of Van Gogh's work.

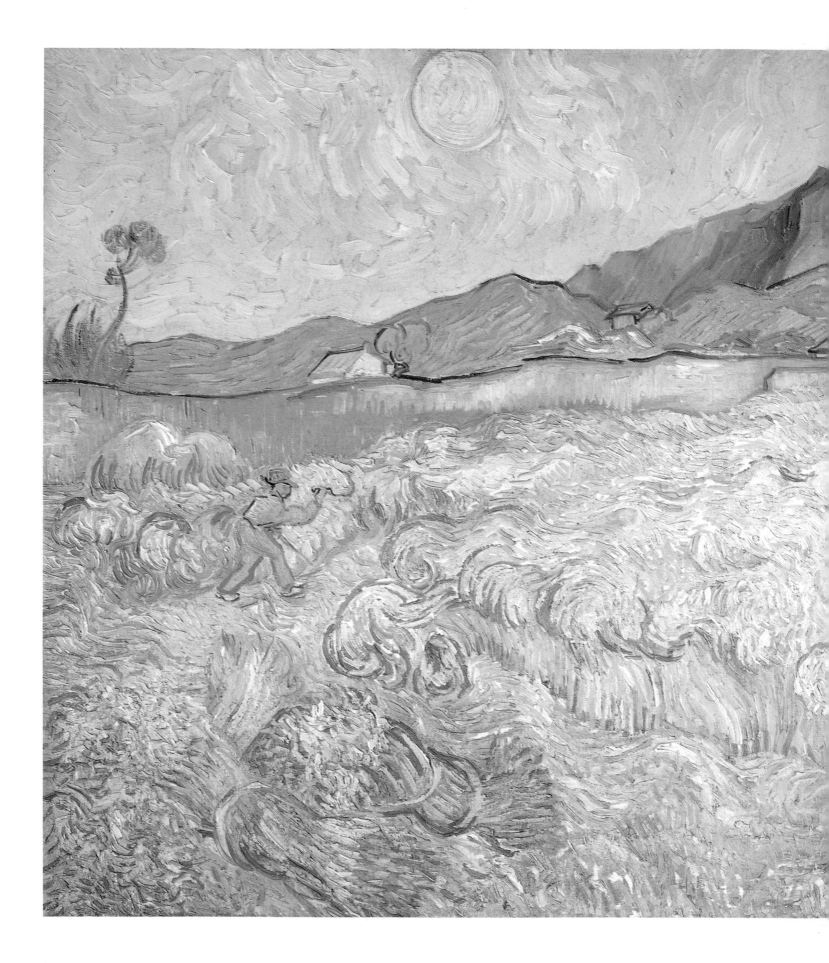

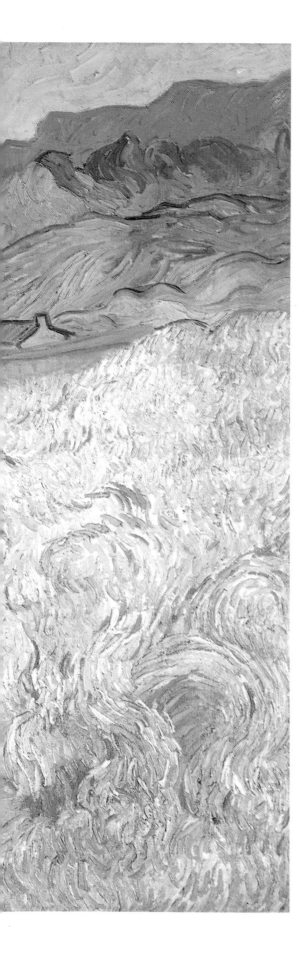

Enclosed Field with Reaper at Sunrise
Saint-Rémy, September 1889
F618 JH1773
Canvas, 74 x 92 cm
Amsterdam, Rijksmuseum
Vincent van Gogh

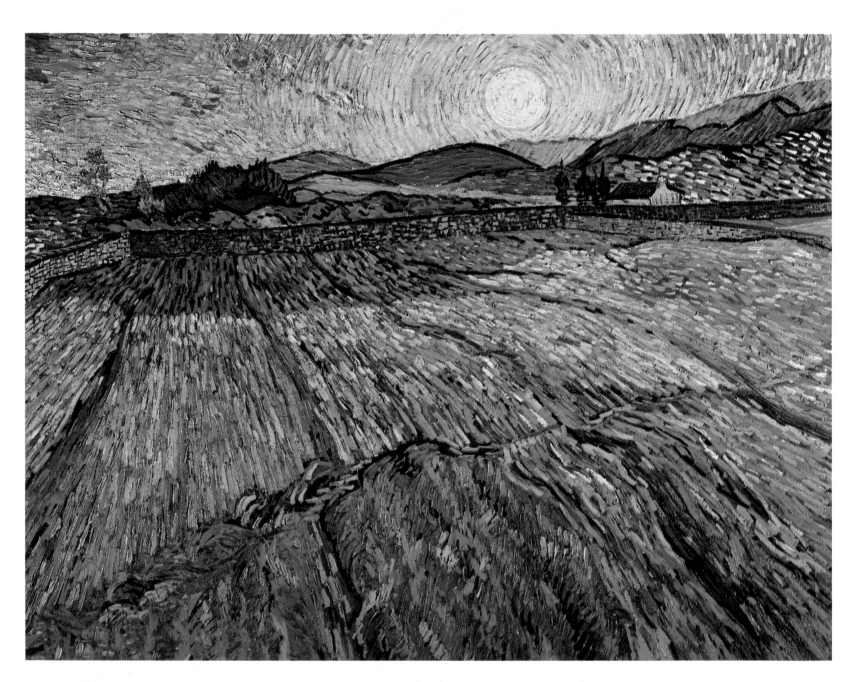

Enclosed Field with Young Wheat and Rising Sun
Saint-Rémy,
November-December 1889
F737 JH1862
Canvas, 71 x 90.5 cm
Private collection

Two Poplars
Saint-Rémy, October 1889
F638 JH1797
Canvas, 61 x 45.5 cm
Cleveland, The Museum of Art,
Leonard C.Hanna Jr.Fund

In May 1890, Van Gogh again took up the theme of the irises, which he had found so fascinating immediately after his arrival a year earlier. *Vase with Violet Irises against a Yellow Background* (JH 1977; see p. 146) is another composition in complementary colours. He was probably inspired to do this painting by one of Hokusai's prints. A *Vase with Purple Irises against a Pink Background*, which also dates from May 1890, is now in the Metropolitan Museum of Art in New York. In June, looking back on his last weeks in Saint-Rémy, Van Gogh wrote from Auvers about these two vases with irises, and about two paintings of a *Vase with Pink Roses* (W 21): 'The last days in St.-Rémy I worked flat out. Large bonquets of flowers, purple irises, large bouquets of roses, landscapes.' And he wrote to his mother about this stage in his work (639): 'In the last fourteen days or three weeks that I was in St.-Rémy I worked from first thing in the morning through to the evening without stopping.'

Little Vincent

In another letter to his mother, Van Gogh wrote about a painting which

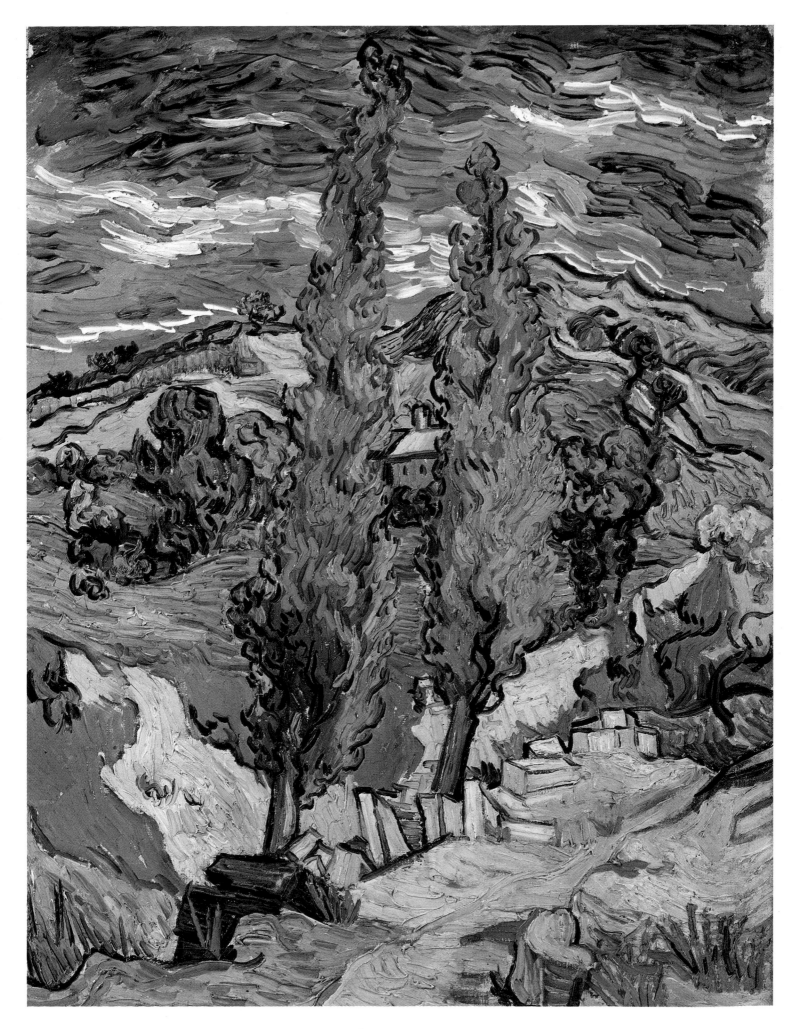

143

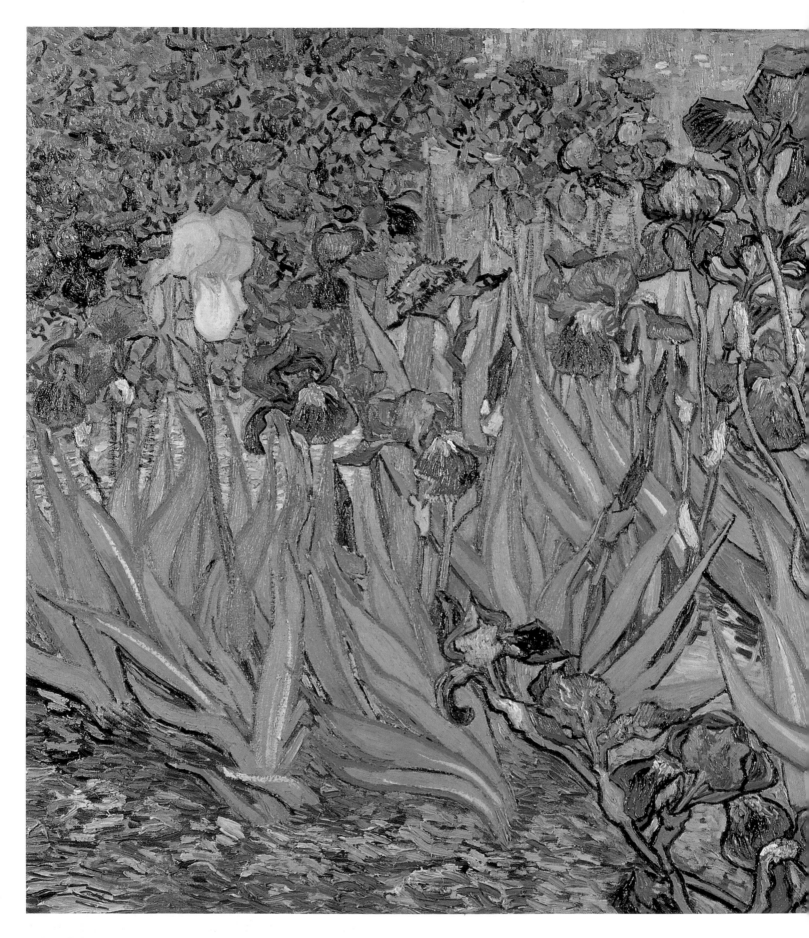

Irises, Saint-Rémy, May 1889
F608 JH1691
Canvas, 71 x 93 cm
Private collection

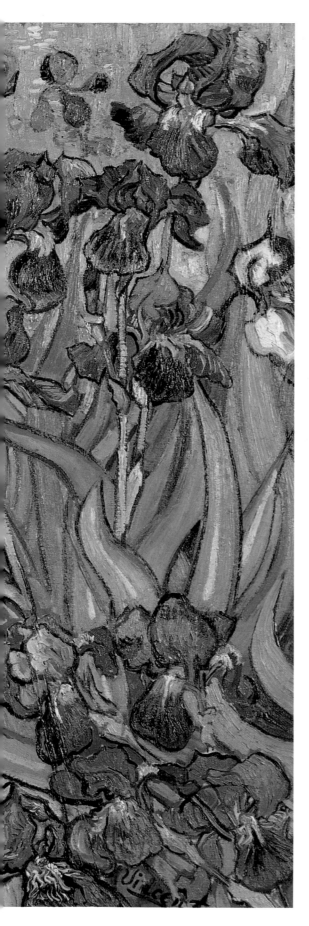

was a harbinger of spring, and a present for his recently born nephew and namesake. On 31 January 1890, Jo had given birth to a baby boy, who was named Vincent after his uncle. Theo wrote to tell him of the glad tidings that very day:

'Jo has given birth to a beautiful little boy, a baby who cries a lot but looks healthy. We will name him after you, and sincerely hope that he will have as much perseverance and be as courageous as you.'

In the letter to his mother, Van Gogh wrote (627): 'I immediately started on a painting for him [the baby], which can hang in their bedroom, large branches of white almond blossom against a blue sky'. This painting, *Branches of an Almond Tree in Blossom* (JH 1891, F6H; see p. 147), is very similar to *Blossoming Almond Branch in a Glass of Water* (see p. 59). But in a letter to his sister Wil, he wrote about the painting for his nephew (W 22): 'White almond blossom - thick branches against a sky blue background.' The words 'sky blue' suggest that he painted the living branch of a tree, and not a cut branch placed in a glass of water. This beautiful work, of which there is only one version, used to hang over the piano in Theo and Jo's house at 9 Cité Pigalle, Montmartre. In little Vincent's room in the same house, there was a painting of a tree in blossom from Arles.

The theme of trees

Trees always fascinated Van Gogh: poplars in Nuenen, trees in parks in Paris and Arles, and flowering fruit trees in the countryside in Provence. In Saint-Rémy there were the pine trees around the asylum, and beyond that, cypresses and olive trees.

Van Gogh painted about fifteen olive groves in Saint-Rémy. These works we completed between June and December 1889. The painting of the *Olive Orchard* (JH 1758; see p. 148) shown here is possibly the first of this series, for it is assumed that it was painted around the middle of June. The work is dominated by the colours blue, green, purple and pink, with forms built up with curved vertical brush strokes. The capricious shapes of the olive trees are continued in the long waving grasses on the ground, and in the blue sky, which is painted with vigorous strokes. It is an extremely dynamic painting, an Expressionist work by a powerfully inspired artist. The same restlessness and tormented tension are also evident to a greater or lesser degree in the other olive groves of 1889.

The plane trees, in a work of mid-December 1889, painted in the village of Saint-Rémy, reveal the same whimsicality as the *Olive Orchard*. Van Gogh painted this work, *Road Menders in a Lane with Plane Trees* (JH 1861; see p. 149), when he was given leave to work outside the asylum. It shows the Cours de l'Est, which was renamed the boulevard Mirabeau eighteen months after the painting was completed. The road menders can be seen working unobtrusively in the centre and also on the right, next to the trees, but our attention is drawn by the plane trees rather than the workers. The women in traditional Provençal dress are very lively, like the Arlésiennes in the nearby town of Arles. The main colours of this gay anecdotal canvas, which depicts so much activity, are greyish green and orange and yellow. Van Gogh often used a great deal of paint and applied it very quickly, but in this work he used paint thinly, and in some places the canvas was even left unpainted, as Monet sometimes did.

Van Gogh had already used the subject of road menders in 1882 in two drawings which he completed in The Hague. This canvas is also reminis-

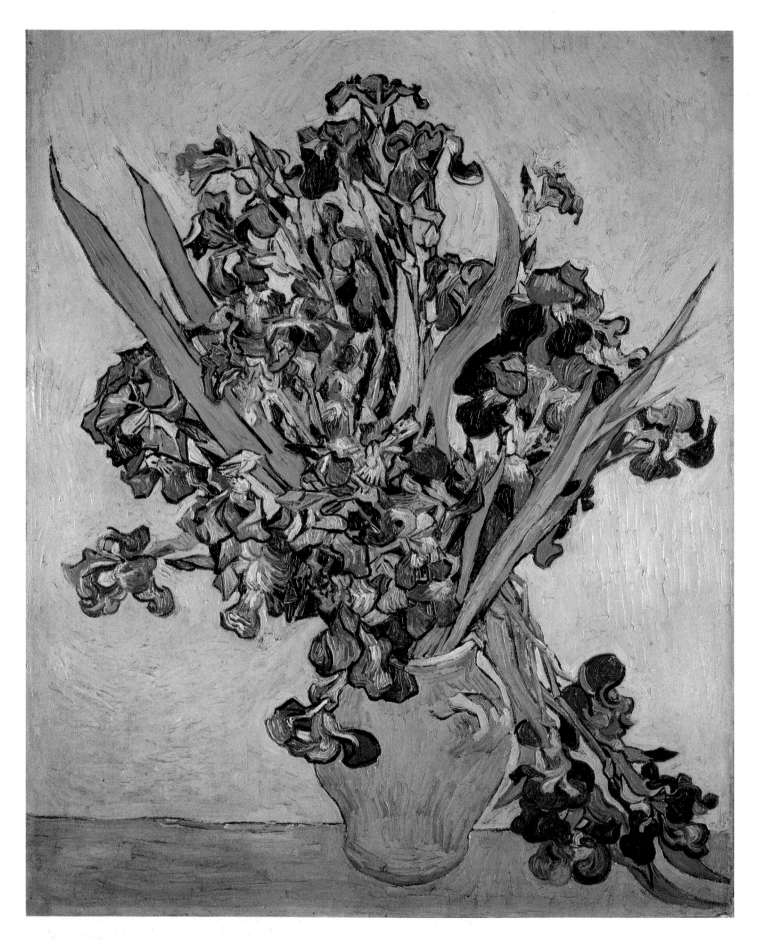

Vase with Violet Irises against a Yellow Background
Saint-Rémy, May 1890 F678 JH1977
Canvas, 92 x 73.5 cm
Amsterdam, Rijksmuseum Vincent van Gogh

146

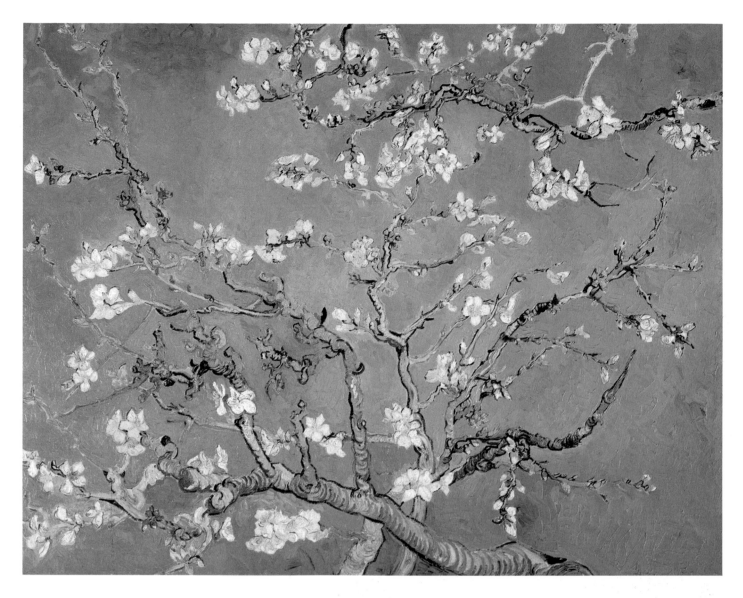

Branches of an Almond Tree in Blossom
Saint-Rémy, February 1890
F671 JH1891
Canvas, 73 x 92 cm
Amsterdam, Rijksmuseum
Vincent van Gogh

cent of a painting by Edouard Manet of the rue Mosnier with road menders, although we do not know if Van Gogh ever saw that painting.

Starry night

The extremely turbulent and almost apocalyptic painting, *The Starry Night* (JH 1731; see p. 150), also dates from June 1889. In this work Van Gogh moved a long way away from the Impressionism of his Parisian period. It is an Expressionist work, the style of which is reminiscent of the paintings of Edvard Munch made ten to fifteen years later. In the representation of the swirling starry sky, there is also an element of Surrealism. The village at the foot of the mountains is painted fairly realistically (its location is unknown, but it is not Saint-Rémy). Van Gogh's imagination is given full rein in the night sky. He does not tell us himself why he painted it in such a wild and dramatic way, but it reminds us of the Bible's predictions about the end of time. It could almost be an illustration for Matthew 24: 'The stars shall fall from heaven, and the powers of the heavens shall be shaken'. Or for Luke 21: 'And there shall be signs in the sun, and in the moon and in the stars.' Finally, the work reminds us of John 8, verse 10, which reads: 'And there fell a great star from heaven, burning as if it were a lamp.' (In the painting there is a large star left of centre.) These comparisons probably seem less far-fetched when one re-

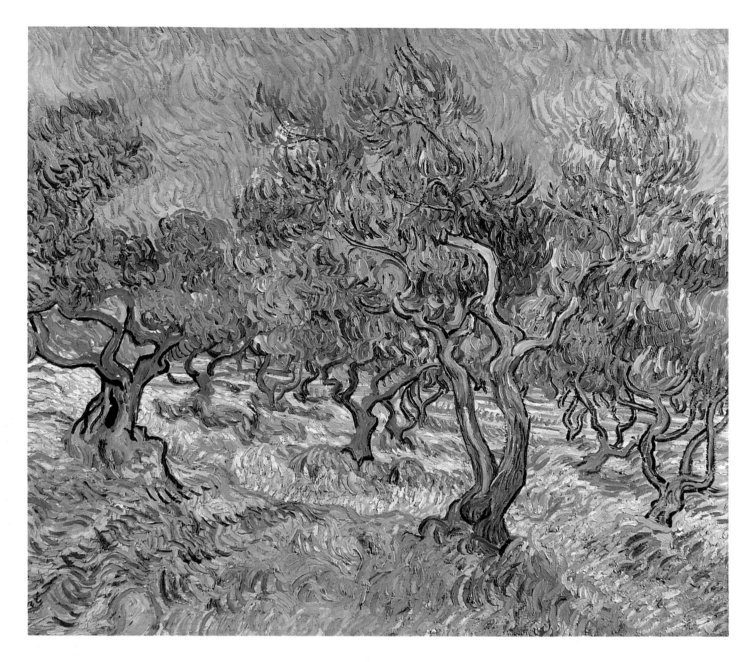

Olive Orchard
Saint-Rémy, June 1889
F585 JH1758
Canvas, 72 x 92 cm
Otterlo, Rijksmuseum
Kröller-Müller

members how familiar Van Gogh had become with the Bible during his evangelical studies.

It is easy to understand why people who saw this painting a hundred years ago felt that it was the work of a madman. They saw this work as confirmation that Van Gogh should be in an asylum. (The painting is now in the possession of the Museum of Modern Art in New York, one of the most popular works in the entire collection.)

Van Gogh added depth to his painting of the starry night by means of the cypress in the foreground on the left. During the Saint-Rémy period he was as fascinated by cypresses as he was by olive trees. In *The Starry Night* the cypress is a dark green silhouette against the night sky, and in *Wheat Field with Cypresses* (JH 1790; see p. 151), we see this green cypress by day against a cloudy summer sky. Each painting can be viewed as the other's counterpart. Van Gogh painted and drew the scene with the wheat field a number of times. The painting shown here was done in October for his mother and his sister Wil, a smaller version of a painting he had done in June. As in this case, the many versions and copies of subjects that Van Gogh produced make his work difficult to classify, and determining the chronological order is equally problematic.

Why Van Gogh repeated a subject several times is a question of psychological interest. He was highly self-critical and a perfectionist; he felt he could always improve on his own work, and that others painted better than he did: Delacroix, Millet and Monticelli, for example, though to most eyes Monticelli is a less interesting artist than Van Gogh. In fact, it is quite astonishing that he actually felt great admiration for an artist of such sentimental religious scenes as Ary Scheffer.

The cypress which emerges from the ground like a dark green burst of flame is also the main motif in the painting *Green Wheat Field with Cypress* (JH 1725; see p. 152). This work was painted from a very low viewpoint with ears of wheat in the foreground to create an effect of depth, a perspective that is intensified by the warm yellow of the wheat field seen against the cool blue-white sky.

The real Provence

Van Gogh painted another flaming cypress in May 1890, right at the end of his stay in Saint-Rémy, and just before his departure for Auvers: *Road with Men Walking, Carriage, Cypress, Star and Crescent Moon* (JH 1982;

Road Menders in a Lane with Plane Trees
Saint-Rémy, December 1889
F658 JH1861
Canvas, 73.5 x 92.5 cm
Washington, D.C.,
The Phillips Collection

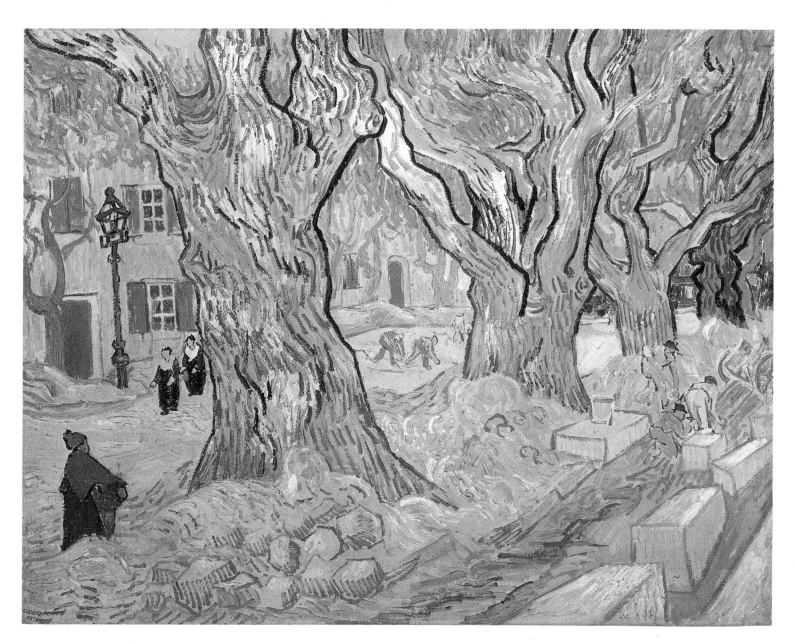

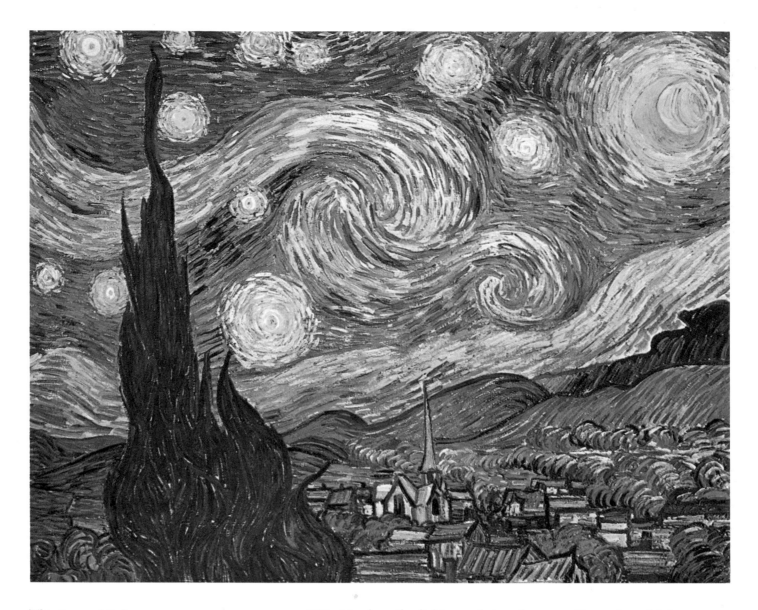

The Starry Night
Saint-Rémy, June 1889
F612 JH1731
Canvas, 73 x 92 cm
New York, The Museum of
Modern Art, Lillie P.Bliss Bequest

see p. 153). He described this work in a letter to Gauguin, which was not completed and was never sent (643):

'A night sky with a moon with no rays, the small crescent moon appears through the transparent shadow of the earth, a star glittering exaggeratedly, a soft pink and green brilliance in the ultramarine sky with a few clouds scudding along. Below this the road is bordered by tall yellow reeds with the low blue range of the Alpilles visible behind it, an old inn with orange lit-up windows and a very tall cypress, very straight and very dark. On the road there is also a yellow carriage drawn by a white horse, and you can see two people walking out late. It is very romantic, but I believe that this is the real Provence.'

This painting is in the Kröller-Müller Museum in Otterlo, as is the work *Cypresses with Two Women*. In the Museum of Sao Paulo in Brazil there is a painting of a crescent moon, a cypress and a couple taking a walk, in which Van Gogh painted himself as one of the figures. In a letter of 25 June 1889, he discusses the theme of the cypresses (596):

'I am constantly fascinated by cypresses. I would like to do something with them, like the canvasses of the sunflowers, for it surprises me that they have not yet been painted as I see them. They have a beautiful line and proportions, like an Egyptian obelisk. And the green is of a highly distinctive quality. A black mark in a sunny landscape, a black note which is extraordinarily interesting, but extremely difficult to convey as I imag-

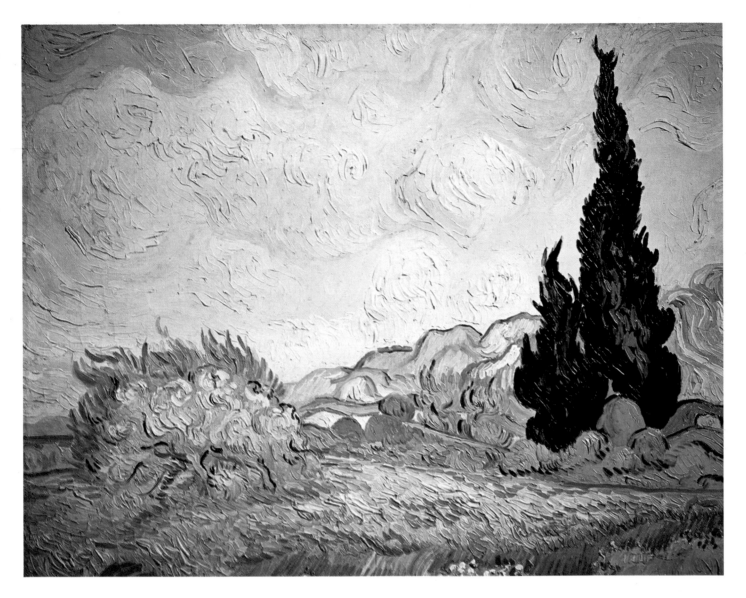

Wheat Field with Cypresses
Saint-Rémy, September 1889
F743 JH1790
Canvas, 52 x 65 cm
Private collection

ine it. Well, you should see them here against the blue - or in the blue, I should say. In order to paint nature here - as anywhere - you really have to be there a long time.'

Van Gogh wished to make a series of cypresses, just as he had planned to do a series of sunflowers. Each series would be a counterpart to the other; sunflowers as the symbol of day and life, cypresses as the symbol of night and death. (In the South of France there are nearly always cypresses to be seen in churchyards.)

It is worth noting that in his letter he wrote about cypresses 'as I see them.' Anyone who examines a cypress in the Midi will find it difficult to recognize Van Gogh's interpretation of this tree, with its wild, violent powerful brush strokes in swirling lines, very dynamic and often highly emotional. This applies particularly to his pen and ink drawings of cypresses. Together with the paintings, they are a spiritual expression of a restless and tormented man. They were painted between his bouts of illness, but they are not the works of a mentally disturbed man for amongst them are masterpieces.

Colourful pine bark

At the end of his stay in Saint-Rémy, Van Gogh painted more trees: two pine trees or fir trees in a wood full of wild flowers. Towards the end of

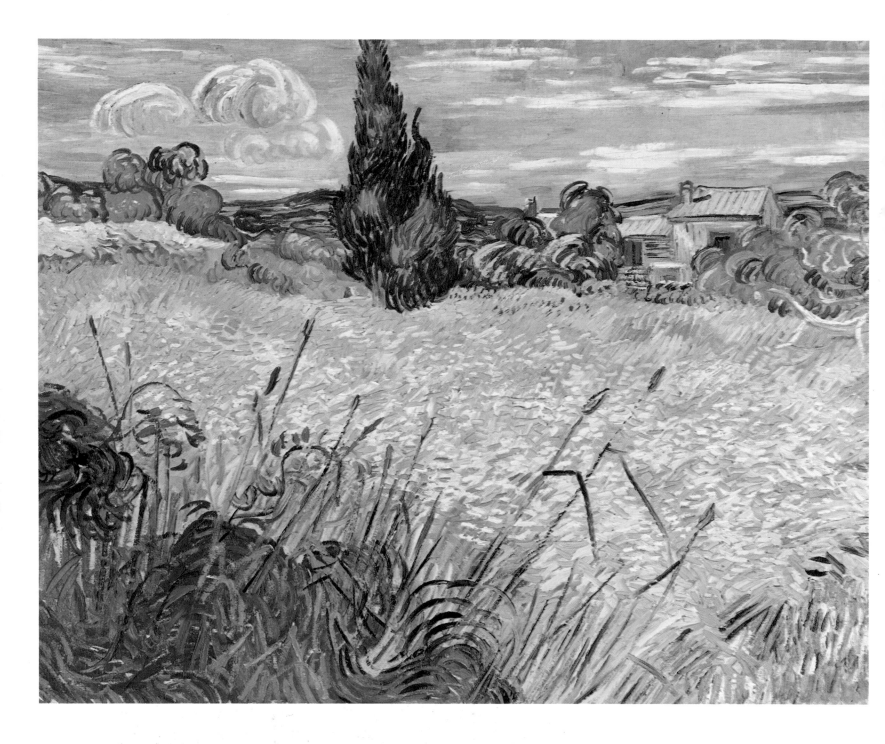

Green Wheat Field with Cypress
Saint-Rémy, June 1889
F719 JH1725
Canvas, 73.5 x 92.5 cm
Prague, Národní Galerie

April 1890 he wrote to his mother (629a): 'For a few days I've been painting a lawn in the full sunlight with yellow dandelions.' And he wrote to Theo (631): 'I have done two canvasses of the fresh grass in the park. The trunk of a pine tree in purplish pink and the grass with white flowers and dandelions, a small rosebush, and other tree trunks in the background.'

In this canvas, *Field of Grass with Dandelions and Tree Trunks* (JH 1970; see p. 154), which was painted in the garden of the asylum, the two trees on the left attract the most attention for the highly original style in which the tree trunks have been painted. The imaginative play of colour, which Van Gogh observed in the bark, captures all the nuances of a sundrenched pine forest. The white flowers have been painted in thick dots of paint with the whole brush, a very static subject that has been painted dynamically. There is no activity in the painting, and yet it is an extremely lively composition.

Fieldscapes

This splendid work shows that Van Gogh had recovered from his serious crisis. He had been overcome by an attack in February 1890, having been given leave to go to Arles, and had to be taken back to Saint-Rémy by coach. He was still not well in the middle of April - as is revealed by a letter to Theo - but two weeks later, towards the end of the month, he recovered. In a birthday letter to Theo he sent a large order for tubes of paint, brushes and 7-10 metres of canvas. Thus he had big plans once again, and wrote (629): 'I have just completed a painting of a sunny lawn and I believe it is quite strong.' This was *Field of Grass with Dandelions and Tree Trunks*, which is extraordinarily forceful.

Out in the open he also painted *Enclosed Field with Ploughman* (JH 1768; see p. 155), a little known painting, now in a private collection. Like the works depicting the lawn and the trunks of fir trees, this painting was also produced after a serious breakdown, a crisis which made it impossible for him to work for six weeks. This work, which was done at the end of August 1889, was produced during the characteristic period of enormous activity that followed these bouts. In less than a month he painted twenty paintings, including several works of a very high standard.

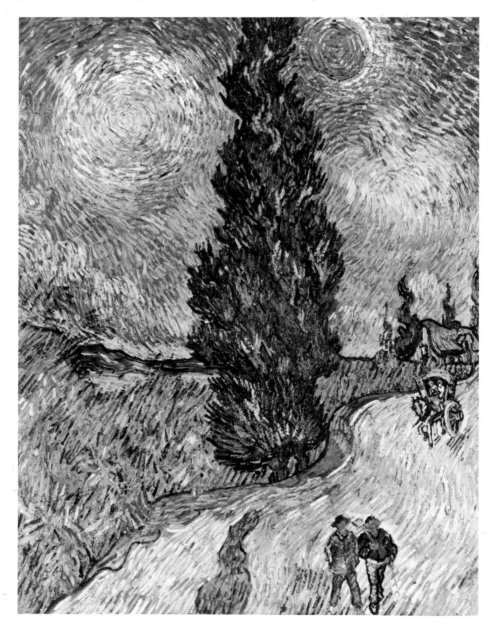

Road with Men Walking, Carriage, Cypress, Star and Crescent Moon
Saint-Rémy, May 1890
F683 JH1982
Canvas, 92 x 73 cm
Otterlo, Rijksmuseum
Kröller-Müller

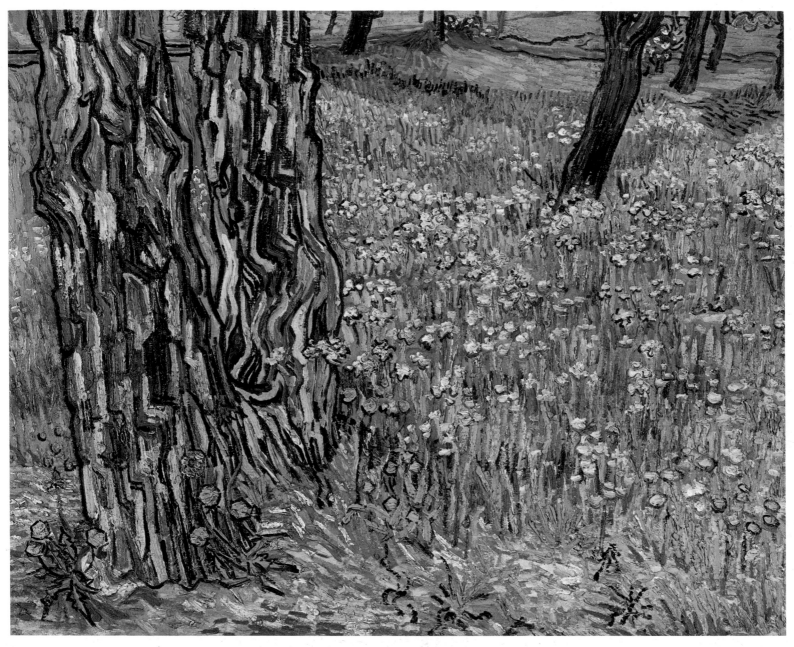

Field of Grass with Dandelions and Tree Trunks
Saint-Rémy, May 1890
F676 JH1970
Canvas, 72 x 90 cm
Otterlo, Rijksmuseum
Kröller-Müller

Thus it is clear that in Saint-Rémy during 1889 and 1890, Van Gogh was incapacitated by illness several times for a month or more, after which he returned to work each time with renewed energy and clarity. During the periods when he was strong enough to draw and paint or to write letters, he was by no means insane. Sometimes he produced works of genius and wrote highly intelligent letters which bore witness to his great powers of observation.

An example of such a painting is *Enclosed Field with Ploughman*. He painted this landscape as he saw it from the window of his bedroom, but it is not an accurate topographical representation. The farmer is in the centre behind his horse-drawn plough. A yellowish field of stubble is being ploughed and the purple earth turned over as the morning sun rises. Van Gogh referred to the work in a letter to Theo in which he enclosed a sketch of the painting.

Religious themes

One of the few religious works that Van Gogh painted was completed in September 1889, the well-known and often reproduced *Pietà (after Dela-*

154

croix) (JH 1775; see p. 156). This is a faithful copy of a lithograph by Célestin Nanteuil after the painting by Delacroix. Van Gogh also produced a smaller version of this work for his sister Wil. In a letter to her, dated 19 September 1889 (W 14), he described the painting as follows:

'The Delacroix is a pietà, i.e., the dead Christ with the Mater Dolorosa. The exhausted dead body lies curved in front of the entrance to a cave on the left, with the hands towards the front, and the woman stands behind it. It is the evening after a thunderstorm, and the inconsolable figure, dressed in blue, stands out against a sky with scudding purple, gold-edged clouds, while her clothes flap in the wind. In a great gesture of despair she stretches out her empty arms, and you see her hands, the strong hands of a woman who has to work hard. Because of the flapping clothes the figure is almost as broad as it is tall.

'While the face of the body is in the shadow, the pale face of the woman is brightly outlined against a cloud. Because of this contrast, the two heads look like a dark and a pale flower which have been deliberately placed next to each other so that they show up better.'

The figure of Christ with his red beard is actually a self-portrait, while Mary was given the face of the Mother Superior of the asylum, Mère Epiphanie (Madame Deschanel). Van Gogh had apparently offered to paint her before. After consulting with the other sisters, she is supposed to have refused, but in this work he immortalized her after all.

Enclosed Field with Ploughman
Saint-Rémy, September 1889
F625 JH1768
Canvas, 49 x 62 cm
Private collection

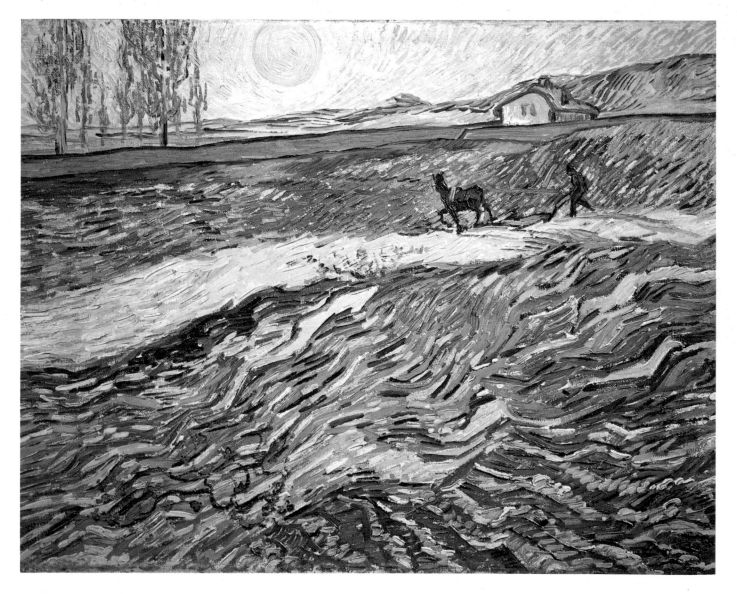

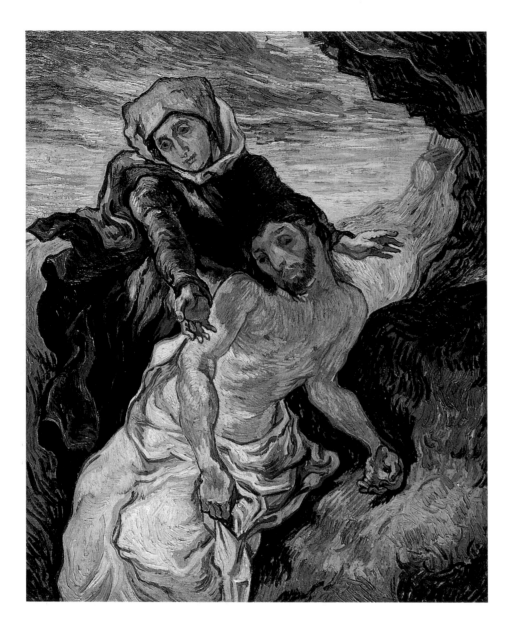

Pietà (after Delacroix)
Saint-Rémy, September 1889
F630 JH1775
Canvas, 73 x 60.5 cm
Amsterdam, Rijksmuseum
Vincent van Gogh

Ten days before this letter to Wil, he wrote to Theo that he felt it was no longer beneficial for him to live in either the old monastery in Saint-Rémy or in the hospital in Arles, even with the care of the Reverend Sisters (605): 'I am not indifferent, and during the illness itself, religious thoughts are often a great consolation.'

Conversely, he complained in a somewhat naive outburst that he felt imprisoned 'in one of those institutions which like to encourage unhealthy religious aberrations, while in fact people should be cured of them ... I reproach myself that I was so cowardly. I should have defended my studio better, and if necessary I should have fought the gendarmes and the neighbours. Others in my situation would have used a revolver. As an artist I could have killed some of these busybodies and have been acquitted. That would have been better. But I was cowardly and drunk.'

He then wrote that he had dropped the lithograph of the Pietà into oil paints so that the print was spoiled, but that he had immediately started to paint a copy.

Van Gogh's 'translations'

During his time in Saint-Rémy, Van Gogh made a large number of copies of other artists' work in his studio, always based on prints. He never

Prisoners' Round
(after Gustave Doré)
Saint-Rémy, February 1890
F669 JH1885
Canvas, 80 x 64 cm
Moscow, Pushkin Museum

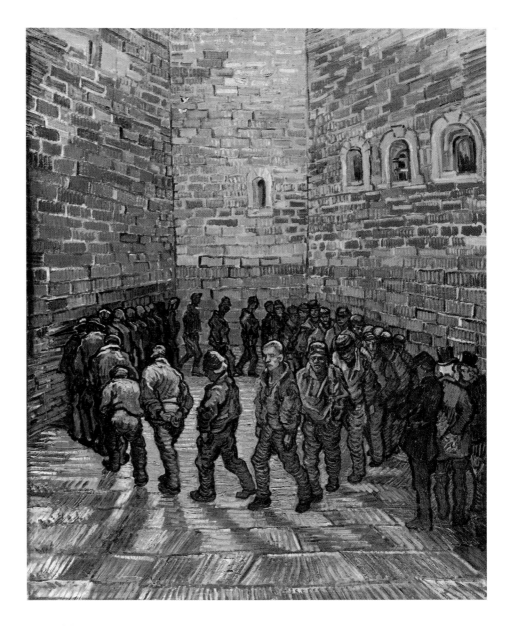

placed his easel in museums to paint a copy, as did many other artists. His *Pietà* and the *Good Samaritan* are after Delacroix; he also copied many works by Jean François Millet, and also Gustave Doré, Honoré Daumier and Rembrandt. There were at least thirty-six copies in all: twenty-eight paintings and eight drawings.

The illustration shown here is of Van Gogh's painting after Gustave Doré, *Prisoners' Round* or *The Prison Yard* (JH 1885; see p. 157) which he copied from a woodcut. The scene probably attracted him because he saw himself as a prisoner, as indicated in his last letter to Theo.

Van Gogh had already started to copy works by Millet in 1880, including *The Angelus*. Now, nine years later in Saint Rémy, he copied a total of twenty works by Millet, whose views of the life and work of the peasant appealed to him. He was particularly impressed by a series of ten drawings, *Travaux des Champs* (Working on the Land) which Millet had done in 1852. In 1889 Van Gogh copied all ten without interruption. (Theo had sent him the set of wood engravings by Jacques-Adrien Lavieille, which were based on Millet's drawings.) Throughout the series Van Gogh used the two primary colours, blue and yellow: blue for the peasants' clothes and for the sky, yellow for the wheat. The blue is used in numerous shades.

Van Gogh himself did not think of these paintings, based on Millet's work, as being copies at all, more a translation into another language ('*les traduire dans une autre langue*').

Freehand Rembrandt

Van Gogh was inspired to paint *The Raising of Lazarus* (JH 1972; see p. 160) in green and yellow, by a Rembrandt etching. 'I improvised the colours', he wrote, but he allowed his imagination to go much further, as is shown by a comparison with the original. The figures of Lazarus and the two women, Mary of Bethany and her sister Martha, are based on Rembrandt's etching, but Van Gogh replaced the figure drawing back, and the man next to him, by a radiant sun. Thus again he used the sun as a religious, life-giving symbol. It is a heathen version of the Biblical story told in the Gospel according to St. John, chapter 11. Van Gogh strongly emphasizes his fundamental change to the evangelical theme by painting the sun thickly as a strongly outlined round disc.

In a letter to Theo dated May 1890 (632), he wrote about the three figures taken from Rembrandt's etching: 'The dead man and his two sisters. The cave and the body are purple, yellow, white. The woman who is removing the shroud from the face of the risen Lazarus is wearing a green dress, and she has orange hair. The other woman has black hair and is wearing a striped green and pink garment. The yellow sun rises behind the blue hills. The combination of the colours is self-evident in the same way as the chiaroscuro effect in the etching.' It is worth noting that in this letter Van Gogh does not give any explanation for his dramatic alteration.

Self-portraits

In September 1889, when Van Gogh painted the Travaux des Champs series, he also did some self-portraits. Most of his self-portraits were painted in Paris, followed by a further six painted in Arles. In Saint-Rémy he returned to this theme with a further three self-portraits, his last. He wrote to Theo (604): 'It is said - and I am prepared to believe it - that it is difficult to know yourself, nor is it easy to paint yourself.'

A letter to Wil, dated 19 September, contains the following interesting reflection on photography, which he utterly deplored (W 14): 'I think photographs are always dreadful, I don't want to have any, especially of people I know and love. Portrait photographs fade more rapidly than we do ourselves, while a painted portrait is good for generations. Anyway, a painted portrait is done with feeling and made with love and respect for the person being painted.'

This condemnation is surprising in view of the fact that Van Gogh's friend from his period in The Hague, the artist George Hendrik Breitner (1857-1923), made several thousand photographs, including a number of very fine portraits which have survived in perfect condition. Félix Nadar too was making beautiful and very sensitive portrait photographs of well-known people in France.

The *Self-portrait* (JH 1772; see p. 159) shown here was a gift from Van Gogh, the grateful patient, to his doctor, Paul Gachet, who had treated him in Auvers-sur-Oise. The orange beard, moustache and sideburns, and the reddish hair, contrast strikingly with the blue of the swirling background. Blue is the predominant colour in this portrait, and our attention is first drawn to the eyes, deep in their sockets, which have a penetrating

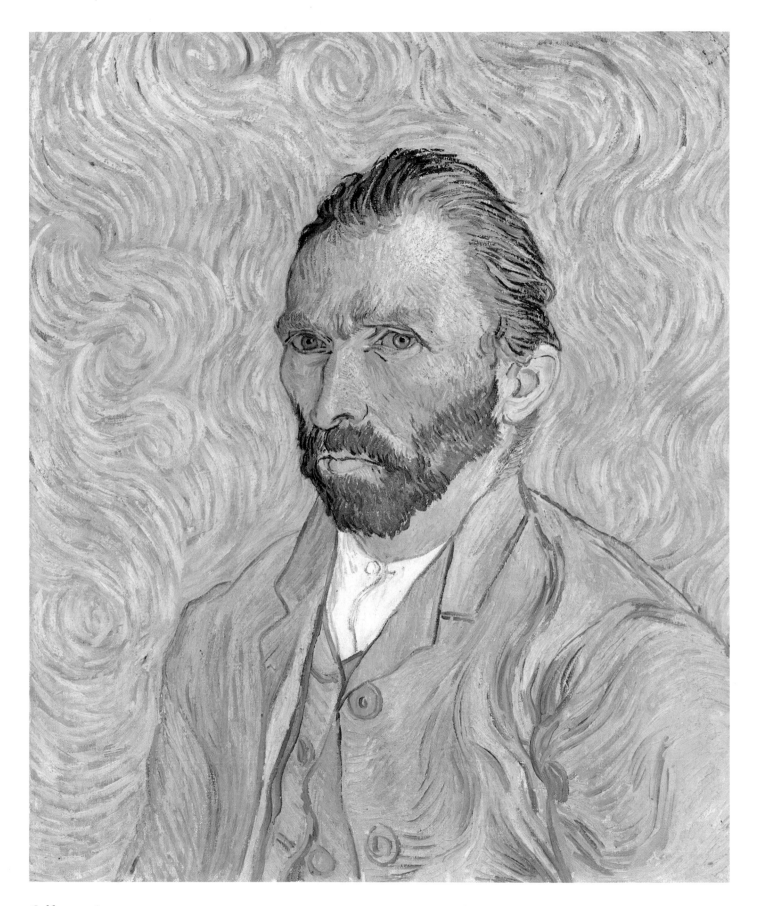

Self-portrait
Saint-Remy, September 1889
F627 JH1772
Canvas, 65 x 54 cm
Paris, Musée d'Orsay

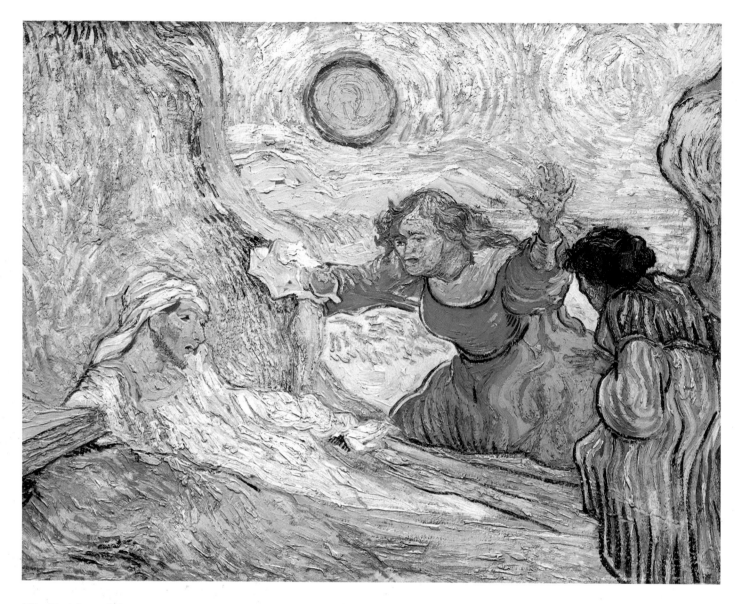

*The Raising of Lazarus
(after a detail from an etching
by Rembrandt)*
Saint-Rémy, May 1890
F677 JH1972
Canvas, 48.5 x 63 cm
Amsterdam, Rijksmuseum
Vincent van Gogh

glance. The painting is very different from the two other self-portraits which Van Gogh made at that time, one of which has a purple background, while the other is painted green.

Times of day

After the Travaux des Champs series of September, Van Gogh did a few more copies of works by Millet in Saint-Rémy. These works include *The Evening Hour*, *The Sower*, *End of the Day*, *Two Diggers*, and *Morning on the Way to Work*. In the witty, anecdotal *Noon Rest* (JH 1881; see p. 161), Van Gogh uses contrasting tones of purple and yellow. One can imagine him being attracted by this peaceful representation by Millet of a young peasant couple, enjoying a nap in the heat of the day after a morning's hard work. The peasant has taken off his clogs, next to which lie two scythes. The bright colours in the painting convey the effect of a hot summer's day more strongly than the original pastel by Millet, which was executed in much softer shades.

At the beginning of 1890, Van Gogh painted *The First Steps* after Millet (JH 1883; see p. 162/3). This is a very attractive rendering of a household scene. A young peasant wife is teaching her child to walk across the yard of her cottage. The father leaves his wheelbarrow and places his spade on the ground so that he can sit on his haunches and stretch out his arms to

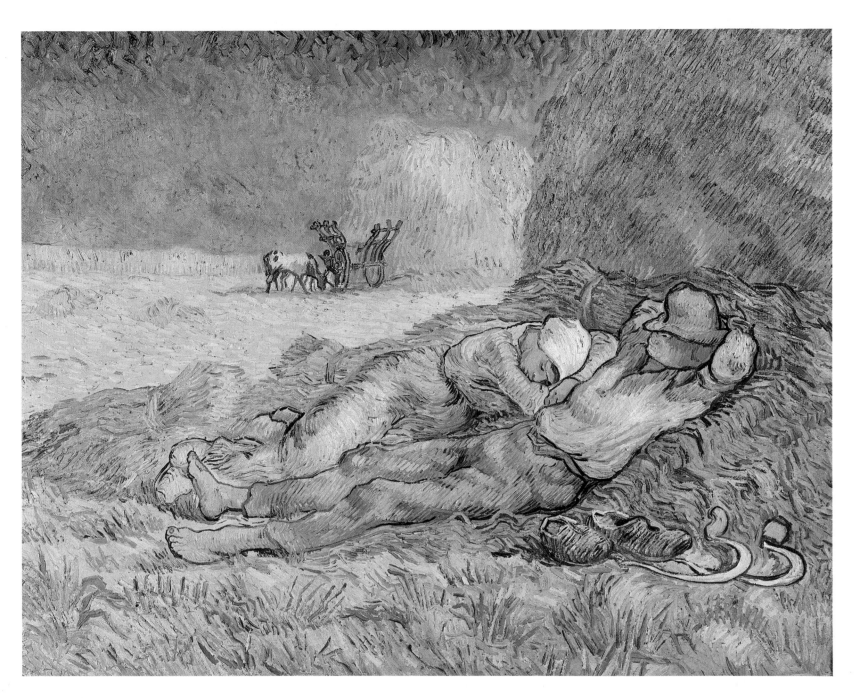

Noon Rest (after Millet)
Saint-Rémy, January 1890
F686 JH1881
Canvas, 73 x 91 cm
Paris, Musée d'Orsay

the toddler, who is enthusiastically waving to her father. The blossoming tree in the background heightens the sense of spring. Van Gogh painted the happy scene from a photograph of Millet's drawing, first dividing the photograph into twenty-four squares with a ruler so that he could enlarge the scene square by square. In other words, it is a close copy, though we must conclude that the colours are Van Gogh's own.

The subject and style of this painting are very similar to *The Evening Hour* (JH 1834), which was painted in the autumn of 1889, also after Millet. In this work, a man and a woman sit opposite each other, with their child in a cradle in the background. The two paintings are also the same size (73 x 92 cm), and together with *Noon Rest* and *On the Way to Work* formed a series, *Les Heures de la Journée* (Times of Day), in Van Gogh's mind, though the relation between them is unclear as the subjects are rather different. In fact, the only similarity lies in the size of the works.

Although he felt that he was doing more than simply copying, Van Gogh always thought of these works after Millet as studies or exercises rather than as his own creations. He wrote to Theo (623): 'The more I

161

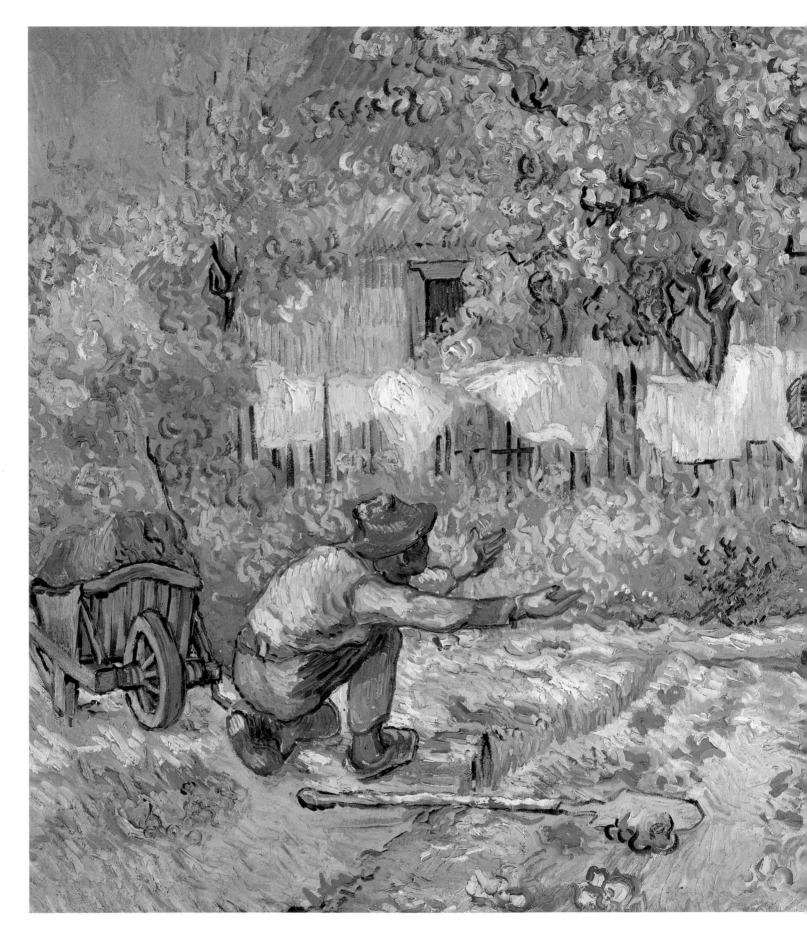

The First Steps (after Millet), Saint-Rémy, January 1890
F668 JH1883 - Canvas, 73 x 92 cm
New York, Metropolitan Museum of Art,
Gift of George N. and Helen M. Richard

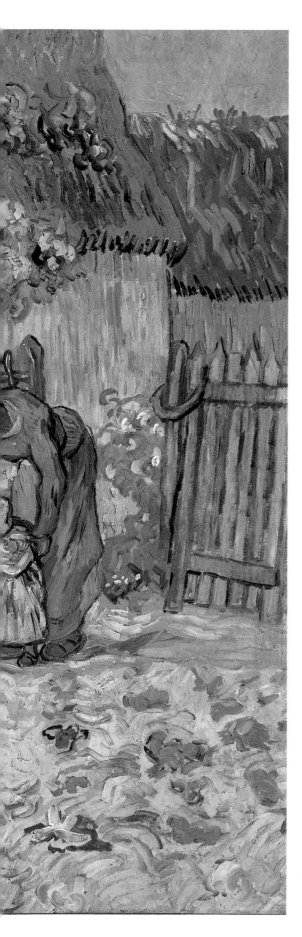

think about it, the more I think that there is a point in reproducing Millet's drawings which he did not have time to paint in oils. Thus when I am working on his drawings or on his woodcuts, this is not merely a matter of copying. It is rather a matter of translating Millet's chiaroscuro impressions into another language, the language of colour.'

Theo replied with a letter dated 3 May 1890, confirming that he had received the Millet copies (T 33):

'The copies of Millet are possibly the most beautiful work you have done, and I believe that we are in for a big surprise once you start to do compositions of figures.' This was not a tactful remark, nor was it very fair with regard to an artist who had clearly painted some very original masterworks, even in Nuenen, but especially in Paris, Arles and Saint-Rémy. Perhaps the young father, Theo, was so moved by the painting of *The First Steps* that he did not stop to think that it might not be an entirely original work.

George H. Breitner considered the paintings of his former friend Van Gogh to be 'crude and repellent'. Nor did he appreciate his copies. Breitner referred to this work as 'goods stolen from Millet and others.'

Nostalgia

Such a sentimental subject as *The First Steps* is not really typical of Van Gogh. It is a more likely theme for an Impressionist artist such as Berthe Morisot or the American, Mary Cassatt.

On 29 April 1890 Van Gogh wrote to his mother and his sister Wil (629a): 'Although I was extremely ill, I still managed to paint, amongst other things a memory of Brabant, huts with mossy roofs and beech hedges on an autumn evening with a stormy sky, the red sun setting in the pink clouds.' This is a description of *Cottages and Cypresses at Sunset with Stormy Sky* (JH 1921; see p. 164), also known as *Souvenir du Nord*. It is a nostalgic work.

During his illness in March and April he brooded about his Brabant background and his childhood spent in Zundert, and later in Etten and Nuenen. At this time he did many drawings of peasant life in Brabant, including some scenes of peasants having a meal. He even considered painting from memory another version of his Nuenen work, *The Potato Eaters*. The sombre and melancholy *Souvenir du Nord* reveals how he felt at times in the early spring of 1890. He wrote (629 Q): 'I have not been able to work during the very best days of spring.' And then he added: 'I am really longing to leave here.'

During this period, he also painted a poignant image entitled *Old Man with his Head in his Hands* (JH 1967; see p. 165), a figure with whom Van Gogh no doubt identified. His source was a lithograph by an unknown English artist, *At Eternity's Gate*. He had already made several copies of this print: a pencil drawing, a drawing in chalk, and a lithograph more than seven years before in November 1882, when he was still living in The Hague.

A good review

During the last year of his life Van Gogh was at least able to read one highly flattering discussion of his work. The first issue of a new magazine called *Mercure de France*, published in January 1890, contained a review by the 35-year-old critic G. Albert Aurier, in which he praised Van Gogh as a worthy successor of the old Dutch masters and a true artist:

'Vincent is not only a great artist, enthusiastic about his art, his palette and nature, he is also a dreamer, a man with a fanatical belief, who sees a beautiful world in the future and lives on ideas and dreams... Will this strict true painter, an authentic true blooded artist with the brutal hands of a giant, the neuroses of an hysterical woman, the soul of a prophet, so original and so different from the impoverished art of the present, will he ever - for anything is possible - know the joy of rehabilitation, the repentance of the vagaries of fashion?'

This article, '*Les isolés. Vincent Van Gogh*', is significant because it focused attention on Van Gogh at a time when he desperately needed some public recognition and appreciation. However, Van Gogh's reaction to this article was rather strange. Several letters to his mother, to Wil, Theo and Aurier himself, express his surprise that the author should tell him how to paint. He felt that the praise awarded him here should go to artists such as Monticelli and Gauguin instead, and he continued to have a feel-

Cottages and Cypresses at Sunset with Stormy Sky
Saint-Rémy, March-April, 1890
F675 JH1921
Canvas on panel, 29 x 36.5 cm
Amsterdam, Rijksmuseum
Vincent van Gogh

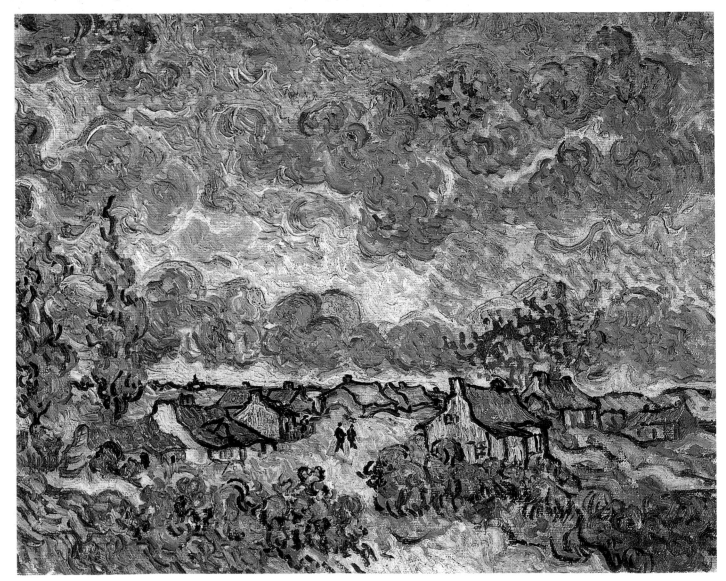

*Old Man with his Head
in his Hands (after the lithograph
'At Eternity's Gate', 268)*
Saint-Rémy, March-April 1890
F702 JH1967
Canvas, 81 x 65 cm
Otterlo, Rijksmuseum
Kröller-Müller

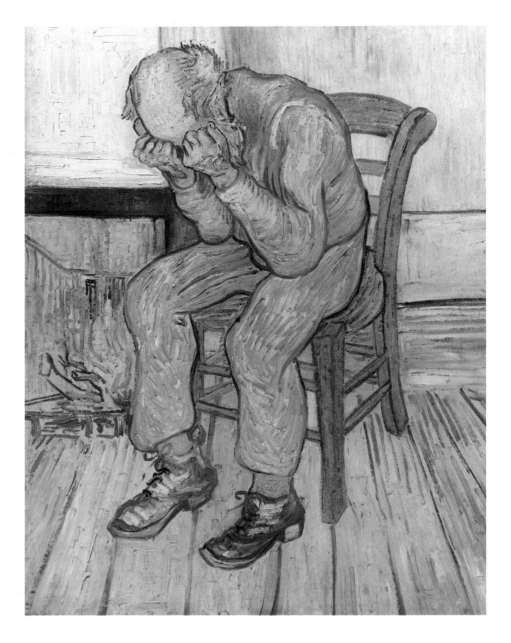

ing of inferiority when compared to other artists of his time. He suffered from a surfeit of self-criticism, and did not dare to consider Aurier's article simply as encouragement.

Leaving the asylum

Van Gogh was a voluntary patient at the asylum in Saint-Rémy, and the register shows that he was released on 16 May 1890 with the note: 'Guérison' (Cured). The patient, who had been admitted on 16 May 1889, was described in the notes of Dr Théophile Peyron, the physician, as someone who was usually calm, but who had suffered a number of attacks lasting between two weeks and a month during his stay in the asylum.

'During these attacks the patient suffered terrible fear and repeatedly tried to poison himself, either by swallowing the paint which he used for his work, or by drinking the petroleum which he managed to steal when the attendant filled the lamps. He had his last attack when he made a trip to Arles. The crisis lasted about two months. Between attacks the patient was very calm and applied himself energetically to his painting. He asked to be dismissed because he wishes to live in the north of France, in the hope that the climate there will be good for him.'

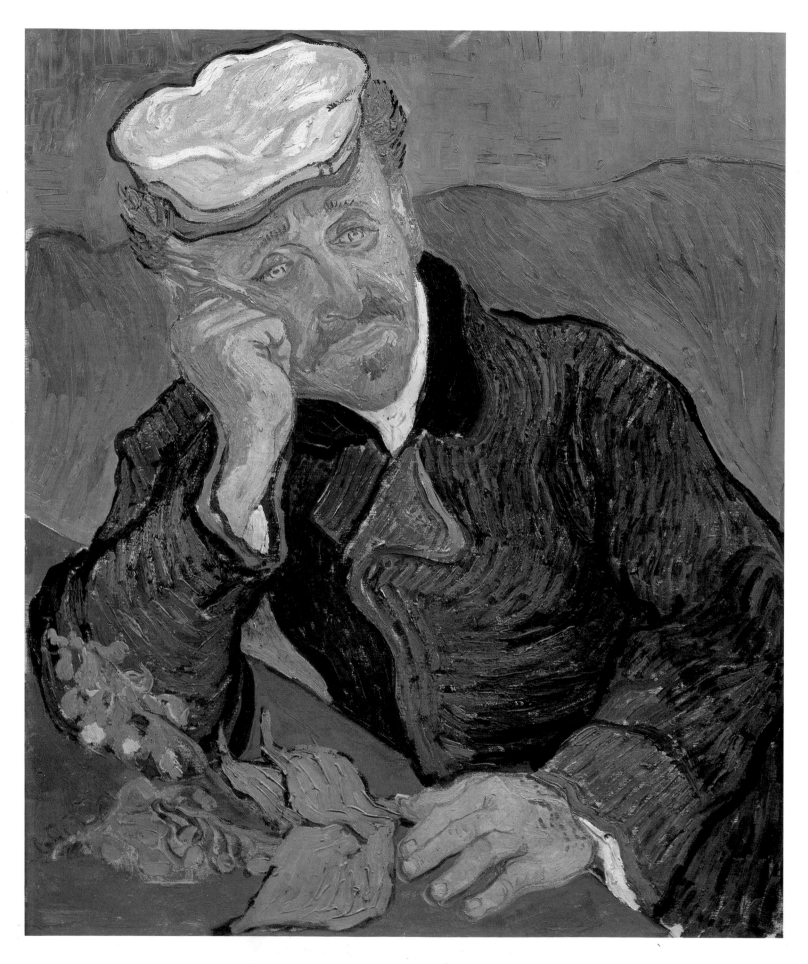

Doctor Gachet with a Sprig of Foxglove
Auvers, June 1890 F754 JH2014
Canvas, 68 x 57 cm Paris, Musée d'Orsay

166

Chapter VI
Wheat field with crows
Auvers-sur-Oise

After bidding farewell to Dr Peyron, Van Gogh left Saint-Rémy by train on the evening of 16 May 1890. At Tarascon, he had to catch the night train for Paris. He had sent most of his luggage on ahead, but he carried his easel and a few frames himself. The next morning he arrived at the Gare de Lyon at ten o'clock, where he was met by Theo. Together they took an open carriage to Theo's apartment on the fourth floor of 8 cité Pigalle, where Jo was waiting for them with baby Vincent.

About her first meeting with Van Gogh, after his discharge from the asylum, Jo wrote (*Collected Letters*, Introduction): 'I had expected to see a patient, and there stood before me a strong, broad-shouldered man with a healthy colour, a smile on his face, and a very resolute expression.' And: 'He stayed with us for three days and was cheerful and lively all the time.'

Van Gogh found quite a lot of his work in his brother's house. *The Blossoming Orchards* hung in the bedroom, *The Potato Eaters* hung above the mantlepiece in the dining-room, the large *Landscape from Arles* and *Night View on the Rhone* were in the living-room. In addition, there were piles of unframed canvasses all over the house - under the bed, under the sofa, under the cupboards and in the guest room. Furthermore, a large number of paintings were stored at the premises of the dealer, Tanguy. All this work was unsold, and at that time, clearly unsaleable.

On Tuesday 20 May, Van Gogh travelled from Paris to the village of Auvers-sur-Oise, about 30 kilometres north-west of Paris. This village, where Corot, Daubigny, Daumier, Gauguin, Cézanne and Pissarro worked, has a picturesque location in the valley of the River Oise. Van Gogh decided to move there on Camille Pissarro's recommendation, away from the bustle of the city, which he could no longer tolerate. Thus artists of the Barbizon School, as well as Impressionists, had worked in Auvers before Van Gogh set up his easel there.

Dr Gachet

In Auvers Van Gogh was put into the care of Dr Paul-Ferdinand Gachet, who was twenty-five years older than his young patient. Gachet had lived for some time in Mechelen, Belgium, before coming to Auvers in 1872, so he was able to converse in Dutch with Van Gogh.

With regard to this move to Auvers, Jo wrote: 'One of the first portraits he made was of Doctor Gachet, who was immediately attracted to Vincent, so that they spent most of the time together and became great friends.' In Gachet's view, Van Gogh was not merely a sympathetic and interesting character, but also a great painter.

Van Gogh painted two portraits of the doctor. The portrait shown here, *Doctor Gachet with a Sprig of Foxglove* (JH 2014; see p. 166), is the first and was donated to the French nation by Paul Gachet, the doctor's son,

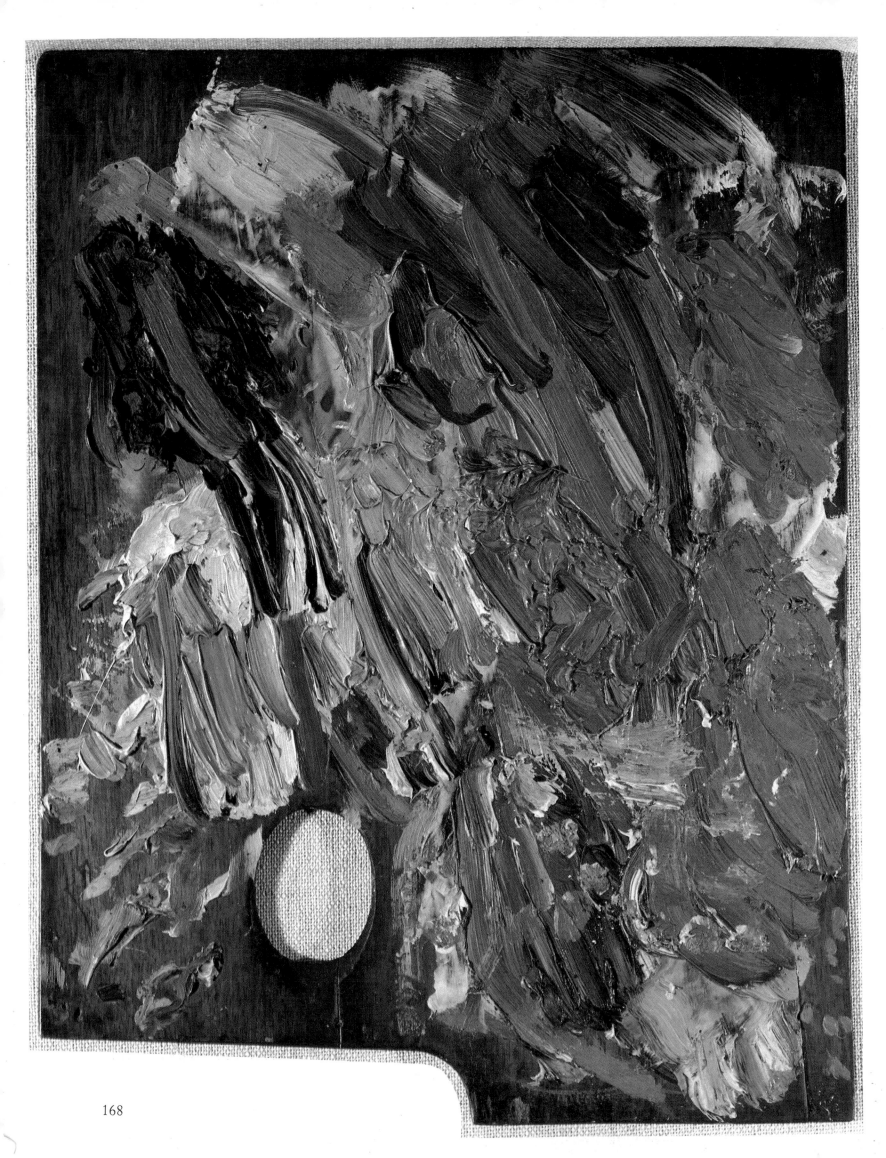

Marguerite Gachet at the Piano
Auvers, June 1890
F772 JH2048
Canvas, 102 x 50 cm
Basel, Öffentliche Kunstsammlung,
Kunstmuseum

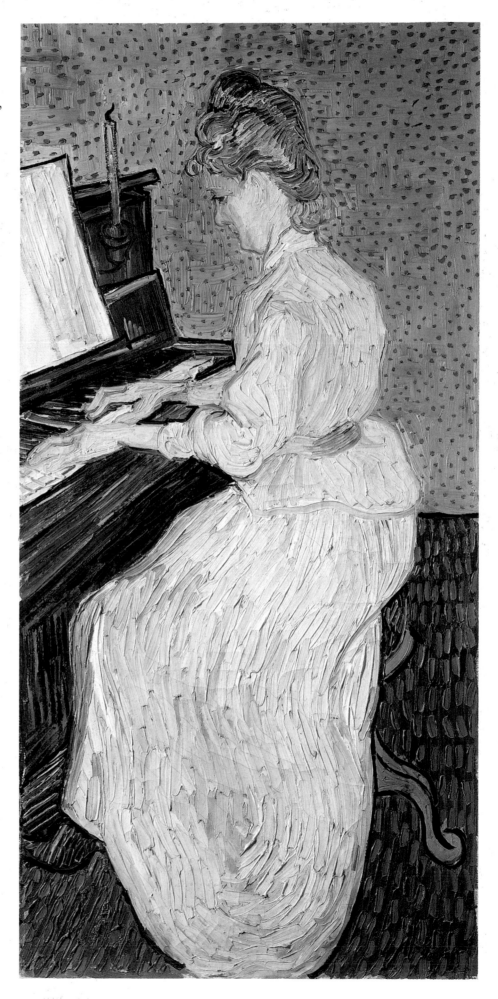

Vincent's Palette, used for the
portrait of Marguerite Gachet
Auvers, June 1890

in 1951. Again, it is a portrait in complementary colours, red for the table and green for the foxglove leaf; orange for the hair and blue for the suit in the background. Van Gogh himself described the portrait as follows (W 22): 'The portrait of Doctor Gachet shows a face with the colour of an overheated stone, and it was tanned by the sun, with reddish hair and a white cap against a background of a blue hilly landscape, and his clothes are an ultramarine blue, so that his face shows up more and looks paler, even though it is brick coloured. The hands - the hands of an obstetrician - are paler than the face.' In his next letter to Wil (W 23), he wrote: 'I have done the portrait of M. Gachet with a melancholy expression, which sometimes looks like a grimace when you look at it. And yet this is what you must paint. Because in this way you realise that in comparison with the old calm portraits, there is an expression and passion in the faces as we paint them now, and a sense of expectation and a cry. Sad, but soft, clear and intelligent. Many portraits should be done like this.'

In this portrait Dr Gachet is revealed as a melancholy figure. He had formerly gained his doctorate at the medical faculty of the University of Montpellier with a thesis entitled *Study of Melancholia*, a subject which clearly attracted him. He was a homeopathic doctor, and had a practice in Paris a few days a week. Van Gogh thought that Gachet was just as neurotic as he was himself, and wondered what happens when the blind lead the blind. But they soon became close friends, and during the months in Auvers the doctor showed great concern for Van Gogh. Gachet was a free thinker and a Darwinist, and politically he was a fervent Republican and socialist. He was used to the company of artists, having struck up friendly relationships with Cézanne, Sisley, Renoir and Manet, and was a passable artist and etcher himself.

The modern portrait

Gachet was 'definitely enthusiastic' about a new portrait, *The Arlésienne*, which Van Gogh had painted of his friend, Madame Ginoux, in Saint-Rémy in February. The doctor also greatly admired one of his self-portraits. For Van Gogh, painting portraits was most important at this stage of his development.

He confided this in a letter to his sister Wil (W 22):

'What I am most involved with, more than any other aspect of my painting, is the portrait, the modern portrait. I am attempting this in colours, and am certainly not the only one trying to do it in this way. This is how I would like to do it you know; I don't say that I can, but I am trying. I would like to do portraits which would seem like apparitions to people in a hundred years' time. I am not aiming for a photographic likeness, but I explore the possibilities of expressing the passions. I would like to heighten the expression of character by means of our modern knowledge and feeling for colour.'

A hundred years on, it is actually possible to say that Van Gogh's dream has come true, in the sense that his portraits of nineteenth-century characters such as Dr Gachet, Madame Ginoux, and above all, the artist himself, appear to come alive, even as apparitions or spirits. These portraits also show how he was ahead of his time, anticipating the works of Fauvist artists such as Matisse in the early 1900s.

In addition to the portraits of Dr Gachet, Van Gogh also painted a portrait of the doctor's 21-year-old daughter, *Marguerite Gachet at the*

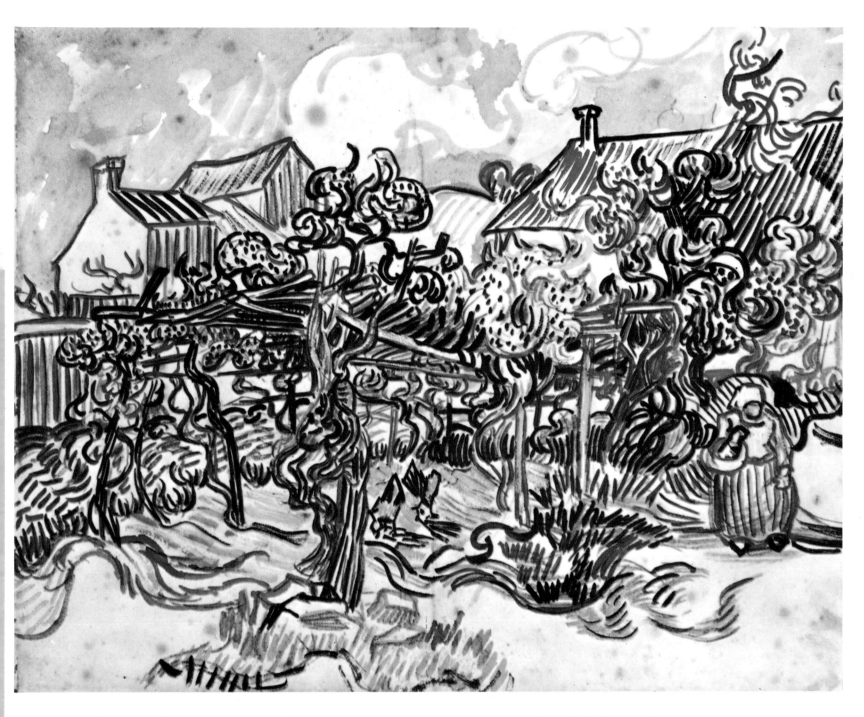

Old Vineyard with Peasant Woman
Auvers, May 1890
F1624 JH1985
Pencil, washed, blue, red and
white gouache, 43.5 x 54 cm
Amsterdam, Rijksmuseum
Vincent van Gogh

Piano (JH 2048; see p. 169). He described the colours of this painting, which he worked on from 24 to 25 June in Auvers, as follows (645): 'The dress is pink, the wall in the background green with orange dots, the carpet is red with green dots and the piano a dark violet colour.'

These colours are also found in the palette used for *Young Woman Playing the Piano*, which is reminiscent of Toulouse-Lautrec's *Mademoiselle Dihau au Piano*, which Van Gogh saw and admired at a later date. The style of Van Gogh's work is quite distinct from that of Manet and Renoir, whose works also show women playing the piano.

Picturesque village

The first drawing he made of the village of Auvers in May 1890 was the *Old Vineyard with Peasant Woman* (JH 1985; see p. 171). A work in pencil, watercolour and gouache, the swirling lines are typical of Van Gogh's Auvers style. It is possible that he did the drawing outside in the open air,

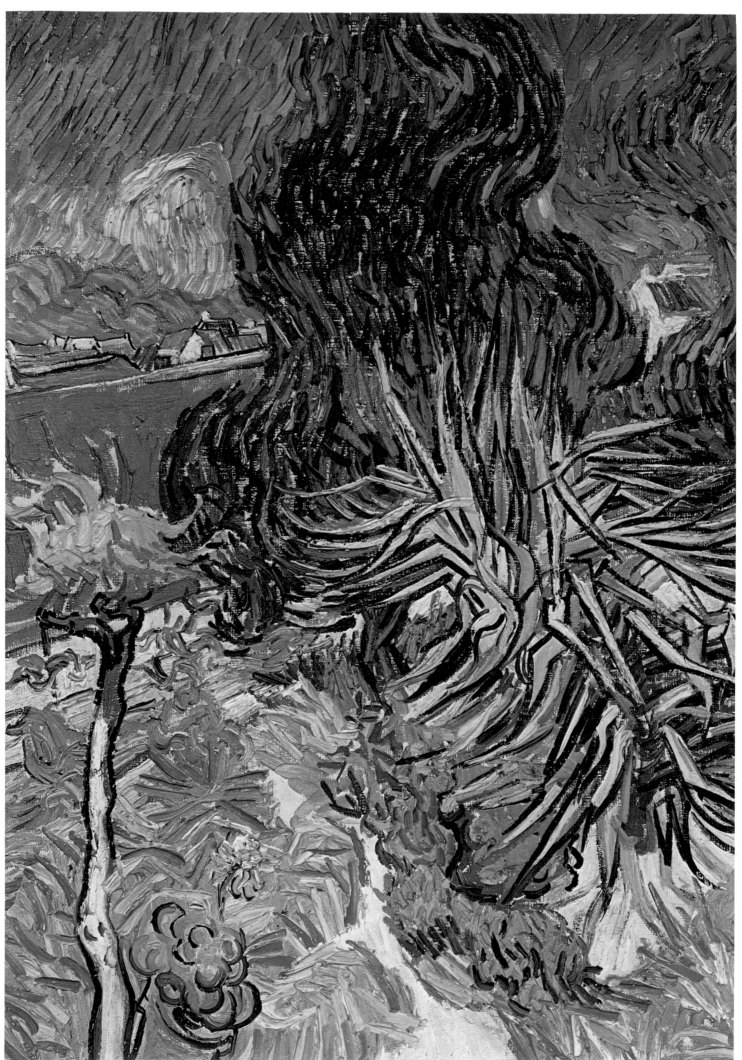

172

and added the colours later at home. He was struck by the old thatched roofs of the farms which he depicted in a very Expressionist style. During this period he did a whole series of drawings and paintings of the village.

For the last three months of his life Van Gogh lived at the inn of Arthure Gustave Ravoux on the Place de la Mairie in Auvers. It is still possible to see the town hall, which stood opposite Van Gogh's last home.

There is a beautiful sculpture by Ossip Zadkine in the park nearby, unveiled in 1961, which shows Van Gogh as a thin man on his way to the wheat fields that he wanted to paint, with his easel on his back, a sketchbook in his left hand, and a brush in his right hand.

Although Van Gogh considered portrait painting to be the highest art form, he did mainly landscapes while he was in Auvers. To do portraits he had to paint in his model's house, for there was absolutely no space in his tiny room on the second floor of Ravoux's inn, where the only light source was a skylight. He paid only three and a half francs per day for this humble room, so there was some money left over for other expenses from the hundred and fifty francs per month that Theo sent him. Usually he received this sum in three installments of fifty francs.

Symphony in blue

The oldest daughter of the innkeeper Ravoux, Adeline, was thirteen years old in 1890, and in June Van Gogh painted her portrait three times. The first canvas shows the girl in profile, looking to the right. Sixty-six years later, Adeline Ravoux remembered how she had posed for Van Gogh: 'I sat on a chair dressed in blue. I wore a blue ribbon in my hair. As I have blue eyes and Van Gogh painted the background blue, it was a symphony in blue.'

The original portrait of Adeline Ravoux was not particularly appreciated by the girl herself or her parents, and in 1905 her father sold it together with another canvas by Van Gogh, *The Decorated Town Hall*, for the total sum of forty francs. A virtually identical portrait of Adeline, a copy for Theo (JH 2037), was sold at an auction by Christie's in New York on 11 May 1988, where it made $ 13.75 million.

In a letter to Theo dated 4 June 1890 (638), Van Gogh wrote that his health was good and that he usually went to bed at nine o' clock in the evening and got up at five o' clock in the morning. He worked hard all day on his drawings and paintings. Altogether Van Gogh painted about seventy oil paintings during his stay in Auvers, on average one a day. In addition, he did a large number of drawings and wrote numerous letters to Theo and others.

Van Gogh and Monet

In 1890, while Van Gogh was living in dire poverty in his garret in Auvers, Claude Monet was working not far away on his beautiful estate of Giverny near Vernon, which he had been able to buy as a result of his success as an artist. A few years previously, between 1886 and 1888, Theo had sold no fewer than twenty of Monet's paintings for the firm Boussod, Valadon et Cie, while he had not been able to sell any of Van Gogh's work. On 14 July 1890 Theo visited Monet in Giverny with Valadon, a member of the firm. Initially Monet also had financial problems, but eventually he was able to enjoy fame and a high income, while Van Gogh

Doctor Gachet's Garden
Auvers, May 1890
F755 JH1999
Canvas, 73 x 51.5 cm
Paris, Musée d'Orsay

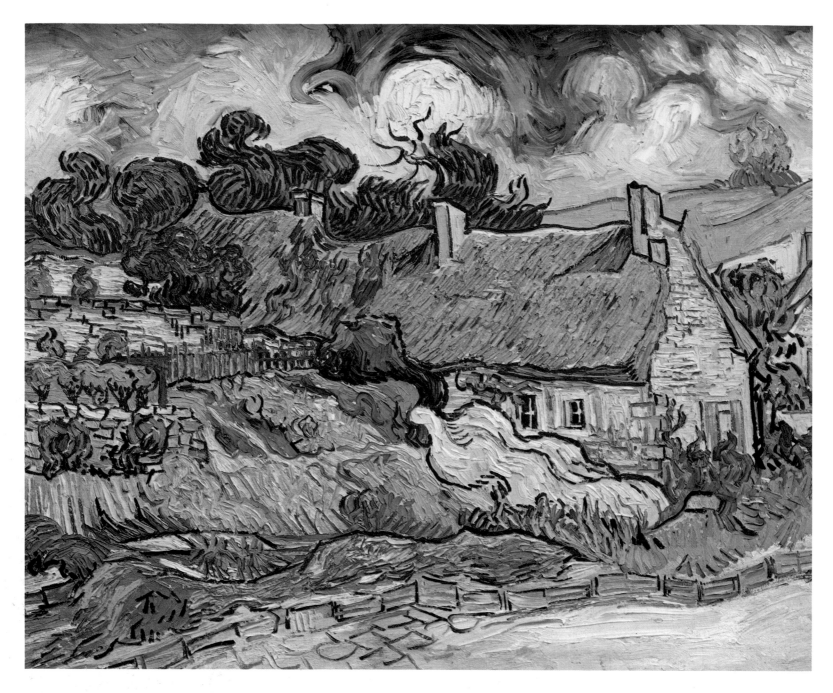

Cottages with Thatched Roofs
Auvers, May 1890
F792 JH1987
Canvas, 72 x 91 cm
Paris, Musée d'Orsay

did not live to see his success. Van Gogh died an unknown artist in Auvers, aged thirty-seven; Monet, who reached the age of eighty-six, was visited in Giverny by the prime minister of France, Clemenceau, who admired the artist's work. What a contrast between the painter of sunflowers and the painter of water lilies. It was only many years later that Van Gogh was given proper recognition.

Theo and Vincent

During the early summer of 1890 Van Gogh lived under almost unbearable tension. For quite a while, Theo had been considering the prospect of leaving Boussod, Valadon et Cie to set up on his own. Vincent realized the consequences for him if the business venture turned out to be a fiasco. How would he be able to live if his brother were no longer able to support him? In a letter to Theo, he wrote (649): 'It is a matter for anxiety if we all see our daily bread becoming jeopardized. I was afraid - not completely, but a little bit - that I would be a burden to you because you have to look after me, but Jo's letter made it clear to me that you realise that I am also working and making an effort, just like you. I have gone back to work, although the paintbrush is nearly falling from my hands.'

Clearly Jo had written an encouraging letter to her brother-in-law, and it was admirable of her to agree that part of Theo's modest salary should continue to support him. Nor could Theo and Jo expect Van Gogh's canvasses to bring in any money in the near future. Theo was clearly unable to sell them himself; nor were his employers impressed by Vincent's work - in fact, these authoritative art dealers considered him to be a 'madman'. When Theo fell sick later in 1890, Boussod's only comment was that 'he had stored repulsive works which were a disgrace to this house'. This did not refer in particular to Van Gogh's work, although Boussod did not share Theo's enthusiasm for the art of avant-garde painters in general, but this view did reflect the tense relationship which existed between Boussod and Theo.

Landscape with Trees and Houses
Auvers, May 1890
F815 JH2000
Canvas, 64 x 78 cm
Otterlo, Rijksmuseum
Kröller-Müller

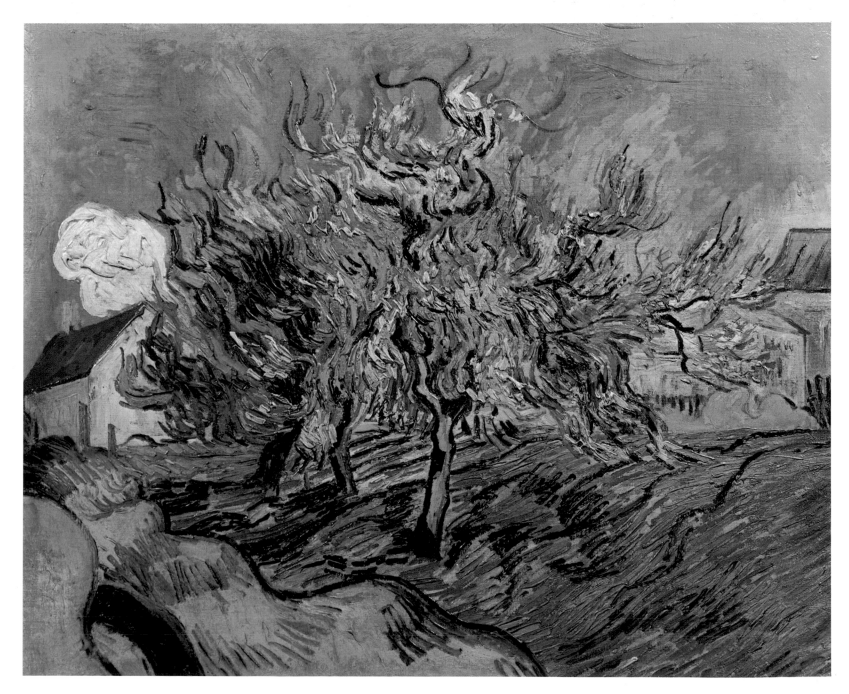

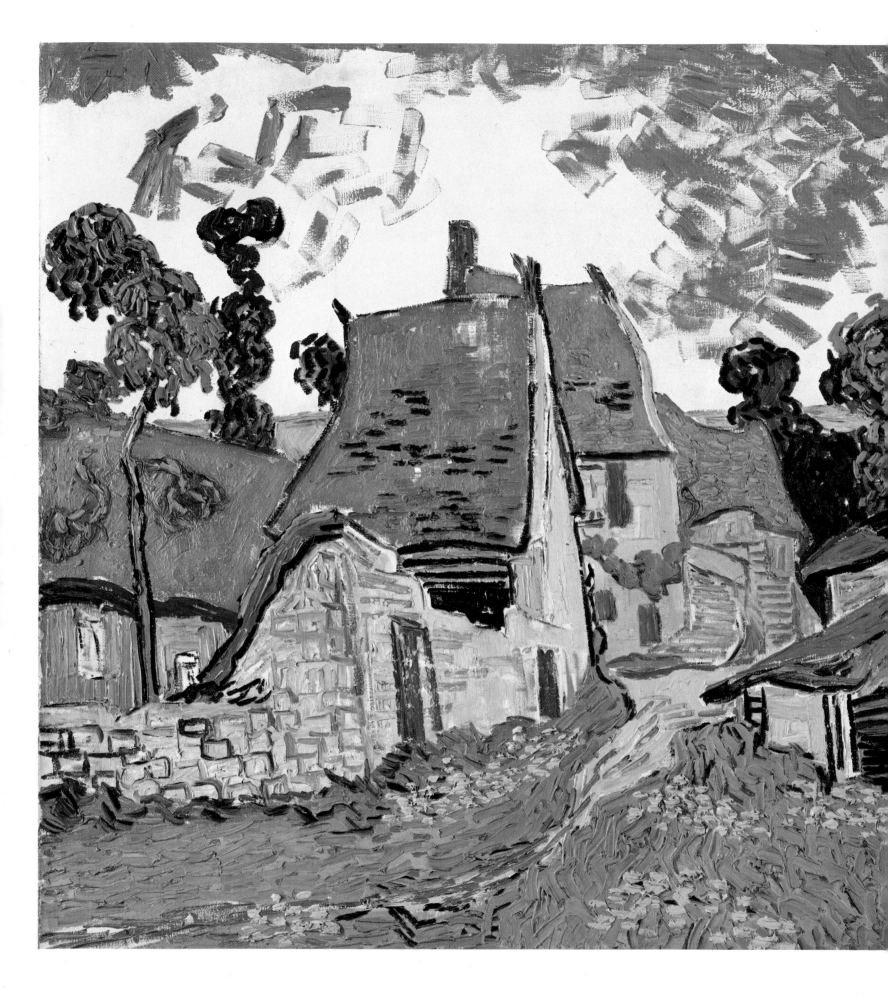

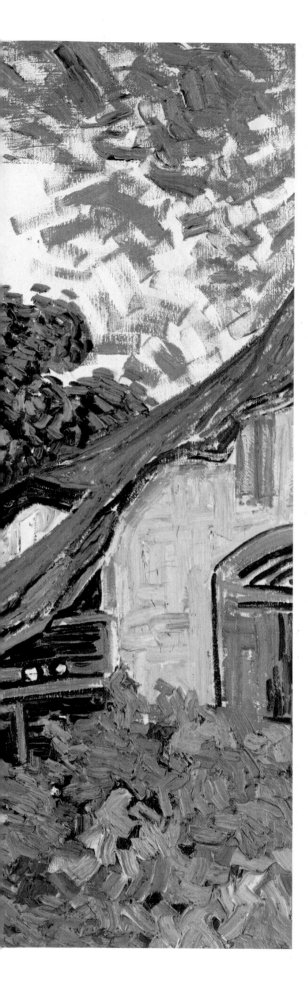

Village Street
Auvers, May 1890
F802 JH2001
Canvas, 73 x 92 cm
Helsinki, Ateneumin Taidemuseo

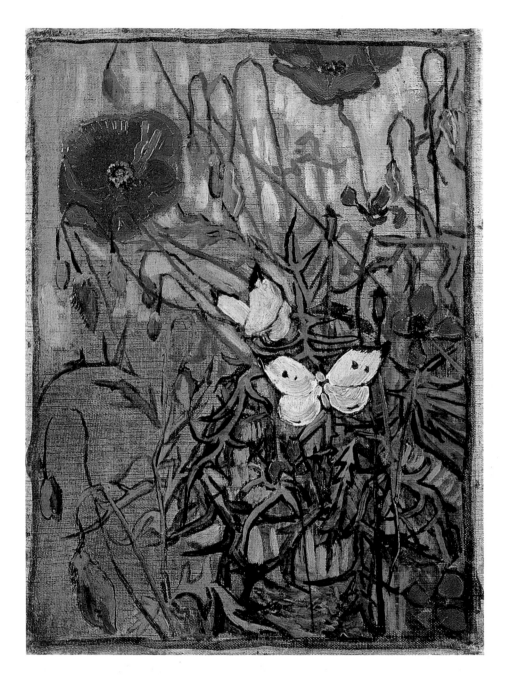

Poppies with Butterflies
Auvers, June 1890
F748 JH2013
Canvas, 33.5 x 24.5 cm
Amsterdam, Rijksmuseum
Vincent van Gogh

Theo and Jo continued to believe in Van Gogh as an artist. They also tolerated his impossible character, and Theo supported his older brother for years. In nearly every letter Van Gogh wrote about money matters. Again and again he asked to be paid more quickly, or for extra money. He considered that he was repaying them by sending quantities of painted canvases to Paris from Arles and Saint-Rémy. But these works remained piled up, usually unframed and unsold.

Returning to Van Gogh's work in Auvers, *Doctor Gachet's Garden* (JH 1999; see p. 172) was painted during Van Gogh's first visit to the doctor's house. The garden is actually hardly visible in the painting because of the large green cypress in the foreground which dominates this work, with its characteristic use of complementary colours - red and green. The garden was a real menagerie: eight cats, eight dogs, chickens, rabbits, ducks and pigeons (641a), all greatly enjoyed by little Vincent when he visited his uncle at Dr Gachet's house one Sunday with his parents.

After this same visit, Van Gogh wrote of the interior of Gachet's house: 'The house was full of antiques, especially black objects, but there were also works by the Impressionists Renoir, Pissarro and Cézanne, who were

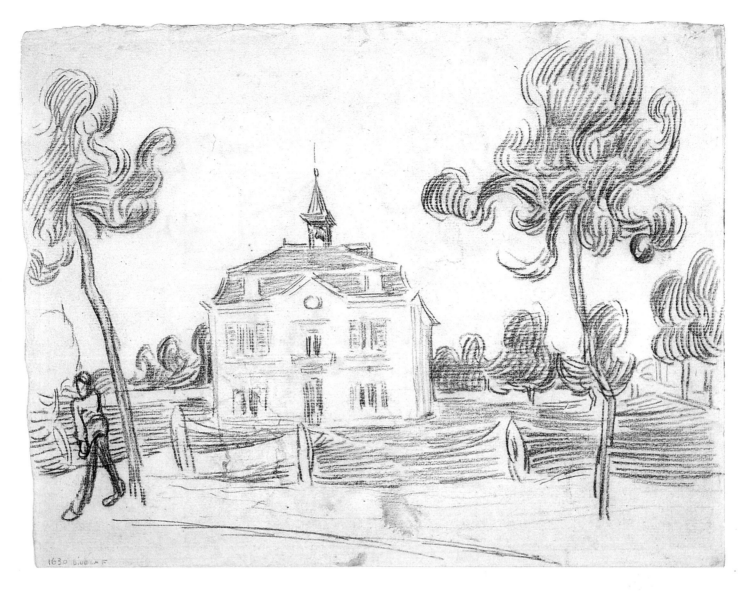

Town Hall with a Man Walking
Auvers, July 1890
F1630 JH2080
Black chalk, 23.5 x 31 cm
Amsterdam, Rijksmuseum
Vincent van Gogh

old friends of the doctor.' He was particularly struck by a painting by Armand Guillaumin of a nude lying on a bed, with a fan in her left hand, now in the Musée d'Orsay, Paris. This work gave rise to an incident in the spring of 1890. Van Gogh looked at the painting, noticed angrily that it was not framed, and told the doctor that he should immediately order the carpenter to make one. A few days later he returned to find that the canvas was still on the wall without a frame, and he became very agitated. A dramatic account of the events that followed states that Van Gogh had a revolver in his pocket, which he then aimed at Gachet. But the doctor never mentioned a weapon, which he certainly would have done after Van Gogh's suicide with a firearm on 27 July. A mental tussle of wills seems more likely than any physical violence.

Van Gogh and Gauguin

Paul Gauguin, who had left Arles and Van Gogh hurriedly at Christmas in 1888, wrote to his former friend in June 1890 from Le Pouldu in Brittany, complimenting him on his portrait of Madame Ginoux and telling him about his plan to set up a studio in Madagascar. Gauguin saw himself as 'St. John the Baptist of the art of the future'. Van Gogh answered promptly with his familiar enthusiasm and naivety, and announced that he wished to go to Brittany for a month to paint seascapes. Gauguin replied that he thought Van Gogh's idea of visiting him in Brittany was

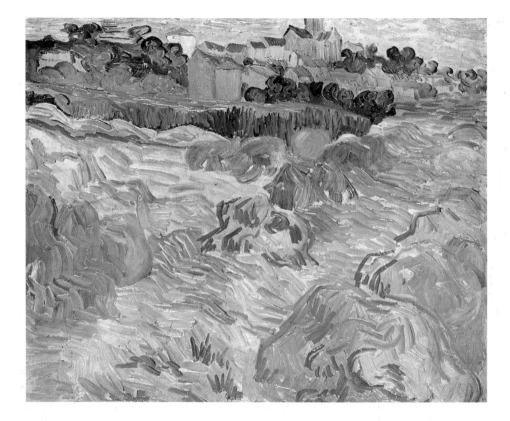

Group of Houses and Church
Auvers, July 1890
F801 JH2123
Canvas, 43 x 50 cm
Switzerland, private collection

excellent *if only it were possible*. In other words, it didn't suit Gauguin at all. Van Gogh then wrote a letter to Theo, saying he might follow Gauguin when he left for Madagascar.

But these were all wild fantasies. In these last months he did not go any further than Paris. In 1891 Gauguin left for Tahiti, following the sale of thirty paintings which made almost 10,000 francs altogether, giving him sufficient means to fund his trip.

More landscapes

Meanwhile, Van Gogh completed more landscapes in Auvers, such as *Cottages with Thatched Roofs* (JH 1987; see p. 174). His characteristic swirling and tormented brush strokes are indicative of his mental state, a sense of having to produce a great deal in a short while.

He also painted a *Landscape with Trees and Houses* (JH 2000; see p. 175) in which the red roof contrasts with the green trees, while a white cloud painted above the cottage draws the eye to it. This landscape was followed immediately by the *Village Street* (JH 2001; see p. 176/7), which was painted with thick brush strokes. It is strange how this time the blue sky is composed of separate short brush strokes or blocks of colour, very different from the thickly painted blue sky of his previous work. In the previous work red had been contrasted with green, and this time there is again a contrast of complementary colours, the blue of the sky with the orange of the roofs. These works show how, towards the end of his life, Van Gogh continued to develop his unique personal style. He took great liberties with the laws of perspective, and both his use of colour and his brush technique were extremely daring.

Paintings of flowers

In June 1890, Van Gogh painted various close-up views of flowers,

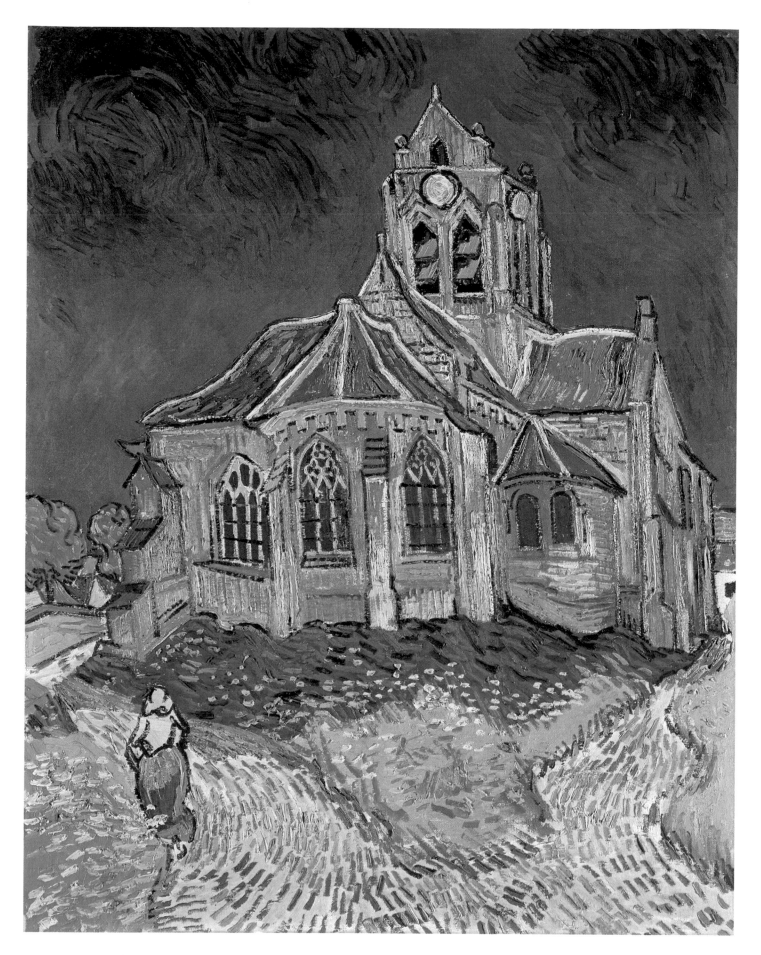

The Church in Auvers, Auvers, June 1890
F789 JH2006 - Canvas, 94 x 74 cm
Paris, Musée d'Orsay

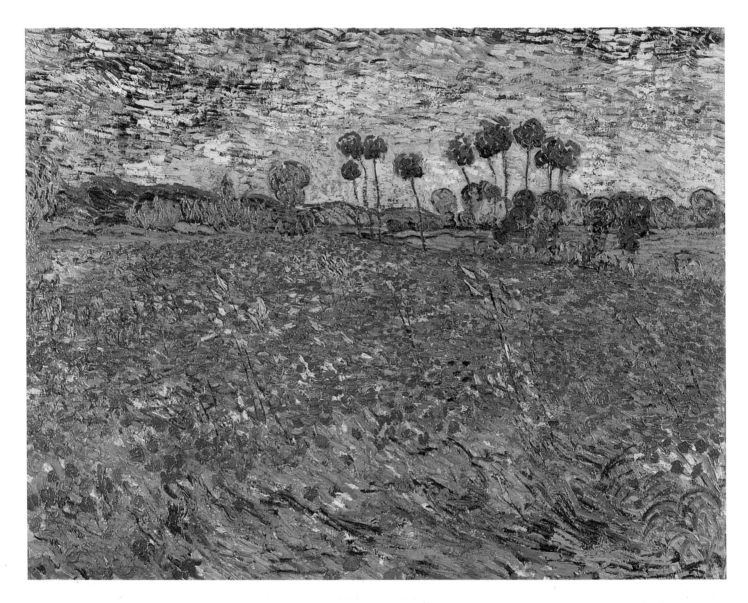

Field with Poppies
Auvers, June 1890
F636 JH2027
Canvas, 73 x 91.5 cm
The Hague, Gemeentemuseum
(on loan from The Netherlands
Office for Fine Arts)

branches of wild roses, wild roses with a beetle and the beautiful, intimate painting, *Poppies with Butterflies* (JH 2013; see p. 178). The lemon-yellow butterfly is wonderfully striking amongst the green leaves, seen below the orange-red hearts of the poppies.

The vases of flowers painted during this period also belong in this series as regards their subject matter. There are bouquets of cornflowers and poppies, roses and anemones, and flowers with thistles. Van Gogh was strongly affected by the beauty of the spring and summer in the Oise valley, painting the wealth of white candles on a flowering chestnut tree with visible enthusiasm. But it was in his last impressive landscapes that he expressed his most passionate feelings.

Auvers and Zundert

The drawing of the *Town Hall with a Man Walking* (JH 2080; see p. 179) shows the town hall of Auvers, immediately opposite Ravoux's inn, which is very similar to the town hall of Zundert in the Netherlands, where Van Gogh was born. Van Gogh also did a lively and colourful painting of the same subject, now in a private collection in America. The building and the square in front of it are exuberantly decorated with flags and lanterns for the French national holiday, le quatorze juillet. Thus we know exactly when this work was painted - two weeks before his death. It was given to the innkeeper Ravoux, from whose café terrace it had been painted, as a present. In 1905 Ravoux sold it for twenty francs to a passing American art dealer, Harry Haranson.

Church of Auvers

The views of the village church at Auvers, which Van Gogh painted several times, date from the last days of his life. *Group of Houses and Church* (JH 2123; see p. 180), which shows the village church in the distance, is possibly his penultimate work. Another work, also entitled *Group of Houses and Church* (JH 2124), now owned by Elizabeth Taylor in the United States, was until recently considered to be a view of Auvers. According to John Rewald, it is actually Saint-Rémy.

Van Gogh did one painting of *The Church in Auvers* (JH 2006; see p. 181) in close up. It is one of the greatest works of the Auvers period. In 1951 it was given to the Jeu de Paume by Paul Gachet, the doctor's son. When the museum was closed, it was moved to the new Musée d'Orsay, together with all the other Van Goghs and Impressionists. The building is Romanesque, dating from the twelfth century, with later Gothic additions and a sixteenth-century chapel, dedicated to the Virgin Mary. The church tower with its ridged roof must have reminded Van Gogh of Dutch medieval churches, especially those still found in the north of the country.

On 5 June 1890 he wrote a letter to his sister Wil (W 22), describing 'a painting of the village church, the effect is as though the building is violet, outlined against a simple deep cobalt-blue sky, the stained glass windows look like ultramarine stains, the roof is violet and partly orange. In the foreground there is some greenery and flowers and sand in the pink light of the sun.' He went on to compare this work with the studies which he had done in Nuenen in May 1885, over five years earlier: 'Only now the colour is probably more expressive.'

Village Street
Auvers, May 1890
F791 JH1995
Canvas, 49 x 70 cm
Private collection

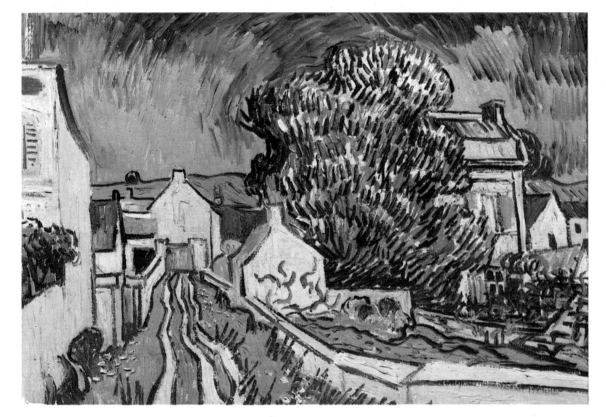

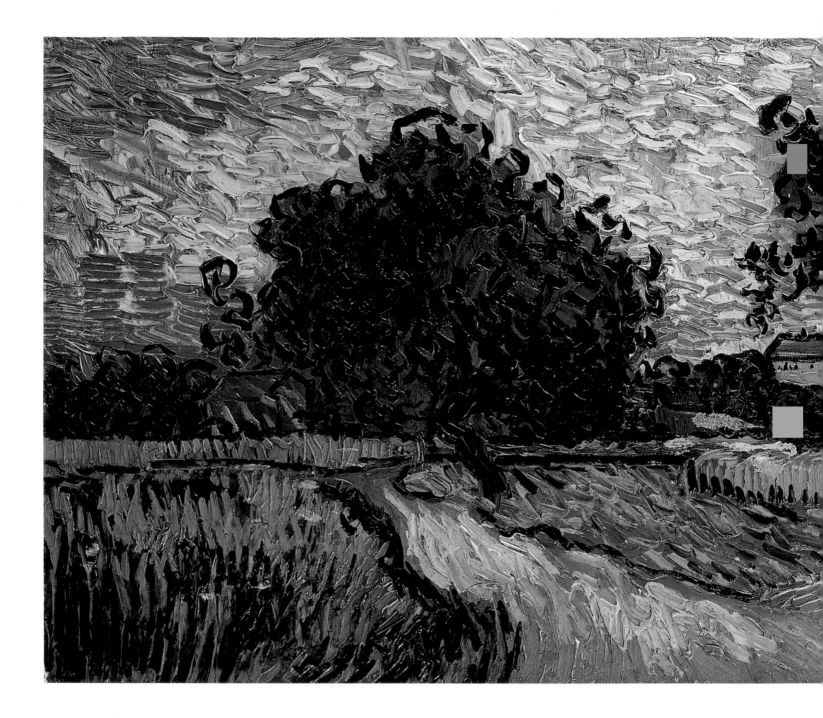

Field with Trees and the
Castle of Auvers at Sunset
Auvers, June 1890
F770 JH2040
Canvas, 50 x 100 cm
Amsterdam, Rijksmuseum
Vincent van Gogh

The church in Auvers is still there, on the hill by the road which leads to the churchyard. When you look at the building from the same angle as Van Gogh did a hundred years ago, his vision seems astonishing. Where did he get his colours from? In the painting the church is bathed in light against a deep blue sky. Although it is a fairly accurate representation of the tower, the chancel, the nave and the transept with the gothic windows and buttresses on the left, it is much more of an Expressionist work rather than a realist painting. Several times Van Gogh said that he did not wish to paint photographically, and this is certainly more of a vision. The short separate brush strokes in the foreground and extremely challenging use of colour in the roofs are characteristic of Van Gogh's work during his Post-Impressionist period.

Fields with poppies

Van Gogh left the village for the fields in the late spring of 1890, when

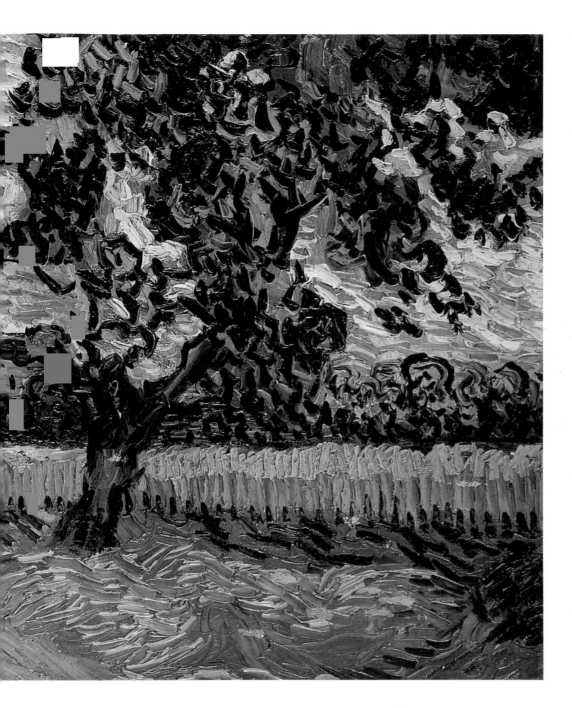

he painted *Field with Poppies* (JH 2027; see p. 182). The subject of this painting is reminiscent of a work by Claude Monet, dating from 1873, showing a field of poppies, and of a painting by Renoir, dating from 1875, again of the same subject. In contrast with these two paintings, Van Gogh's painting of poppies is certainly not an Impressionist work, and it does not have any of the easy charm of the works by Monet and Renoir in which figures of elegant ladies with parasols, and well-dressed children playing, liven up the scene. Van Gogh painted an uncompromising work in complementary colours of red and green. Again, there is a blue sky painted with short separate brush strokes, while the hearts of the poppies are painted as thick red dots.

Villas and castles

Dating from the spring of 1890 is another *Village Street* (JH 1995; see p. 183), an Auvers scene also known as *La Maison de Père Pilon*, after the

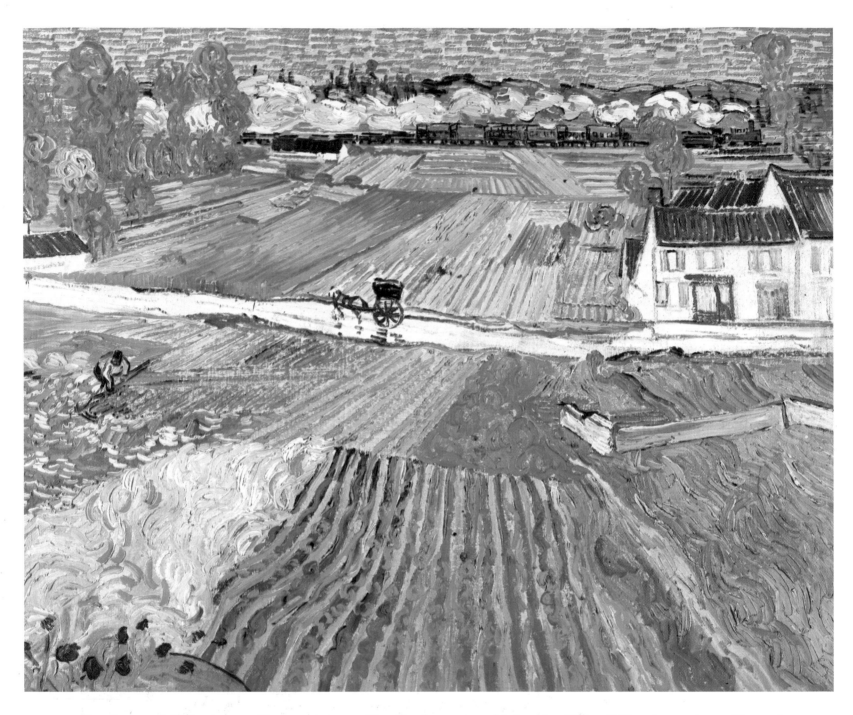

*Landscape with Carriage and
Train in the Distance*
Auvers, June 1890
F760 JH2019
Canvas, 72 x 90 cm
Moscow, Pushkin Museum

owner. Van Gogh wrote to his brother Theo: 'I like the modern villas and country houses of the affluent townspeople almost as much as the dilapidated farms with their thatched roofs.' This house at 18 rue François Villon was one of the large modern villas. The house is partly concealed by a large flowering chestnut tree with white candles, perhaps the same tree as that painted earlier. The work entitled *Street and Staircase with Five Figures* is a counterpart to this painting, with its straight lines and geometric shapes.

In the painting of June 1890, *Field with Trees and the Castle of Auvers* (JH 2040; see p. 184/5), the two trees in the foreground are predominant, while the seventeenth-century castle can barely be seen in the distance. The dark green trees are sharply outlined against the greenish-yellow evening sky. This painting, 50 x 100 cm, is the same size as *Field with a Blue Sky* and *Wheat Field with Crows*, dated July 1890. But as regards the use of colour, it differs considerably from the two other works, in which the atmosphere is much more highly charged, with blue skies above and a green and a yellow field respectively. By contrast, the painting of the castle exudes a tranquil feeling; it is a scene of serenity. Van Gogh mentioned the painting briefly in a letter to Theo (644): 'an evening effect - two totally black pear trees against the yellowish sky with wheat, and in the purple background the castle is surrounded by dark green.' The painting was probably finished very quickly in a single session. The sunset is suggested by heavy orange and yellow brush strokes in the sky. During the Auvers period Van Gogh never painted the sun, such a recurring symbol in his work from Arles and Saint-Rémy.

Landscape with train

The *Landscape with Carriage and Train in the Distance* (JH 2019; see p. 186) is a cheerful painting with a great deal of activity. The colours are lively and the perspective beautiful. Like Monet, Van Gogh repeatedly included steam trains in his paintings, but in Van Gogh's work they are always in the distance. This train has a large number of carriages and is fairly clearly delineated. The red of the roofs of the houses contrasts with the green of the fields, while the sky at the top of the painting is painted in separate short horizontal blue brush strokes. The eye is drawn into the distance by the more or less vertical lines of the various fields. Exactly in the centre, the canvas is divided by the broad white horizontal line of the road against which the small horse-drawn wagon is clearly outlined. In a letter to Wil dated 12 June (W 23), Van Gogh wrote about this painting: 'I have painted a large landscape which shows endless fields seen from a

Wheat Fields
Auvers, July 1890
F782 JH2099
Canvas, 73.5 x 92 cm
Munich, Neue Pinakothek

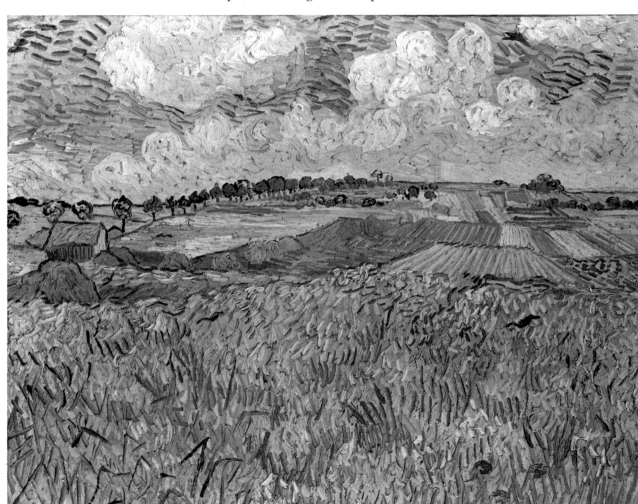

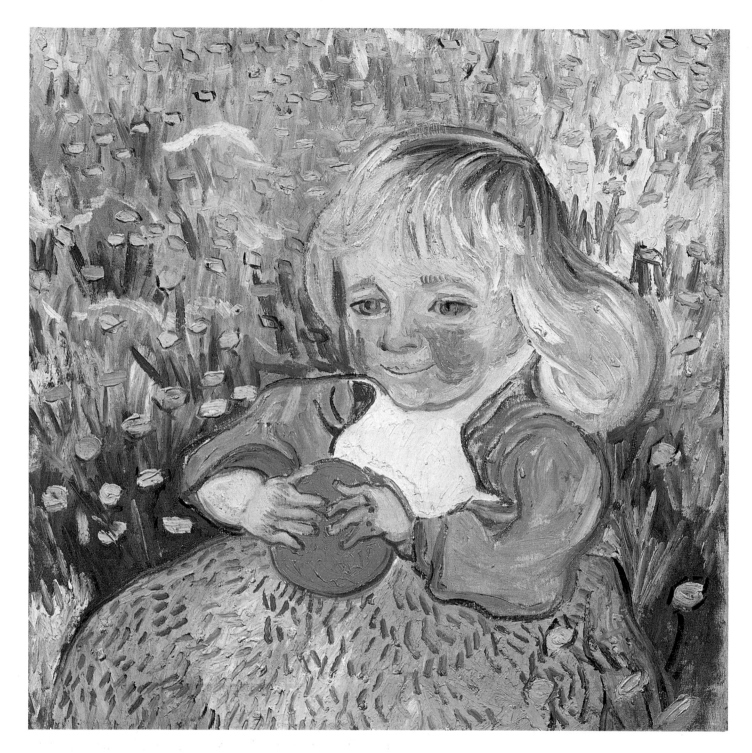

*Child, Sitting in the Grass
with an Orange*
Auvers, June 1890
F785 JH2057
Canvas, 50 x 51 cm
Switzerland, private collection

high vantage point in different shades of green, and a dark green potato field. Between the regular blocks of colour there is a heavy violet patch of earth, to the side a field of beans with white flowers, a field of clover flowering pink, a figure of a mower, a field of long ripe, faded red grass, and then wheat fields, poplars, a final line of blue hills on the horizon, where a train is passing by, leaving an endless plume of white smoke behind it in the green.'

Infinite space

Wheat Fields (JH 2099; see p. 187) is a similar work of approximately the same size, painted more than a month later in July. On 13 July Van Gogh wrote to his mother and his sister Wil (650): 'I am completely absorbed in this infinite space with wheat fields against the hills, as big as the sea, a

Girl, Standing in the Wheat
Auvers, June 1890
F788 JH2055
Canvas, 66 x 45 cm
Washington, National Gallery
of Art, Chester Dale Collection

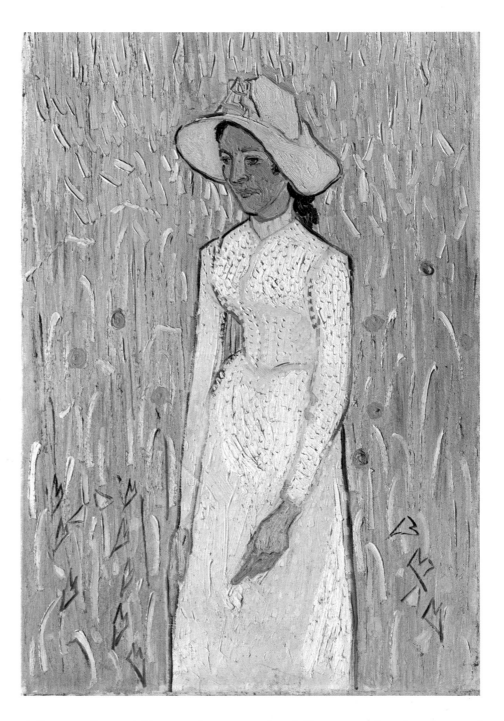

delicate yellow, delicate pale green, the delicate purple of a dug and weeded patch of earth with the regular dots of green of flowering potato plants, all under a sky of delicate shades of blue-white, pink and violet. I am completely in a mood of almost too much calm, a mood to paint this.'

If all the details of this description, written in advance of the painting, cannot be seen in the final work, it is due to Van Gogh's poetic licence with which he sometimes changed reality. After all, he did not claim to make, or intend to paint, topographically accurate landscapes, but wished to express the feeling of a landscape, his own completely original artistic reality.

Children

The paintings of children which Van Gogh painted during the last weeks of his life form quite a different subject. He did not paint sentimental portraits in the manner of Berthe Morisot or Renoir. His double portrait,

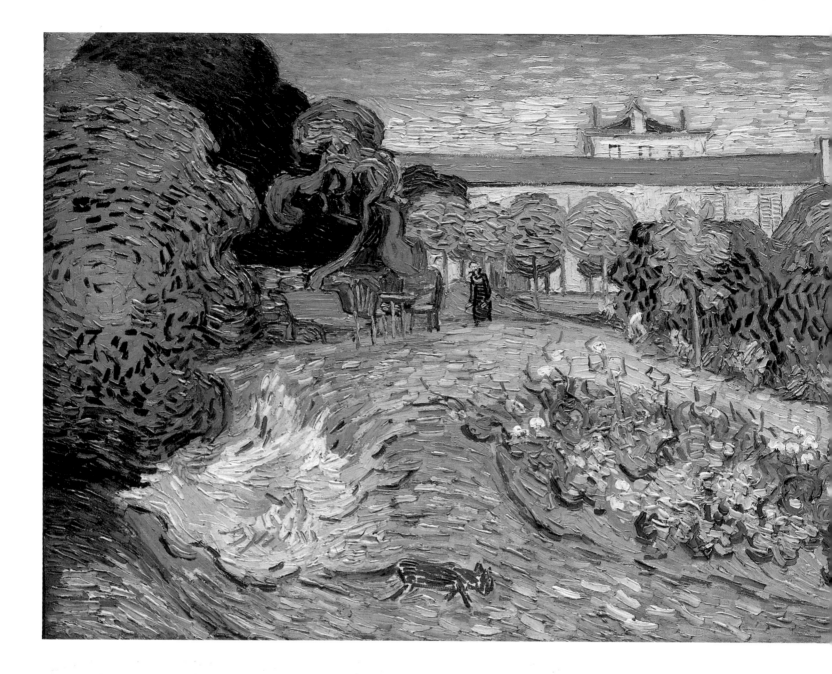

Daubigny's Garden with
Black Cat
Auvers, July 1890
F777 JH2105
Canvas, 56 x 101.5 cm
Basel, Kunstmuseum,
Rudolf Staechelin Foundation

Landscape in the Rain
Auvers, July 1890
F811 JH2096
Canvas, 50 x 100 cm
Cardiff, National Museum
of Wales

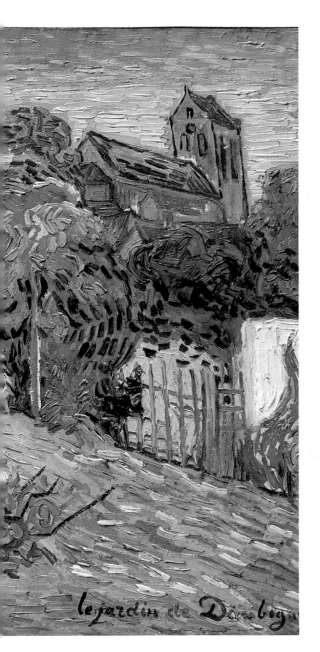

Two Children (JH 2051), now in the Musée d'Orsay, is a work of uncompromising realism. *Child, Sitting in the Grass with an Orange* (JH 2057; see p. 188) shows an effective use of complementary colours, as in most of Van Gogh's portraits. The very bright orange, which the little girl is grasping with both hands, contrasts effectively with her light blue blouse and striped blue skirt. This happy toddler, with her round pink cheeks and long blonde hair, surrounded by the wild flowers of the meadow, is without doubt the best portrait of a child that Van Gogh ever painted.

Another charming work is the painting of the *Girl, Standing in the Wheat* (JH 2055; see p. 189). In a letter to Theo and Jo dated 1 July 1890, Van Gogh wrote about this work (646): 'A peasant girl, a large yellow hat with a sky blue ribbon tied in a bow, a very red face, a coarse blue jacket with orange dots, all against a background of ears of wheat.' He painted the girl again with the same background, this time sitting down, and included a sketch of her in the letter quoted here.

Van Gogh and Daubigny

Charles-François Daubigny (1817-1878), an artist of the Barbizon School, is commemorated in Auvers-sur-Oise with a splendid bust in the park. He had come to live in Auvers in 1861 at the age of 44. With the arrival of the Impressionists, Cézanne, Pissarro, Gauguin and Van Gogh, Auvers became an artists' village, as Barbizon had been previously. Daubigny built a house, the Villa Ida, in the centre of the village, surrounded by a beautiful garden and he also had a boat on the River Oise which he used as a studio. By the time Van Gogh came to Auvers in 1890, Daubigny had been dead for twelve years, but his widow still lived in the village.

In July 1890 Van Gogh painted *Daubigny's Garden with Black Cat* (JH 2105; see p. 190/91), of which he also painted a copy. He described this painting in a letter to Theo (651): 'Daubigny's Garden: in the foreground there are green and pink plants, to the left a green and lilac shrub and the stem of a plant with whitish leaves; in the middle there is a bed of roses, to the right a fence, a wall, and above the wall, a nut tree with violet

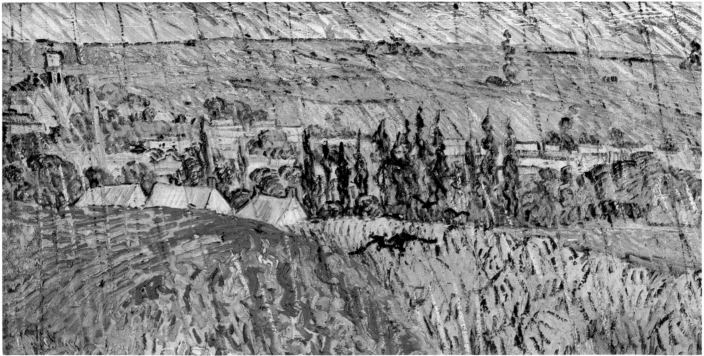

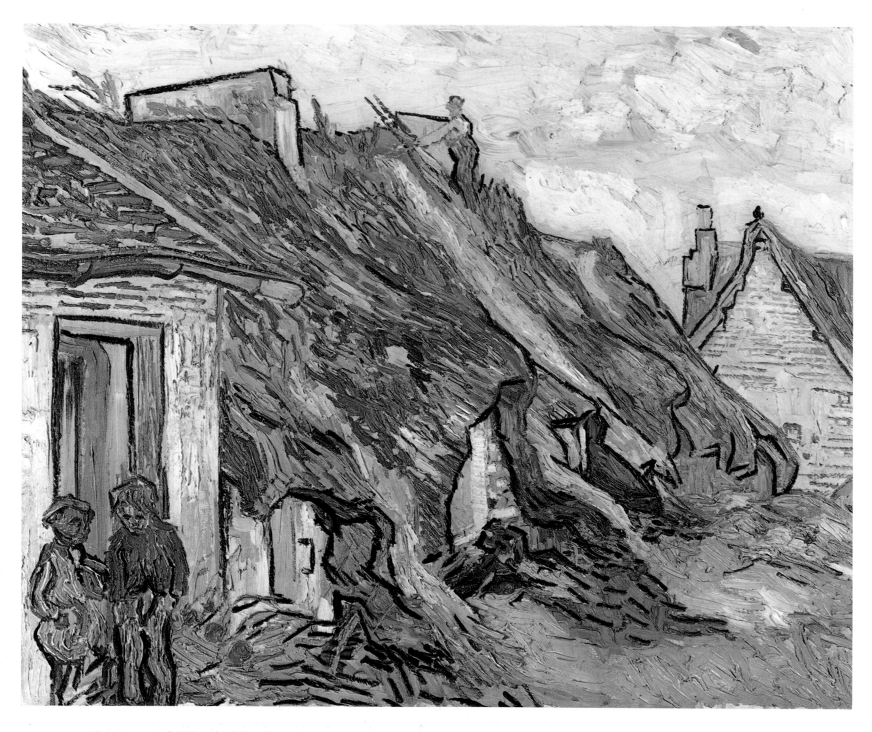

*Cottages with Thatched Roofs
and Figures*
Auvers, July 1890
F780 JH2115
Canvas, 65 x 81 cm
Zurich, Kunstmuseum,
Dr.Hans Schuler Legacy

foliage. There is a lilac hedge, a line of round yellow lime trees, the house in the background, pink with a roof of bluish tiles, a bench and three chairs, a black figure with a yellow hat, and in the foreground a black cat. The sky is pale green.' This description is accompanied by a drawing which shows the composition of the painting.

This was the last letter that Van Gogh wrote to his brother Theo. It was dated 24 July. Three days later he shot himself, and the injury was to result in his death. An unfinished letter to Theo was later found in a pocket of his clothes. It contains the following significant passage, which reveals Van Gogh's appreciation of, and gratitude to, Theo (652): 'Through my mediation you have played your part in the production of some of the canvases which retain a sense of tranquillity, even in the midst of disaster.'

This was the quotation - in the original French - that was inscribed under the impressive monument by Ossip Zadkine in Zundert, Van Gogh and Theo's birthplace. The sculpture shows the two brothers standing next to each other.

Last landscapes

Another work which dates from the last weeks of Van Gogh's life is *Landscape in the Rain* (JH 2096; see p. 191). This work, 50 x 100 cm, is notable for the way in which the rain is painted. During the last period of his life Van Gogh made quite a few paintings of this size, such as the famous *Wheat Fields under Clouded Skies*, which is probably the most beautiful landscape he ever painted. Another late work, *Cottages with Thatched Roofs and Figures* (JH 2115; see p. 192), was painted in the rue du Gré in Chaponval, to the west of Auvers. It is extremely thickly painted, a typical example of an almost three-dimensional style of painting which Van Gogh used on several occasions. A thatcher is shown working on the roof of one of the houses, and to the left in the foreground a boy and a girl are talking to each other. The subject matter is reminiscent of the *Cottages with Thatched Roofs* (see p. 174) which was painted in May, just after Van Gogh's arrival in Auvers, while the composition of this late painting is strikingly similar to that of the *Street in Saintes-Maries* (JH 1462) of June 1888.

In conclusion, the work which has sometimes been referred to as Van Gogh's last painting was *Wheat Field under Threatening Skies with Crows* (JH 2117; see p. 194/5). It was probably not his final work, and is now assumed to have been painted between 7 and 10 July, at the same time as the painting *Wheat Fields under Clouded Skies*, which is the same size (50 x 100 cm). These paintings belong together and both hang in the Van Gogh Museum in Amsterdam.

The *Wheat Field under Threatening Skies with Crows* is a fascinating painting with its ink-black sky above a golden yellow wheat field and the silhouettes of crows flying upwards. Was it an intimation of Van Gogh's imminent suicide? Does it reflect his tortured soul during the last weeks of his life? Is there no way out of the field on the three paths criss-crossing the wheat? Are the crows flying at us threateningly to instill a sense of fear and increase the feeling of being trapped?

On the evening of Sunday 27 July, Van Gogh returned to Ravoux's inn later than usual. He did not say a word and stumbled up the steep wooden staircase to his garret. When the innkeeper Ravoux went to investigate, it

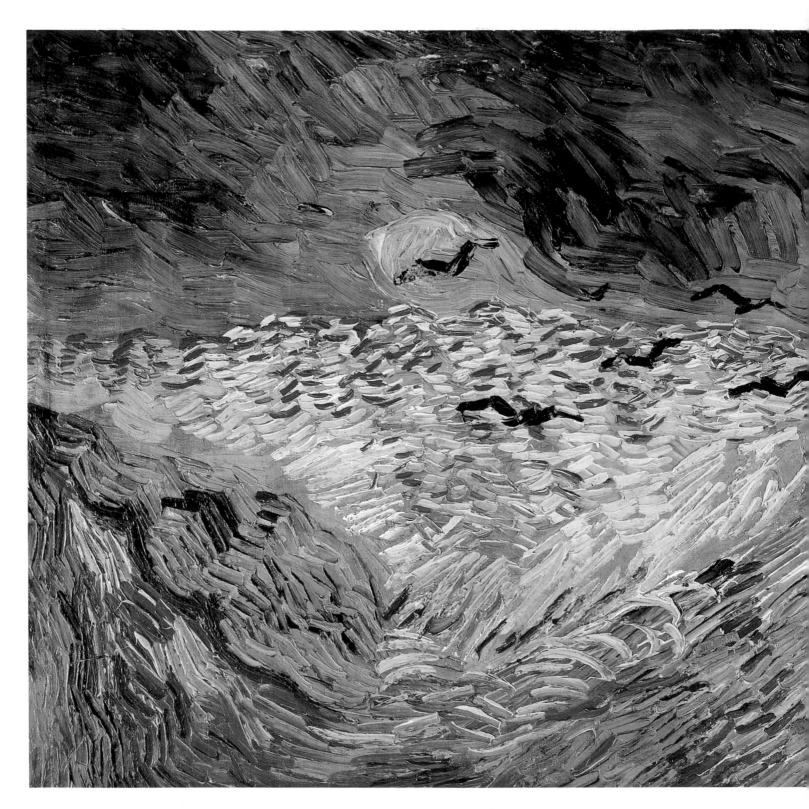

Wheat Field under
Threatening Skies with Crows
Auvers, July 1890
F779 JH2117
Canvas, 50.5 x 100.5 cm
Amsterdam, Rijksmuseum
Vincent van Gogh

was clear that Van Gogh had tried to kill himself. In the field he had tried to shoot himself through the heart, but the bullet went into his side. The local doctor and Dr Gachet were called immediately, but they did not dare remove the bullet. A message was sent to Theo, but it was delayed so he did not arrive until Monday morning. Theo stayed by his brother's bedside all day while Vincent smoked his pipe. The heavy internal bleeding continued to sap his strength. His last words were: '*La tristesse durera toujours*' (Sadness will last forever). Then he died, not long after midnight on Tuesday, 29 July 1890.

Van Gogh was laid out in the bar, and his paintings were hung on the walls. Sunflowers were put in vases, the sunflowers he loved so much. The

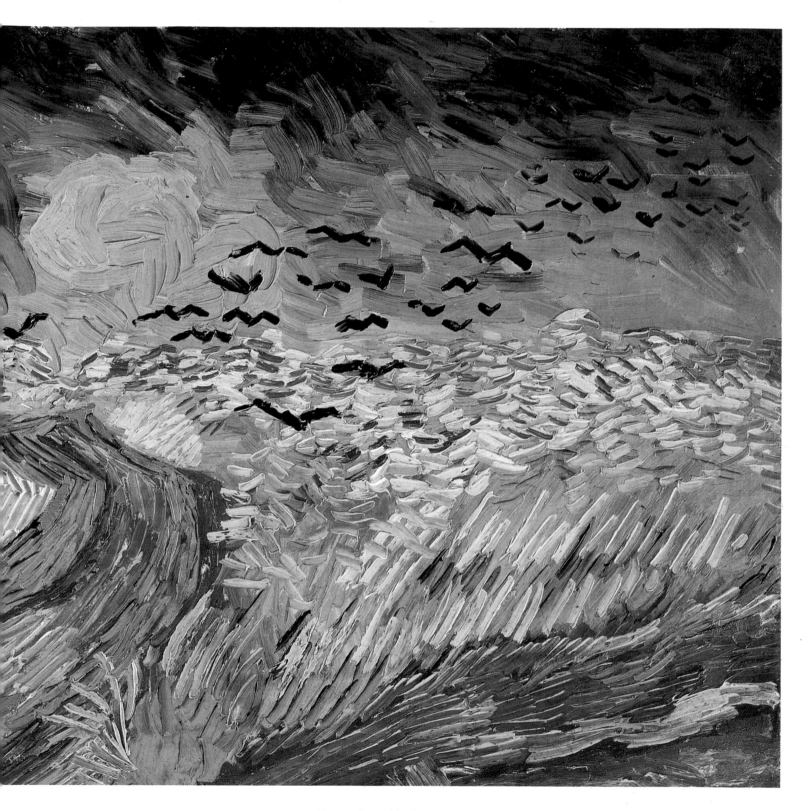

funeral took place on Wednesday, 30 July. The pastor in Auvers would not allow the hearse to be used for a suicide, so a carriage had to come from another village. The cortège comprised Theo, his brother-in-law Andries Bonger, Dr Gachet, and artist friends Charles Laval, Emile Bernard and Lucien Pissarro, son of Camille. Père Tanguy, the seller of artists' materials in Paris, also came. When Dr Gachet tried to give his speech of farewell in the churchyard, he burst into tears. Van Gogh was buried on the edge of the churchyard by the wall, and the standing headstone on his grave bore the simple inscription: '*Ici repose Vincent Van Gogh, 1853-1890*'.

Bibliography

List of books consulted and recommended

Jean-Francois Barrielle, *La Vie et l'oeuvre de Vincent Van Gogh*, ACR édition internationale, Paris, 1984.

Ton de Brouwer, *Van Gogh in Nuenen*, Van Spijk, Venlo, 1984.

Jean-Paul Clébert et Pierre Richard, *La Provence de Van Gogh*, Edisud, La Calade, Aix-en-Provence, 1981.

Marie-Paule Défossez, *Auvers ou le regard des peintres*, Editions du Valhermeil, Paris, 1986.

J.B. de la Faille, *The Works of Vincent Van Gogh*, Meulenhoff International, Amsterdam, 1970.

Walter Feilchenfeldt, *Vincent Van Gogh and Paul Cassirer, Berlin. The reception of Van Gogh in Germany from 1901 to 1914*, Waanders, Zwolle, 1988.

Viviane Forrester, *Van Gogh ou l'enterrement dans les blés*, Seuil, Paris, 1983.

A.M. Hammacher and Renilde Hammacher, *Van Gogh, een documentaire biografie*, Meulenhoff/Landshoff, 1982.

Van Gogh in Brabant, Waanders, Zwolle, 1987.

Jan Hulsker, *Van Gogh en zijn weg. Al zijn tekeningen en schilderijen in hun samenhang en ontwikkeling*, Meulenhoff, Amsterdam, 1979.

Lotgenoten, het leven van Vincent en Theo van Gogh, Agathon/Unieboek, Weesp, 1985.

Verzamelde brieven van Vincent van Gogh, Wereldbibliotheek, Amsterdam-Antwerp, 1974.

Vincent van Gogh. Een leven in brieven. Keuze, inleiding en toelichtingen, Meulenhoff Pocket Editie, Amsterdam, 1988.

Tsukasa Kodera, *Christianity versus Nature. A Study of the Thematics in Van Gogh's Oeuvre*, Dissertation, University of Amsterdam, 1988.

Paulo Lecaldano, *Tout l'oeuvre peint de Van Gogh*, Flammarion, Paris, 1971.

Ronald Pickvance, *Van Gogh in Arles*, Metropolitan Museum of Art, New York, 1986.

Van Gogh in Saint-Rémy and Auvers, Metropolitan Museum of Art, New York, 1978.

E.H. du Quesne, *Van Gogh, Persoonlijke herinneringen aan Vincent van Gogh*, J.F. van de Ven, Baarn, 1910.

John Rewald, *Post-Impressionism. From Van Gogh to Gauguin*, The Museum of Modern Art, New York, 1978.

Marinus Schroevers and Dirk de Herder, *Van Gogh achterna*, Het Spectrum, Utrecht/Antwerp, 1975.

Benno J. Stokvis, *Nasporingen omtrent Vincent van Gogh in Brabant*, S.L. van Looy, Amsterdam, 1926.

A. Tellegen-Hoogendoorn, *Vincent van Gogh. De waardering van zijn werk*, AO-boekje 1466.1.6.1973.

Richard Thompson, *Van Gogh in Paris. The fortification drawings of 1887*, in Jong Holland, September 1987.

Marc-Edo Tralbaut, *De gebroeders van Gogh*, Uitgave van het Gemeentebestuur van Zundert, 1964.

Vincent van Gogh, The Viking Press, New York, Macmillan, London, 1969.

Prof. Dr. H.F.J.M. van den Eerenbeemt, *De onbekende Vincent van Gogh. Leren en tekenen in Tilburg, 1866-1868*, Bergmans, Tilburg, 1972.

Dr. J.G. van Gelder, *De aardappeleters van Vincent van Gogh*, Wereldbibliotheek Amsterdam-Antwerp, 1949.

Van Gogh Bulletin, publication of the National Museum Vincent Van Gogh, Amsterdam.

Louis van Tilborgh, *Van Gogh en Millet*, Waanders, Zwolle, 1988.

Evert van Uitert, *Vincent van Gogh, leven en werk*, Landshoff, Amsterdam, 1976.

Vincent van Gogh. Tekeningen, Landshoff, Bentveld, 1977.

Vincent van Gogh. A detailed catalogue of the paintings and drawings by Vincent van Gogh in the collection of the Kröller-Müller National Museum, Otterlo, 1980.

Evert van Uitert and Michael Hoyle, *Catalogue of Paintings and Drawings of the National Museum Vincent van Gogh*, Amsterdam, 1987.

Johannes van der Wolk, *De schetsboeken van Vincent van Gogh*, Landshoff, Bentveld, 1977.

Vincent, publication of the National Museum Vincent Van Gogh, Amsterdam.

Kenneth Wilkie, *Het dossier Van Gogh*, Het Wereldvenster, Baarn, 1978.

Index

PHOTO CREDITS

Artothek, Peissenberg - Jochen Remmer
Bridgeman Art Library, London
Christie's/Bridgeman Art Library, London
Tom Haartsen, Ouderkerk
Hans Hinz, Allschwill
R.M.N., Paris
Sotheby's, Amsterdam
Stedelijk Museum (Reproduction Dept.), Amsterdam
and the photo libraries of the collections mentioned in the captions.

The author and publisher wish to thank the museums, galleries and private collectors for the permission to reproduce in this volume paintings from their collections.